CW00794407

'Nadir Lahiji's *Kōjin Karatani's Philos*
moment in the understanding of th
and architecture. Taking Kōjin Karataɴɪ ꜱ ᴡᴏʀᴋ ᴀᴛ ᴀ ꜱᴛᴀʀᴛɪ⸱⸱⸱ɢ ᴘ⸱⸱⸱ , ⸱⸱⸱ ,
shows how theorizing architecture in philosophy allows us to discover
precisely how theory and practice intersect in our ethical being.'
Todd McGowan, *author of* Emancipation After Hegel

'Nadir Lahiji's book is the kind of brilliant, erudite study of Kōjin
Karatani's work that we have long needed. A groundbreaking reassessment of the role played by the architectural metaphor in the history of
philosophy, Lahiji shows how, in a series of radical new readings of Kant
and Marx, Karatani compellingly defends a thought of architectonic reason against its various postmodern critics.'
David Cunningham, *University of Westminster*

'Lahiji, one of the sharpest theorists of architecture today, permits us to
rethink the philosophical system of Kojin Karatani, from the standpoint of the
will to architecture. While insisting on his "theoretical system," Lahiji recon-
structs Karatani's system in a way that goes well beyond the very complicated
and not much discussed relation between architecture and philosophy.'
Agon Hamza, *coauthor of* Reading Hegel

'In our postmodern era, philosophy is often denounced as the expression
of some underlying will—the will to power, the will to rationalize and
dominate the world, the will to ground ordinary and scientific knowledge in a deeper wisdom. Kōjin Karatani proposes a radically different
approach: philosophy as the expression of a will to architecture, a desperate effort to formulate the hidden architecture of our universe. In his
outstanding elaboration of Karatani's insights, Lahiji analyses the strength
and the limit of this architectural metaphor. He follows Karatani in focus-
ing on Kant who was the first to deploy the structure of philosophy as the
architecture of pure reason immanently divided into three domains: pure
reason, practical reason, and their unity in the theory of judgment. But
Kant was also the first to clearly perceive the abyss which condemns
every such architecture of reason to its ultimate failure. Lahiji thus avoids
the trap of providing a "philosophy of architecture": he does the exact
opposite, using architecture to formulate the shaky foundations of philosophy itself. The combination of philosophy and architecture works as
an explosive mixture which revolutionizes not only our notion of philosophy but also our elementary idea of reason. *Kōjin Karatani's*
Philosophy of Architecture enables us to understand the roots of the crisis
of reason which characterizes our historical epoch. It is a book for everyone who wants to *think* today.'
Slavoj Žižek, *Hegelian philosopher and communist political activist*

KŌJIN KARATANI'S PHILOSOPHY OF ARCHITECTURE

In this book, Nadir Lahiji introduces Kōjin Karatani's theoretical-philosophical project and demonstrates its affinity with Kant's critical philosophy founded on 'architectonic reason'. From the ancient Greeks we have inherited a definition of the word 'philosophy' as Sophia—wisdom. But in his book *Architecture as Metaphor* Kōjin Karatani introduces a different definition of philosophy. Here, Karatani critically defines philosophy not in association with Sophia but in relation to foundation as the Will to Architecture. In this novel definition resides the notion that in Western thought a crisis persistently reveals itself with every attempt to build a system of knowledge on solid ground. This book reveals the implications of this extraordinary exposition. This is the first book to uncover Kōjin Karatani's highly significant ideas on architecture for both philosophical and architectural audiences.

Nadir Lahiji is an architect. He is most recently the author of *Architecture in the Age of Pornography* (Routledge, 2021), *Architecture, Philosophy and the Pedagogy of Cinema* (Routledge, 2021), *Architecture or Revolution: Emancipatory Critique after Marx* (Routledge, 2020), and *An Architecture Manifesto: Critical Reason and Theories of a Failed Practice* (Routledge, 2019). His previous publications include, among others, *Adventures with the Theory of the Baroque and French Philosophy* and the coauthored *The Architecture of Phantasmagoria: Specters of the City*.

KŌJIN KARATANI'S PHILOSOPHY OF ARCHITECTURE

Nadir Lahiji

Routledge
Taylor & Francis Group

LONDON AND NEW YORK

Designed cover image: 'The Fall of the Tower of Babel' (1547) by
Cornelis Anthonisz. Rijksmuseum, Amsterdam.

First published 2024
by Routledge
4 Park Square, Milton Park, Abingdon, Oxon OX14 4RN

and by Routledge
605 Third Avenue, New York, NY 10158

*Routledge is an imprint of the Taylor & Francis Group, an informa
business*

British Library Cataloguing-in-Publication Data
A catalogue record for this book is available from the British Library

ISBN: 978-1-032-64757-9 (hbk)
ISBN: 978-1-032-64759-3 (pbk)
ISBN: 978-1-032-64761-6 (ebk)

DOI: 10.4324/9781032647616

Typeset in Optima
by SPi Technologies India Pvt Ltd (Straive)

CONTENTS

FRONTISPIECE

'The Fall of the Tower of Babel' (1547)
By Cornelis Anthonisz[1]

Building Hubris: The Tower of Babel

If I regard the sum total of all cognition of pure and speculative reason as an edifice for which we have in ourselves at least the idea, then I can say that in the Transcendental Doctrine of Elements we have made an estimate of the building materials and determined for what sort of edifice, with what height and strength, they would suffice. It turned out, of course, that although we had in mind a tower that would reach the heavens, the supply of materials sufficed only for a dwelling that was just roomy enough for our business on the plane of experience and high enough to survey it; however, that bold undertaking had to fail from lack of material, not to mention the confusion of languages that unavoidably divided the workers over the plan and dispersed them throughout the world, leaving each to build on his own according to his own design.[2]

Kant, *Critique of Pure Reason*

Human reason so delights in constructions that it has several times built up a tower and then razed it to examine the nature of foundation. It is never too late to become reasonable and wise; but if the insight comes late, there is always more difficulty in starting the change.[3]

Kant, *Prolegomena to Any Future Metaphysics*

The story of the Tower of Babel goes back to Genesis 11. As the story goes, God at first visited the Earth and witnessed the construction of this structure as a sign of the unity of the people speaking one language. God saw this as the intervention of the Earth into the affairs of Heaven. He therefore decides to cause confusion and tumult by scattering people across the surface of the Earth and make them speak different languages. As a result of not understanding each other's tongue, people had to stop constructing the Tower, leaving it incomplete. 'Men could no longer understand each other, and the project of finishing the tower was put to rest for good. The humans then separated from each other as they could no longer live peacefully. And since the term "Babel" in Hebrew means confusion, the place was called Babylon, and the tower Babel'. Sibyl recounts the story: 'When all men were of one language, some of them built a high tower, as if they would thereby ascend up to heaven; but the god sent storms of wind and overthrew the tower, and gave everyone a peculiar language, and for this reason, it was that the city was called Babylon'.[4] The Greek historian Herodotus claimed to have seen the Tower during his visit to Babylon. He reported it as a tall Tower with twenty stories and eight levels.

Building the Tower of Babel was considered to be both 'an accomplishment and a sign', as Daniel Purdy writes. 'The construction of the Tower parallels the compilation of a metaphysical system', which Kant demonstrated to be untenable.[5] It became a metaphor in the eighteenth century for the *hubris* of metaphysics and the absolutist state power. Yet, mankind – starting with the tyrannical King Nimrod who was said to be responsible for building the Tower of Babel by manipulating his people to turn them against God – has tried desperately to reach Heaven over and over again, thus repeating the hubris of trying to build the Tower.

Significantly, it was Fritz Lang who, in his film *Metropolis* (1927), presented a *filmic* critique in the twentieth century that can be taken as a counterpart to Kant's *philosophical* critique of the Tower of Babel. Recall the *technological* imagery that stages the 'completed' version of the 'Tower of Babel' in *Metropolis* with designers behind the work causing the revolt by the workers that would lead to the destruction of the Tower.[6] It is the division, or better, the *conflict* between 'hands' and 'brains'. As Andreas Huyssen, invoking this conflict in the film, writes, 'The imagery of the tower of Babel (the machine center of Metropolis is actually called the New Tower of Babel) relates technology to myth and legend. The biblical myth is used to construct the ideological message about the division of labor into the hands that build and the brains that plan and conceive, a division which, as the film suggests, must be overcome'.[7] And further, 'The capital/labor conflict is present in the sequence showing the Master of Metropolis in his control and communications center and the workers in the machine room, with the machines being subservient to the master but enslaving the workers'.[8]

All the *unreasonable* attempts at building a Tower of Babel will have to be submitted to a Kantian philosophical scrutiny—The 'nature' of its 'foundation' must be re-examined all over again: 'It is never too late to become reasonable and wise'.

Notes

1 Cornelis Anthonisz, a Dutch painter, engraver and mapmaker, was born in Amsterdam around 1505. His 'The Fall of the Tower of Babel', dated 1547 is credited to Rijksmuseum Amsterdam. He is well known for his detailed maps of medieval Amsterdam. 'The text in the top right reads "Babelon/Genesis 14". Originally it read Genesis 11, which makes more sense as that is the chapter where the construction of the tower and the punishment are described. The number 14 probably refers to the chapter about the Last Judgment in the Book of Revelation. The tower is destroyed by winds and fire from heaven, announced on trumpet by an angel. In the foreground people lay mortally wounded by falling masonry while others flee in all directions. The text in the top left banner is somewhat strange: "When it was at its highest / it should not do fall". The stone in the bottom left is inscribed with the date 1547'. https:// www.artbible.info/art/large/619.html. Compare Anthonisz's depiction of the Tower of Babel with that by Brueghel the Elder's 1563 depiction which portrays the Tower as a complete and a magnificent structure standing on the ground.
2 Immanuel Kant, *Critique of Pure Reason* (Cambridge: Cambridge University Press, 1998), 627.
3 Immanuel Kant, *Prolegomena to Any Future Metaphysics* (Indianapolis/ Cambridge: Hackett, 1977), 2.
4 For the quoted passages see *Tower of Babel: The Biblical Legend of Babylon*, copyrighted, 2020 (no author and no publisher's names), 46–47.
5 See Daniel Purdy, *On the Ruins of the Babel, Architectural Metaphor in German Thought* (Ithaca: Cornell University Press, 2011), 55.
6 As mentioned in *Tower of Babel: The Biblical Legend of Babylon*, 55.
7 See Andreas Huyssen's excellent analysis in his 'The Vamp and the Machine: Fritz Lang's *Metropolis*', in *After the Great Divide: Modernism, Mass Culture, Postmodernism* (Bloomington: Indiana University Press, 1986), 67.
8 Andreas Huyssen, 'The Vamp and the Machine: Fritz Lang's *Metropolis*', 67.

PREFACE

In 'Transcendental Doctrine of Method', the last part of *Critique of Pure Reason*, Kant employed a 'building metaphor' for a most 'pedestrian understanding of architecture'.[1] The *hubris* of building the Tower of Babel had to be confronted with a simple 'plan' of building, with the materials readily available, with what is at humanity's disposal—no more, no less. This had been lost to the philosopher and the architect both. Hence the reason for a Kantian *transcendental critique*. As there is a *limit* to reason, so there is a *limit* to building. This is the fundamental necessity of Kant's critical philosophy in any investigation into the relationship between *philosophy* and *architecture*—a much misconceived relation. Kōjin Karatani is a prodigious thinker who has brought out the Kantian *critique* to expose the *limits* of architecture *as* metaphor by invoking Kant's *architectonics* as *transcendental* structure. In the present work I take up Karatani's thesis for an expanded analysis.

My first exposure to the work of Kōjin Karatani began with reading his *Architecture as Metaphor* when it was published in 1995.[2] The central thesis of his book goes as follows: Philosophy as the *will to architecture* exposes the limits to architecture *as* metaphor, which is omnipresent at the foundation of Western thought. Karatani informs us that his works have been 'interventions' that critically examine 'architecture as metaphor in order to expose its limits'.[3] In the 'Introduction to the English Edition' of the book, Karatani reveals that it was by looking back at his previous works that he realized that he was 'unwittingly' engaging in 'a kind of Kantian critique all along'.[4] He tells us that he became aware of Kant only when he targeted the dominant modernist ideology of a 'grand narrative'. With the fall of the grand narrative, all other alternative narratives or ideologies appeared on the scene, as he notes, under the rubric of the 'end of history', and an ensuing cynicism when the 'metaphor of architecture' collapsed. He became aware of Kant, he informs us, only after 'architecture as metaphor' collapsed. Therefore, 'it is the Kantian transcendental critique that is called for', which led him to reevaluate his previous work.[5] This Kantian transcendental critique will include Marx. Marx appears on the stage unambiguously to be named as a *transcendental* thinker whose *Capital* is in essence nothing but a *transcendental* critique. Kant and Marx are conspicuously present in Karatani's *Architecture as Metaphor*.

With *Architecture as Metaphor*, Karatani proclaimed his arrival at Kant's critical philosophy. A more comprehensive exposition on Kant had to wait until his later book *Transcritique: On Kant and Marx*, published in 2003.[6] In the latter he offers a novel interpretation of the 'Kantian Copernican turn' and transcendental philosophy and a rigorous reading of Marx with Kant through a conceptual category he coined as *transcritique*. In his work, Karatani renews the much-forgotten 'Kantian Marxism'. In *Architecture as Metaphor*, he would nevertheless use the occasion to foreground the much-contested Kantian notion of the 'thing-in-itself' that he will treat more comprehensively in *Transcritique*. However, it is in the earlier book that we come to understand Kant's philosophy as the 'critique' of a long tradition of the old 'architecture metaphor' in philosophy.

In the present book I am mainly concerned with the theses in *Architecture as Metaphor* on Kant and Marx later enriched in *Transcritique: On Kant and Marx*. Here I should point out that Karatani referred back to *Architecture as Metaphor* only in *Transcritique: On Kant and Marx*. The central argument here is that Kant inaugurated a break in the traditional notion of the 'metaphor of architecture' in philosophy. We owe this insight mainly to Karatani. On this point, today, we must read Kant through Karatani, not only for the idea of the relation of philosophy to architecture but more importantly for an interpretation of Kant that bypasses most of the academic interpretations, which are abundant and copious. We must grant it to Karatani that he is an *architectonic* thinker. By his own admission in his later work, not discussed in the present book, Karatani becomes a '*systematic* thinker'. He once declared that 'We must never give up the "will to architecture"'.[7] This very statement constitutes 'Karatani's philosophy of architecture'. He never claimed that his *Architecture as Metaphor* is a text for architects. For that matter, I aim the present work primarily at philosophers and only secondarily to scholars in the field of architecture.

Architecture as Metaphor and *Transcritique: On Kant and Marx* were both written, as Karatani says, in his capacity as a 'literary critic'. In this regard, his important book on Marx first published in Japanese in 1974, translated into English in 2020, entitled *Marx: Towards the Center of Possibility*, was also written when he was still a literary critic.[8] It is only

with his major 'monumental' work (as Fredric Jameson calls it) entitled
The Structure of World History, published in 2014, that Karatani abandoned his academic position as a 'literary critic' to become, as mentioned, a *systematic* thinker writing as a theorist.[9] In the Preface to the
latter work he writes:

> Accordingly, in taking up the problem of the structure of the world
> history, I felt the need to construct my own theoretical system. I have
> always disliked systematic undertakings and was never particularly
> good at them. Nonetheless, I am now for the first time in my life
> venturing to construct a theoretical system. This is because the prob-
> lem I am wrestling with here can only be explicated systematically.[10]

Karatani later published his *Isonomia and the Origins of Philosophy*. This
book was intended to clarify and expand on the notion of '*Isonomia*' that
he had mentioned only in passing in *The Structure of World History*.[11] It
is a work which stands on its own in posing an enormous challenge to
the reception of Plato at the origin of Western philosophy and has radical
political implications. In between these works, Karatani published
Nation and Aesthetics: On Kant and Freud in 2017, a book of collected
essays he had published in previous years, in which he applies his *transcritique* to read Freud through Kant in order to shed light on the notion
of nation in relation to aesthetics.

In the present work I am mainly concerned with *Architecture as
Metaphor* with occasional references to *Transcritique: On Kant and
Marx*. To reiterate, this is an investigation into the relation of philosophy
to architecture and the concept of architectonics in a sustained reference
to Kantian philosophy as read and interpreted by Karatani.[12]

Notes

1 See Immanuel Kant, *Critique of Pure of Reason*, trans. and eds. Paul Guyer
and Allen W. Wood (Cambridge: Cambridge University Press, 1998).
2 Kōjin Karatani, *Architecture as Metaphor: Language, Number, Money*, trans.
Sabu Kohso, ed. Michael Speaks (Cambridge: The MIT Press, 1995).
3 Kōjin Karatani, *Architecture as Metaphor*, xl.
4 Kōjin Karatani, *Architecture as Metaphor*, xl.
5 Kōjin Karatani, *Architecture as Metaphor*, xli.
6 Kōjin Karatani, *Transcritique: On Kant and Marx*, trans. Sabu Kohso
(Cambridge: The MIT Press, 2003).
7 Graciously responding to my invitation, Karatani made this statement in an
article that I asked him to contribute to the book I was editing; see Kōjin
Karatani, 'Rethinking City Planning and Utopianism', in Nadir Lahiji, ed. *The*

Political Unconscious of Architecture: Re-opening Jameson's Narrative (Surrey: Ashgate, 2011), 170.

8 See Kōjin Karatani, *Marx: Towards the Center of Possibility*, ed., trans., with an intro. Gavin Walker (London and New York: Verso, 2020).

9 See Kōjin Karatani, *The Structure of World History: From Modes of Production to Modes of Exchange*, trans. Michael K. Bourdaghs (Durham and London: Duke University, 2014).

10 Kōjin Karatani, *The Structure of World History*, xvi.

11 See Kōjin Karatani, *Isonomia and the Origins of Philosophy*, trans. Joseph A. Murphy (Durham and London: Duke University Press, 2017).

12 This book is to be followed by a forthcoming one which will be devoted to Karatani's singular reading of Marx, tentatively titled *Kōjin Karatani's Reconstruction of Marx, An Introduction*.

ACKNOWLEDGEMENT

The publication of this book was initially supported by Francesca Ford, the senior publisher at Routledge, to whom I am indebted.

I enjoyed the help of the editorial assistant Hannah Studd throughout in preparation of the manuscript for its production. Many thanks for her diligent work through this process.

Kristina Wischenkamper went through the early draft of the manuscript. I am grateful to her for the thorough and meticulous editorial intervention she made.

INTRODUCTION

From *Sophia* to the *Will to Architecture*

From the Ancient Greeks we have inherited an understanding of the word *philosophy* as *Sophia*—'wisdom'. Thales, a friend of Anaximander, was known as a sage—*Sophoi*. He was a mathematician and a technologist, but also a politician, and as such it would be wrong to limit his *Sophia* to a technical expertise.[1] At the same time, ancient Greek philosophy was always concerned with what we call the 'theory of knowledge', or *epistemology*, derived from the Greek *epistēmē*, and *logos*. Hence we obtain the 'opposition of knowledge to wisdom'. The theory of knowledge, to put it precisely, is the problem of 'how to formulate a systematic theory of philosophy', which has become central to *critical philosophy*.[2] Aristotle in his *Nicomachean Ethics*, making a distinction between 'philosophical wisdom' and 'practical wisdom', wrote that

> philosophic wisdom is scientific knowledge, combined with intuitive reason, of the things that are highest by nature. This is why we say Anaxagoras, Thales, and men like them have philosophic but not practical wisdom, when we see them ignorant of what is to their own advantage, and why we say that they know things that are remarkable, admirable, difficult, and divine, but useless; viz because it is not human goods that they seek.[3]

'Practical wisdom', Aristotle added, 'on the other hand is concerned with things human and things about which it is possible to deliberate', and further on,

> political wisdom and practical wisdom are the same state of mind, but their essence is not the same. Of the wisdom concerned with the city, the practical wisdom which plays a controlling part is legislative wisdom, while that which is related to this as particulars to their universal is known by the general name "political wisdom"; this has to

DOI: 10.4324/9781032647616-1

do with action and deliberation, for a decree is a thing to be carried out in the form of an individual act.[4]

Under the term '*Wisdom*', Aristotle further wrote that

> (1) in the arts we ascribe to their most finished exponents, e.g. to Phidias as a sculptor and to Polyclitus as a maker of portrait-statue, and here we mean nothing by wisdom except excellence in art; but (2) we think that some people are wise in general, not in some **particular** field or in any other limited respect, as Homer says in the *Margites*, "Him did the gods make neither a digger nor yet a ploughman Nor wise in anything else." Therefore wisdom must plainly be the most finished of the forms of knowledge. It follows that the wise man must not only know what follows from the first principles, but must also possess truth about the first principles. Therefore wisdom must be intuitive reason combined with scientific knowledge—scientific knowledge of the highest objects which has received as it were its proper completion.[5]

Prior to this passage, Aristotle stated the following about architecture:

> Now since architecture is an art and is essentially a reasoned sate of capacity to make, and there is neither any art that is not such a state nor any such state that is not an art, *art* is identical with a state of capacity to make, involving a true course of reasoning.[6]

Still, for the same philosophical notion of *Sophia*, we must go back a bit in time before Aristotle. Jean-Pierre Vernant in his *The Origins of Greek Thought* discusses certain aspects of the 'Mycenean reality', the origin of the search for a 'balance and accommodation between the opposing forces', between the 'silent *demos*' and the 'palace-centered system', between social forces with which the power had to come to terms, the elements indicating a time of troubles that would give rise to 'moral thought and political speculation' that constituted an early form of human 'wisdom'. He explains that

> This *sophia* appeared as early as the dawn of the seventh century, and was associated with a rather odd assortment of figures who came to be clothed with an almost legendary radiance and whom the Greeks continued to revere as their first true sages. *Sophia* was concerned not with the universe of *physis* [nature] but with the human world: the elements that made it up, the forces that divided it against itself, and the means by which they might be harmonized and unified so that their conflict might give birth to the human order of the city.[7]

In Athens, 'democracy' was established and Athenian society was known as a place for the art of rhetoric, oratory. The teachers of this art came to be known as Sophists, persuading people by ruling them. But the art of rhetoric had been developed in Ionia.[8] In Athens, Socrates was labeled a 'sophist'. But Socrates, being such only theoretically, had opposed the sophists. Being more concerned about the moral nature of man he would change the name 'Sophia' to 'Philosophia', *philosophy*, or the love of wisdom. We need not go any further into this etymological history. It is sufficient for my purposes to make the point that it was Kōjin Karatani who some 30 years ago introduced a *different* definition of philosophy in his *Architecture as Metaphor* published in 1995. There, Karatani *critically* defined philosophy, not in association with Sophia, but as the *will to architecture*. In this novel definition resides the notion that in Western thought a *crisis* persistently reveals itself with every attempt to build a system of knowledge. Karatani begins *Architecture as Metaphor* by bringing out a new interpretation of Plato's specific use of the 'architecture metaphor' by pointing out that 'For Plato, architecture meant, more than anything else, an active position that enables one to resist or withstand all "becomings" by reconstructing them as "making"'. He cites Plato from *The Republic*:

> By its original meaning [*poiesis*] means simply creation, and creation, as you know, can take very various forms. Any creation which is the cause of a thing emerging from non-existence into existence might be called [*poiesis*], and all the processes in all the crafts are kinds of [*poeisis*], and all those who are engaged in them [creator].[9]

Plato, Karatani reminds us,

> likened philosophers who took such a position to architects. Yet, like other Athenians of his time, Plato despised the manual labor involved in building. Unlike the substantial materiality of architecture, which belongs to the realm of what we might call 'semi-becoming,' Platonic architecture is metaphorical'.[10]

Karatani makes a central argument with which I will be concerned in this investigation, that is, 'Plato's use of the metaphor of architecture, like that of Descartes, Kant, and Hegel who followed him, should thus be understood as the will to *construct an edifice of knowledge on a solid foundation*'[11] [emphasis mine]. Noting that this 'will to architecture' is attributed to Plato, Karatani briefly describes that in ancient Greek, the term *architectonicé* (architecture) is 'constructed from *architectonicé techné*, which signifies *techné of architechtón, architectón* being a compound of *arché* (origin, [first]principle, primacy) and *tectón* (craftsman [mainly a carpenter])'.[12] As Karatani points out, in his metaphor of architecture Plato 'discovered a figure that under the aegis of "Making" is able to withstand becoming'.[13] However, the etymological account, as Karatani rightly notes, is not adequate to explain why Plato 'regarded architecture as a figure of philosophy par excellence, or to explain why this figure is obsessively repeated in philosophical and theoretical discourse', adding that 'Plato disdained both architecture and the real-life architect'.[14]

After long neglect, we must come to recognize the unique contribution that Karatani has made, not only to the illumination of Kantian critical philosophy but more importantly to Kant's transformative moment on the fate of the 'architecture metaphor' in the philosophical tradition. It is well known, as cited previously, that philosophers since Plato have returned time and again to building analogies to use architectural figures and metaphors 'as a way of grounding and stabilizing their otherwise unstable philosophical system'.[15] This is the crux of the matter. The employment of this analogy after Descartes's extensive uses of it takes a different turn in classical German philosophy. Kant's introduction of the concept *architectonics* located in 'human reason' was later taken up in post-Kantian idealism, from Schelling to Fichte, and to Hegel, who believed that 'knowledge must be systematic, architectonic'.[16]

My point of departure for this study is the key statement made early in *Architecture as Metaphor* where Karatani first notes that Plato miserably failed to implement his idea of the 'philosopher-king'—which actually goes back to Pythagoras—and makes the following remarks:

> All of this demonstrates the impossibility of the *being* of the *ideal* and yet, at the same time, it repeatedly invokes the *will to architecture* by asserting that the impossible, the *being* of the *ideal*, be realized. This *will to architecture* is the foundation of Western thought.[17]

For Karatani, philosophy is just another name for this *will to architecture* when an attempt is made to build the *edifice of knowledge* on a *solid foundation*.[18] But it must be noted that this foundation is never a secure one. For my part, I examine the *idea* of this 'will to architecture' by tracing reason in its center and explore its *ethical* implications. But what is important to keep in mind is that in the history of Western thought, as Karatani informs us, this 'will to architecture' is 'reiterated and renewed at times of crisis'.[19] To illustrate this, Karatani identifies a consequential intellectual moment in the early twentieth century in mathematical thought that he relates to the conception of *architectonics*. He writes: 'Architecture as a metaphor dominated mathematics and even architecture itself until 1931, when Kurt Gödel's incompleteness theorem unvalidated mathematics as the ground for the architectonic'.[20] The implications of this extraordinary exposition are far reaching. They contain the core of Platonism, the problem of *foundationalism* and mathematics. In the following chapters I attempt to examine them in the context of German idealism and the 'authority of reason', and ultimately the 'vindication of reason' in Kant. In conjunction with the foregoing remarks, Karatani makes another statement that is crucial for this study: '*architectonics as metaphor is indispensable to the critique of architecture as metaphor*'[21] (my emphasis). This thesis effectively changes the terms of the 'metaphor of architecture' as traditionally understood in the philosophical tradition from Plato to Descartes, up to Kant. It foregrounds the break effected by Kant with his introduction of *architectonics* in *Critique of Pure Reason*. In the center of it resides the 'limits of reason' linked to *critique*—it can be said that 'reason of critique' is 'critique of reason' by reason itself.[22]

Before I proceed, I pause here to state the scope of my investigation in the present work. Influenced and guided by Karatani's ideas, I will deal with certain aspects in Kant's philosophy into which Karatani does not enter in his *Architecture as Metaphor*. I therefore attempt to expand on his original insights in this work. I examine the relation between the 'faculty' of architecture and the 'faculty' of philosophy, for which I study the last work that Kant published, in 1798, *The Conflict of the Faculties*, where he calls philosophy the 'lower faculty' and discusses its relation to law, theology, and medicine, which he names the 'higher faculties'. I locate the 'faculty' of architecture between them and will examine its particular status. Needless to say, in the center of the division between the faculties lies the idea of 'public reason' that Kant had already discussed in his 'journalistic' essay titled 'What Is Enlightenment?' On the one hand, that division and the question of reason had something to do with the power of the state and the problem of censorship in Kant's time. My intention in this is to advance the thesis that whenever we talk about 'philosophy' we are at the same time talking about 'architecture' before its 'metaphor'. This is because at stake is always, to use Karatani's term, the problem of a 'crisis of foundation'. This foundation persistently remains *unstable*. On the same line of thought I renew an old question: Who is the 'philosopher', and who is the 'architect'? This question leads me to a reading of Paul Valéry's famous dialogues of 'Eupalinos, or the Architect'; this has been never attempted before.

Karatani begins his reflections on the category of *architectonics* with the 'triadic concept' in Kant's *transcendental* philosophy. He writes:

> The fact that Kant's triadic concept [i.e., 'thing-in-itself', 'phenomenon', and *'Schein'*] is replaceable with different triads indicates that it forms a kind of structure that can be grasped transcendentally. Kant called this structure 'architectonics'. While philosophical discourses generally disregard rhetoric in order to achieve their much-desired precision, and philosophers, especially those who emerged after Kant, sought to do away with figurative expression, Kant's critique is marked by the omnipresence of the 'metaphor'.[23]

Citing a passage from *Critique of the Power of Judgement*, Karatani explains how Kant employed architectonics as a metaphor. I quote here the entire paragraph to give it a proper context.

> A critique of pure reason, i.e., of our faculty for judging in accordance with *a priori* principles, would be incomplete if the power of judgment, which also claims to be a faculty of cognition, were not dealt with as a special part of it, e ven though its principles may not constitute a special part of a system of pure philosophy, between the theoretical and practical part, but can occasionally be annexed to either of them in case of need. For if such system, under the general name of metaphysics, is ever to come into being (the complete production of which is entirely possible and highly important for the use of reason in all respects), then the critique must previously have probed the ground for this structure down to the depth of first foundations of the faculty of principles independent of experience, so that it should not sink in any part, which would inevitably lead to the collapse of the whole.[24]

Karatani notes that Kant in this passage might appear to incline toward the 'Platonic use of architecture as metaphor', but in fact the opposite is the case. According to Karatani, Kant claimed in the *Critique of Pure Reason* that his investigation could not 'properly be called a doctrine, but should instead be called *transcendental critique*'[25] (my emphasis). This is the crux of the matter. Because 'Kant's critiques were not intended to construct a system but to reveal that any system "inevitably bring[s] with it the ruin of all" inasmuch as it is upheld under the aegis of the "arrogation of reason"', and further, 'Since "arrogation" is a juridical term, Kant's architectonics might also be substituted by a set of juridical metaphors', and therefore, what must be noted, as quoted previously, is that 'architectonics as metaphor is indispensable to the critique of architecture as metaphor'.[26] The latter point constitutes the main element in Karatani's contribution regarding the *critique* of the 'metaphor of architectonics' in philosophy that would need to be elucidated by a further investigation into the categories of 'reason' and 'foundation'. Suffice it to say here that 'architectonics' must be studied in relation to the 'limit of reason' in Kant.

In the light of the fact that in our time *reason* has entered into a *crisis*, a time characterized as 'postmodern *un*reason', it is all more important that Karatani's invocation of 'the will to architecture' prompted by his *return* to Kant be reiterated. This return is a necessary one, as Terry Pinkard has reminded us, because 'After Kant, nothing would be the same again'.[27]

The *crisis* in its instance in the early twentieth century returned to philosophy in the late twentieth century prompted by certain political and philosophical mutations. It is therefore proper to call for a *reiteration* of the *will to architecture* supported by a *retrieval of architectonics* in philosophy. This reiteration must be directed against the dominant postmodern relativist-deconstructionist tendency, the so-called 'post-philosophical' thought, a trend that Alain Badiou in his *Manifesto for Philosophy* characterized as the age of 'new sophists' that he calls 'antiphilosophy'.[28] Ironically, Badiou, who loathes Kant, has made a clear statement on the necessity of 'architectonics' in philosophy. In *Manifesto for Philosophy* he took Jean-François Lyotard to task for once saying, 'Philosophy as architecture is ruined'. To which Badiou retorts: 'is it however possible to imagine a philosophy that is not in the least architectonic?'[29] In this statement, Badiou unmistakably sounds like a Kantian—perhaps he is a 'Kantian' thinker in spite of himself. What I want to say here is that Badiou, precisely because of his anti-Kantian standpoint, does not go further in bringing up the necessity of 'architectonics' in *any* philosophy worth its name. From the Kantian standpoint, expressed forcefully in the section 'The Architectonic of Pure Reason' of his *Critique of Pure Reason*, *critical philosophy* is grounded in the 'architectonic of human reason'—not 'philosophy as it exists', but philosophy as a 'general delineation or outline' of the system of human reason.[30] Badiou himself, 30 years after his *Manifesto for Philosophy*, declared that in our contemporary world, in 2022, 'philosophy is in crisis'. The 'world', he says, is facing a 'catastrophe'. And he is absolutely right.[31] Departing from the Kantian point of view, I claim that this *crisis* is in fact the crisis in the 'architectonic of human reason'. Here I should point out in passing that I consider Badiou's philosophy, in spite of its anti-Kantian stand, to be one of the strongest statements of the 'will to architecture', which attempts to *systematically* put the edifice of knowledge on a solid foundation through establishing the idea of *truths* stated in his four 'conditions' for philosophy.

Disorientation in much of philosophy in the late twentieth century may be attributed to the eclipse, or better, the *weakening* of the *will to architecture*. Its sources can be traced back to Friedrich Nietzsche and his postmodern followers in the late twentieth century, from George Bataille to Michel Foucault to Gilles Deleuze to Jacques Derrida—with certain reservations on Derrida. Nietzsche, an anti-Kantian and a harsh critic of Socrates and Platonic reason, is the same (anti)philosopher who in his 'On the Truth and Lies in a Nonmoral Sense' wrote the following that would ironically put him in affinity with Kant's 'constructivism'.[32] He wrote:

> *Here one may certainly admire man as a mighty genius of construction*, who succeeded in piling up an infinitely complicated dome of concepts upon an unstable foundation, and as it were, on running water. Of course, in order to be supported by such a foundation, his construction must be like one constructed by spiders' webs: delicate enough to be carried along by the waves, strong enough not to be blown apart by every wind. As a genius of construction man raises himself far above the bee in the following way: whereas the bee builds with wax that he gathers from nature, man builds with the far more delicate conceptual materials which he first has to manufacture from himself. In this he is greatly to be admired, but not on account of his drive for truth or for pure knowledge of things[33] [emphasis mine].

By 'man' Nietzsche of course meant the figure of the philosopher. Interestingly enough, Nietzsche pretended that he did not know that we can actually build a 'foundation' and have the 'running water' around it! Standing with the skeptics against Kant, Nietzsche wanted to undermine the 'grounded building'. The anti-reason thinker, Nietzsche, would not bring himself to cite Kant's famous remarks in the 'Preface' to his *Prolegomena to Any Future Metaphysics*, which goes as follows:

> Human reason, so delights in *constructions* that it has several times built up a tower and then razed it to examine the nature of the *foundation*. It is never too late to become reasonable and wise; but if the insight comes late, there is always more difficulty in starting the change.[34] [emphasis mine]

I will return to this key passage in a later chapter. Here it must be said that we might take Nietzsche's statement as an exposition of 'architectonics' that demands a constant examination when built on an unstable 'foundation'. I might add in passing that perhaps Nietzsche desired to be an 'architect', but alas, he would be a 'failed' one! At the same time, perhaps he was also a 'failed' philosopher, or an 'anti-philosopher' as Badiou names him. Still another kind of 'failure' may be attributed to him, as Karatani notes citing what Nietzsche wrote in *On the Genealogy of Morals* and *Beyond Good and Evil*, where he 'rebuked morals as the ressentiment of the weak'. Karatani writes that 'In the most straightforward interpretation, Nietzsche himself, who failed as scholar and suffered from syphilis, was nothing but "the weak"'.[35] Yet, as Karatani admits, the 'case is not that simple'. 'To him', Karatani writes,

'the strong' or the überman is the one who accepts such a miserable life as one's own creation in the place of attributing it to someone else or to given conditions. This is his formula of *amor fati*. The überman is not an exceptional human. And *amor fati* is the stance to accept one's destiny determined by external causes (nature) as if it were derivative of one's free will (consistent with the principle of *causa sui*), in Kantian terms.[36]

Going back to Nietzsche's 'architectonic-sounding' remarks given previously, we must note his harsh stand against reason with some romantic resonances, which has not escaped Karatani, who writes that 'For Nietzsche, the Greek side of the equation could not be so easily identified as rational', citing paragraph 10 from *Twilight of the Idols* where Nietzsche wrote:

If one needs to make a tyrant of *reason*, as Socrates did, then there must exist no little danger of something else playing the tyrant. Rationality was at that time divined as a *saviour*; neither Socrates nor his 'invalids' were free to be rational or not, as they wished—it was *de rigueur*, it was their *last* expedient. The fanaticism with which the whole of Greek thought throws itself at rationality betrays a state of emergency: one was in peril, one had only *one* choice: either to perish or—be *absurdly rational*. … The moralism of the Greek philosophers from Plato downwards is pathologically conditioned: likewise their estimation of dialectics. Reason = virtue = happiness means merely: one must imitate Socrates and counter the dark desires by producing a permanent *daylight*—the daylight of reason. One must be prudent, clear, bright at any cost: ever yielding to the instincts, to the unconscious, leads downwards …[37]

Karatani comments that 'Nietzsche discovered that the will to architecture, which appears to characterize the West, is itself irrational, despite the appearance that it derives from an ostensibly rational will'.[38] Remarking on the relation between Greek, Christianity, and Hebraic tradition, he notes that 'this commonly held view—that Western thought is a synthesis of *rational* Greek and *irrational* Hebrew—can in no way account for the obsessive recurrence of the will to architecture in philosophy'.[39] And further he notes that

> Nietzsche's assessment of Christianity as a vulgar Platonism is indeed much more aggressive than the more general view that divides the Hellenic and the Hebraic into a clear-cut dichotomy. One wonders if another origin is veiled behind the origins of the Western as such.[40]

On this point Karatani offers the following thoughts:

> I propose the following view: Plato was no doubt in the minority of Greek thinkers. His belief that architecture could stave off becoming must have appeared abruptly and completely out of the context of Greek thought in general—it must have come from Greece's exterior, from Egypt, where immortality of spirit, monotheism, and state-controlled planning originated. The platonic notion of the philosopher/king itself can be traced to Egypt. Signs of Egyptian influence can also be discovered at the origin of Judeo-Christianity. Freud, for example, in *Moses and Monotheism*, argued that Moses, who was raised Egyptian and monotheistic, was murdered en route from Egypt. Moses's murder initiated a kind of structure of repetition that Freud called the 'return of the repressed'. From a Freudian perspective, these two fundamental tenets of Western thought—Judaism and Christianity—originated in Egypt, and it is their origin that has been so strictly repressed and that continues to obsessively return.[41]

He further remarks:

> My concern here, however, is not with these historical retrospections—not least because they are not persuasive enough to be truly fertile—but with pursuing a totally different line of inquiry, one that is compelled by reconsidering the importance of formalism for the major thinkers of this century [the twentieth century]. Nietzsche attempted to restore the pre-Socratic—the 'philosophers in the tragic age' whom Plato had suppressed. Nietzsche established the prototypical critique of Platonism, but Nietzsche's critique overlooked something: the paradoxical fact—revealed unintentionally by Nietzsche's Platonist contemporaries—that the *'will to construct a solid edifice' ultimately does not achieve a foundation, but reveals instead the very absence of its foundation.*[42] [emphasis mine]

'What is overlooked in the return to Nietzsche initiated by poststructuralism', Karatani claims, 'is Nietzsche's internalized romanticist disposition; it is from this reconsideration that we are today reinterpreting him'.[43] And further, 'In opposition to reason, romanticists regard as essential the manifold and contingency—immanent in concepts like body, affect, feeling, and the like'.[44] In sum, in Kantian terms, it comes to this important point that 'it is only reason itself that can deconstruct reason'. This is the point I will reiterate throughout this study. And along with it, I will be following closely Karatani's contention that 'without a formal procedure or method, all critique directed at the will to architecture, no matter how obsessively repeated, will invariably devolve into romanticism'.[45]

My contention throughout is that against the 'post-philosophical thought', Kant's *architectonics* as a 'metaphor' should be upheld as the 'condition of possibility' of philosophy. Slavoj Žižek once reminded us that not only philosophy but 'everything hangs on the answer to this related question: is it possible today, apropos of the postmodern age of new sophists, to repeat mutatis mutandis the Kantian gesture?'[46] Karatani's intention in raising the Kantian question is ultimately a *political* one. What he articulated in the 'Afterword' to *Architecture as Metaphor* attests to it, and also explains why he has devoted important chapters to Marx in the book. His 'Afterword' is central to my investigation, lurking in the background throughout. Karatani brings up the Hegelian *Idee* and notes that Marxism is a variant of it. He asks if 'what has taken place after 1989 is the disintegration of the *Idee*?' He thinks not. As opposed to Hegelian 'world history' we got the 'end of history' and 'cynicism' that denies and scorns *Idee*. Therefore, Karatani argues that 'it is in this context that the reassessment of *Idee* becomes urgent'.[47] It is for this reason that he urges a return to Kant's 'thing-in-itself'. He writes: 'However, what is important is that the concept of the "thing-in-itself" was proposed by Kant, less as an account of the true world, as with Plato's *idea*, than as the basis upon which to criticize all the ideation as *Schein*'.[48] He informs us that Kant did not deny *Idee* only to claim that *Idee* is necessarily a *Schein* that 'functions "regulatively", though it cannot be proven theoretically and must never be realized "constitutively"'.[49] Karatani points out that after Kant, the 'thing-in-itself' was ignored, and instead the Hegelian position emerged in which '*Idee* is realistic and the real is ideation'. I come back to these points in the Epilogue to this work.

The foregoing reflections in *Architecture as Metaphor* are Karatani's attempt to establish a connection between Kant and Marx that more fully was later elaborated in his *Transcritique: On Marx and Kant*. The conclusion that I draw from these reflections will serve as the foundation for the argument in this study centered on the notion that the *Idee*, both in architecture and philosophy, is *Schein*, an illusion, which is nevertheless a *necessary* illusion. Hence I go back to the beginning of Karatani's argument where he stated, as cited previously, 'the impossibility of the *being* of the *Ideal'*, that nevertheless, 'repeatedly invokes the *will of architecture'*, insisting that the 'impossible', that is, '*being* of the *ideal'*, to be realized.

Notes

1 See Kōjin Karatani, *Isonomia and the Origins of Philosophy*, trans. Joseph A. Murphy (Durham and London: Duke University Press, 2017).
2 See Tom Rockmore, *Before and After Hegel: A Historical Introduction to Hegel's Thought* (Indianapolis/Cambridge: Hackett, 1993), 5.
3 See Aristotle, *Nicomachean Ethics*, in *The Basic Works of Aristotle*, ed. Richard McKeon, intro. C. D. C. Beeve (New York: The Modern Library, 2001), 1028.
4 Aristotle, *Nicomachean Ethics*, 1029.
5 Aristotle, *Nicomachean Ethics*, 1027–1028.
6 Aristotle, *Nicomachean Ethics*, 1025. Aristotle adds,

> All art is concerned with coming into being, i.e., with contriving and considering how something may come into being which is capable of either being or not being, and whose origin is in the maker and not in the thing made; for art is concerned neither with things that are, or come into being, by necessity, nor with things that do so in accordance with nature (since these have their origin in themselves). Making and acting being different, art must be a matter of making, not of acting, 1025.

7 See Jean-Pierre Vernant, *The Origins of Greek Thought* (Ithaca: Cornell University Press, 1982), 40.
8 Regarding this point, Karatani in *Isonomia and the Origins of Philosophy* writes that 'It is under democracy (majority rule) that rhetoric becomes a means of ruling over other people. However, this was not the case in Ionia, where the arts of rhetoric were developed', 108. This subject is much more complex, as Karatani has masterfully developed, so that I need not enter into it here.
9 Kōjin Karatani, 'Introduction to the English Edition' in *Architecture as Metaphor, Language, Number, Money*, trans. Sabu Kohso, ed. Michael Speak (Cambridge: The MIT Press, 1995), xxx–xxxi. Also see Plato, 'Republic' in *Complete Works*, ed. John M. Cooper (Indianapolis and Cambridge: Hackett, 1997).
10 Kōjin Karatani, *Architecture as Metaphor*, xxxi.
11 Kōjin Karatani, *Architecture as Metaphor*, xxxi.
12 Kōjin Karatani, *Architecture as Metaphor*, 4. Karatani further explains that 'Among Greeks, architecture was considered not merely a skill of craftsmen but an art practiced by those who possess a principal knowledge and mastery of all technologies, and who therefore plan projects and lead other craftsmen. In this context the term *techné* meant not only technology in a narrow sense but also *poeisis* (making) in general', 4, 5.
13 Kōjin Karatani, *Architecture as Metaphor*, 5.
14 Kōjin Karatani, *Architecture as Metaphor*, 5.
15 Kōjin Karatani, *Architecture as Metaphor*, 4.
16 Kōjin Karatani, *Architecture as Metaphor*, 4.
17 Kōjin Karatani, *Architecture as Metaphor*, xxxv.

18 Kōjin Karatani, *Architecture as Metaphor*, xxxii.
19 Kōjin Karatani, *Architecture as Metaphor*, 5.
20 Kōjin Karatani, *Architecture as Metaphor*, xxxii.
21 Kōjin Karatani, *Architecture as Metaphor*, xliv.
22 This problem of 'reason' called the 'authority of reason' is explored in the excellent study by Frederich C. Beiser, *The Fate of Reason: German Philosophy from Kant to Fichte* (Cambridge: Harvard University Press, 1987).
23 Kōjin Karatani, *Architecture as Metaphor*, xliii
24 Immanuel Kant, *Critique of the Power of Judgment*, ed. Paul Guyer, trans. Paul Guyer and Eric Mathews (Cambridge: Cambridge University Press, 2000), 56. For partial citation of the same passage in which Karatani uses a different translation see Kōjin Karatani, *Architecture as Metaphor*, xliii.
25 Kōjin Karatani, *Architecture as Metaphor*, xliii–xliv.
26 Kōjin Karatani, *Architecture as Metaphor*, xliv.
27 See Terry Pinkard, *German Philosophy, 1760–1860: The Legacy of Idealism* (Cambridge: Cambridge University Press, 2002), 15.
28 See Alain Badiou, *Manifesto for Philosophy*, trans. and ed. with intro. Norman Madarasz (Albany: State University of New York Press, 1999).
29 Alain Badiou, *Manifesto for Philosophy*, 28.
30 See the entry 'Architectonic' in Howard Caygill, *A Kant Dictionary* (Oxford: Blackwell, 1995).
31 See *Badiou by Badiou*, trans. Bruno Bosteels (Sandford: Sandford University Press, 2022). In this respect Badiou writes:

> It is not just the end of the nineteenth and twentieth centuries; it is the end of the world of social classes. Of inequalities, of state power, of the subservience to science and technology, of private property colonizing everything, of senseless and criminal war. […] Our problem therefore is that this world has witnessed the birth and development of the conditions of philosophy, as well as of philosophy itself, and this is a world that is also its nihilistic use. *Philosophy is in crisis, this much is evident*, 27 (my emphasis).

32 I adopt the notion of 'constructivism' in Kant from Tom Rockmore in his *In Kant's Wake, Philosophy in the Twentieth Century* (Malden: Blackwell, 2006).
33 See Freidrich Nietzsche, *Philosophy and Truth: Selections from Nietzsche Notebooks of the Early 1870's*, ed. and trans. Daniel Breazeale (Amherst: Humanity Books, 1999), 85.
34 See Immanuel Kant, *Prolegomena to Any Future Metaphysics*, second edition, and "Letter to Marcus Herz," February 1772, trans. with intro. and notes, James W. Ellington (Indianapolis/Cambridge, 1977), 2.
35 Kōjin Karatani, *Transcritique: On Kant and Marx*, 122–123.
36 Kōjin Karatani, *Transcritique: On Kant and Marx*, 123.
37 In Nietzsche, *Twilight of the Idols and Anti-Christ*, trans. and intro. R. J. Hollingdale (Middlesex: Penguin Books, 1968), 33; also see Kōjin Karatani, *Architecture as Metaphor*, 7.
38 Kōjin Karatani, *Architecture as Metaphor*, 7.
39 Kōjin Karatani, *Architecture as Metaphor*, 7.
40 Kōjin Karatani, *Architecture as Metaphor*, 7.
41 Kōjin Karatani, *Architecture as Metaphor*, 8.
42 Kōjin Karatani, *Architecture as Metaphor*, 8.
43 Kōjin Karatani, *Architecture as Metaphor*, 9.
44 Kōjin Karatani, *Architecture as Metaphor*, 9.
45 Kōjin Karatani, *Architecture as Metaphor*, 9.

46 See Slavoj Žižek, *Tarrying with the Negative: Kant, Hagel, and Critique of Ideology* (Durham: Duke University Press, 1993), 5. Žižek poses his question in a larger context to risk a 'hyperbole' that 'in a sense, *everything*, from the fate of so-called 'Western civilization' up to the survival of humanity in the ecological crisis, hangs on the answer to this question: Is it possible today, apropos of the postmodern age of new sophists, to repeat mutatis mutandis the Kantian gesture?', 5.

47 Kōjin Karatani, *Architecture as Metaphor*, 185.

48 Kōjin Karatani, *Architecture as Metaphor*, 185.

49 Kōjin Karatani, *Architecture as Metaphor*, 185–186.

1

FOUNDATIONALISM, REASON, AND BUILDING METAPHOR

In the philosophical tradition called foundationalism, knowledge must be *systematic*, and its *edifice* must be built on a solid foundation. It is believed that this foundation is secure, firm, and unshakable on which one erects the edifice of knowledge. A significant feature rules over this theory of knowledge. It resorts to a 'building metaphor', over and over again, in an attempt to suggest that its edifice of knowledge is resting on firm ground. In this epistemology, *reason* is believed to be a *self-evident first principle*. Kant's project of a 'critique of pure reason' and his 'vindication of reason' will forever change this metaphysical foundation of knowledge by employing a different notion of 'building analogy'.

A belief rooted in the age of Enlightenment came with its faith in the 'authority of reason', as pointed out by Frederick Beiser in his *Fate of Reason: German Philosophy from Kant to Fichte*.[1] He writes, 'Reason had self-evident first principles; it could criticize all our beliefs; it could justify morality, religion, and the state; it was universal and impartial; and it could, at least in theory, explain everything in nature'.[2] Kant and Spinoza were thought to be the prominent exponents of the Age of Enlightenment, and their philosophies were regarded to be the 'bulwarks of the authority of reason'. As Beiser notes, Spinoza offered a model which defined reason in terms of the principle of *sufficient reason*, which was interpreted in a

> strictly mechanistic fashion, so that it read 'for any event B there must be some prior event A, such that given A, B occurs of necessity'. If this principle is universalized, however, it leads to atheism and fatalism; for God and freedom must be self-causing agencies, causes that act without a prior cause.[3]

In this age, 'Philosophers predicted that the authority of reason would eventually replace the authority of tradition, revelation, and scripture

DOI: 10.4324/9781032647616-2

precisely because they believed that reason was a more effective sanction for moral, religious, and political beliefs'.[4] It must be noted in passing that much of the hostility toward Kant's philosophy in the last decade of the eighteenth century was rooted in hostility to the French Revolution and Enlightenment reason.

However, the age of Enlightenment is not only the age of *reason* but also the age of *criticism*. Kant in his Preface to the first edition of *Critique of Pure Reason* wrote:

> Our age is the genuine age of **criticism**, to which everything must submit. **Religion** through its holiness and legislation through its **majesty** commonly seek to exempt themselves from it. But in this way they excite a just suspicion against themselves, and cannot lay claim to that unfeigned respect that reason grants only to that which has been able to withstand its free and public examination.[5]

With Kant, *reason* must show up in the tribunal established by reason itself in order to set a limit to itself. Hence the Kantian *'critique'*. In critical philosophy, reason has to examine itself. In respect to this legal metaphor, Kant wrote:

> This is evidently the effect not of the thoughtlessness of our age, but of its ripened way of **power of judgment**, which will no longer be put off with illusory knowledge, and which demands that reason should take on anew the most difficult of all its tasks, namely, that of self-knowledge, and to institute a court of justice, by which reason may secure its rightful claims while dismissing all its groundless pretensions, and this not by mere decrees but according to its own eternal and unchangeable laws; and this court is none other than **critique of pure reason** itself.[6]

Kant was in fact responding to a *crisis* facing late eighteenth-century philosophy. This crisis had its origin with David Hume, the skeptic, who almost 50 years earlier had put forward his ideas in *A Treatise of Human Nature*.[7] He saw 'an irresolvable conflict between the claims of reason and faith, philosophy and life'.[8] Hume, with his skeptical reason, had concluded that 'he knew nothing more than his own passing impressions'.[9] According to Karatani, Hume radically questioned the Cartesian *ego cogito*, 'arguing that there are multiple *I*s—multiple egos in one person's being—and that identical subjectivity as such exists only customarily—such as a republic or commonwealth—as an imaginary union of the *Is.*'[10] Karatani cites what Hume wrote at the end of Book I of *A Treatise*. It goes as follows:

> We have, therefore, no choice left but betwixt a false reason and none at all. For my part, I know not what ought to be done in the present case. I can only observe what is commonly done; which is, that this difficulty is seldom or never thought of; and even where it has once been present to the mind, is quickly forgot, and leaves but a small impression behind it.[11]

In the paragraph immediately following the foregoing, Karatani finds a contradiction where Hume wrote:

> But what have I here said, that reflections very refined and metaphysical have little or no influence upon us? This opinion I can scarce forbear retracting, and condemning from my present feeling and experience. The *intense* view of these manifold contradictions and imperfections in human reason has so wrought upon me, and heated my brain, that I am ready to reject all belief and reasoning, and can look upon no opinion even as more probable or likely than another. Where am I, or what? From what causes do I derive my experience, and to what condition shall I return? Whose favour shall I court, and whose anger must I dread? What beings surround me? And on whom have I any influence, or who have any influence on me? I am confounded with all these questions, and begin to fancy myself in the most deplorable condition imaginable, environed with deepest darkness, and utterly deprived of the use of every member and faculty.[12]

Karatani comments that Hume goes on to spell out his

> contradictory feelings about skepticism: It is just empty and frivolous, it results in self-destruction, and so on. These depictions tell us that, for Hume and Descartes, to doubt was never merely some sort of intellectual puzzle. It induced in him an almost morbid state of mind.[13]

Hume wrote:

> Since reason is incapable of dispelling these clouds, nature herself suffices to that purpose, and cures me of this philosophical melancholy and delirium, either by relaxing this bent of mind, or by some

avocation, and lively impression of my senses, which obliterate all these chimeras.[14]

At the end, therefore, he says,

> I dine, I play a game of backgammon, I converse, and am merry with my friends; and when after three or four hour's amusement, I would return to these speculations, they appear so cold, and strained, and ridiculous, that I cannot find in my heart to enter into them any farther.[15]

Hume was invoked by the anti-Enlightenment to confront Kant in the late eighteenth century. They confronted Kant with the dilemma Hume expressed at the end of *A Treatise*: 'either a rational skepticism or an irrational leap of faith'. This was Hume's revenge on Kant, as Beiser puts it. 'The ghost of *le bon David* stood above the twilight of the Enlightenment only to sigh "I told you so"'.[16] Facing this dilemma, to rescue reason against its destruction, Kant resolutely offered his project of 'critique of pure reason', as noted previously, contrasting his critical project with the two tendencies of *skepticism* of the empiricists and *dogmatism* of the rationalists. The word 'dogmatism' derives from the Greek '*dogma*', which means 'belief' or 'opinion'. In Christian theology the word 'dogma' is an article of faith. But Kant uses the word 'dogmatic' in a negative sense to imply 'a belief that is held with insufficient justification, and he regarded rationalist metaphysics, which claimed to provide us with theoretical insight into how things are in themselves dogmatic in this negative sense'.[17] He meant the rationalist philosophers, namely, Descartes, Leibniz, and Wolff, who as dogmatic metaphysicians claimed that they had 'knowledge of nature and existence of God, the soul and the world as it is in itself'.[18] Skepticism, on the other hand, denies the possibility of knowledge. It overturned the rationalist metaphysics. A skeptic like Hume argued that the claims of dogmatic metaphysicians could not be unjustified. Although not satisfied with skepticism, a final resting place for thought, Kant did not advocate a return to dogmatism. He famously said that Hume awakened him from his 'dogmatic slumber'. Instead he advocated *critique*. Yirmiyahu Yovel puts it succinctly:

> dogmatism ascribes to human reason capacities it does not possess, and skepticism denies it the capabilities it does not possess. The first *builds groundless castles in the air, the second undermines all grounded buildings*. Thus dogmatism is flawed by excessive affirmation and skepticism by excessive negation, whereas the *Critique*, after rigorous scrutiny, combines within itself the negation and affirmation in a state of reciprocal and balanced tension.[19] [my emphasis]

And significantly, 'each of those opposing movements also commits its opponent's fallacy: empiricist skepticism is dogmatic since it does not question its own presuppositions, and rationalist dogmatism breeds skepticism because it leads to inner contradictions in reason'.[20] More importantly, for Kant, a dogmatic 'takes it for granted that objects are things in themselves, and that reason can derive existence from mere concepts without the cooperation of experience', and therefore, the dogmatic

> believes that reason can know what lies beyond experience, to pene-trate into the 'interior' of things, as it were, and rise to the knowledge of God, the freedom of the will, immortality, and the cosmos as totality—the traditional queries of metaphysics.[21]

Kantian critical philosophy, to put it in a simplified definition,

> rather than starting with an attempt to understand the nature of the world, begins by examining our capacity of knowledge or cognition with the goal of understanding the scope and limit of human cogni-tion and the *a priori* principles that govern our knowledge of objects.[22]

Going back to the distinction between 'faith' and 'knowledge', it must be pointed out that philosophy and indeed the search for all forms of knowl-edge require 'faith in reason'. This 'reason' is to be properly examined in association with *Idee* (Idea). But in the 1790s, as noted previously, with the *crisis* of Enlightenment reason, the crisis of *Aufklärung* in German philosophy, and the rise of romantic *Sturm und Drang*, the authority of reason came under attack.[23] This was the time of its first instance in the *postmodern* age before its second advent in our own time.[24] Before this crisis in Enlightenment reason, Kant already in 1784 had written a 'jour-nalistic' article as a specific 'response' to the question of 'What is Enlightenment?' that has lost none of its force for us in our confrontation with the 'postmodern *unreason*'. I will come back in a later chapter to Kant's article when I discuss the problem of foundationalism in Kantian *architectonic* philosophy and its unique employment of the 'building metaphor'. Here I am more concerned to provide a background for 'foundationalism', specifically to *rationalist* tradition exemplified in the work of René Descartes and his extensive uses of 'building analogies'. For this examination I turn to Karatani's discussion of Descartes' *cogito* in which he invokes Kant's sophisticated response and criticism. But before I come to that, I should briefly reflect on the word 'reason' (*Vernunft*) in its distinction from 'understanding' (*Verstand*), as they are prominent terms throughout the tradition of German idealism from Kant to Hegel.

The faculty of reason, *Vernunft*, derives from '*vernehmen*' meaning 'to perceive, hear, examine, interrogate'.[25] It generates 'rational' and 'reasonable' in both subjective and objective senses, and 'rationality and reasonableness', which is related to *ratio* in Latin, in the sense of 'faculty of reason, and not of ground'.[26] *Vernunft* is distinct in Hegel when derived from its Latin equivalents, '*ratio: Rationalismus, rational* and *rationell*. These are usually associated with the rationalism of the Enlightenment, and thus have more in common with *Verstand* than with *Vernunft*'.[27] *Verstand*, the faculty of understanding, or intellect, enters in a cluster of combined notions, namely, 'human understanding and common sense'. Above all, '*Verstand* is used for the Latin *intellectus*'. In Hegel, 'intellectuality' and 'intelligible' are 'usually associated with the intelligible world of Plato, Neoplatonism and Leibniz, in contrast to the phenomenal world'.[28] Philosophers have traditionally postulated two intellectual faculties, as Michael Inwood points out.

> In Plato, *dianoia* ('discursive reason') lies between perception and *nous* ('mind, intellect') or *noesis* ('thinking, the activity of *nous*'): *dianoia* deals with mathematics, the more institutive *nous* with philosophy. For Plato's successors, *nous* is usually the higher faculty and is contrasted with dianoia, *logismo* (calculation, ratiocination, in e.g., Plotinus), or *pathētikos nous* ('passive in contrast to active') *nous*, in Aristotle) … *Nous* brings us into contact with intelligible order, the cosmic *nous* or intelligible (*noetos*) world.[29]

Martin Jay in his *Reason after Its Eclipse* traces the history of reason over a large span of time stretching from classical Greek sources to the Enlightenment, to the Frankfurt School, to ultimately Jürgen Habermas, and in between deals with the problematic reason in Kant, Hegel, and Marx, and refers to the distinction between 'noetic' and 'dianoetic'. He points out that '*Noēsis*' 'is the mental operation of nous (mind or intelligence), which differs from the mere sensual perception of an object in the world called *aisthesis*'.[30] He notes that for Plato, it was the function of the 'eye of the soul' as opposed to the 'physical eye of the body'.[31] Mentioning the pre-Socratic Parmenides, Jay writes that he had claimed that thought (*noeîn*) and being (*eînai*) are the same. Noting further that 'Intuition, drawn from the Latin *intueri* (which means to "look on"), implies the ability to know something immediately and directly, through a kind of instantaneous "apperception" […] going beyond the uncertainties of mere sensation and perception'.[32] Jay explains that dianoetic thought, 'more than mere opinion—*doxa*—nonetheless eschews the direct power of noetic intuition to access the absolute, a power that might well be reserved only for gods'.[33] Instead of noetic intuition, dianoetic employs

> syllogistic logic and discursive argumentation, the inferential process of reasoning, in order to come to rational conclusions. The addition of the prefix 'dia' ('through') suggested a temporal process of demonstration, argumentation, and inference, perhaps best exemplified for the Greeks by the successive steps of an inferential geometric proof.[34]

When the distinction between the 'higher faculty' and the 'lower faculty' was introduced into German, *Verstand* (*intellectus*) stood for higher faculty and *Vernunft* (*ratio*) for lower faculty: '*Vernunft* conceptualizes sensory material, while *Verstand* gives non-sensory knowledge of God', but, significantly,

> their positions were reversed by Enlightenment thinkers such as Wolff, who had no place for the supersensory, institutive knowledge of *Verstand*. *Verstand* is still more intuitive than *Vernunft*, but is now connected with concepts and their application to sensory material: it is the 'faculty of distinctly representing the possible'. *Vernunft* retains its link with inference and argument: it is the 'faculty of seeing into connection of truths'.[35]

Kant intertied this distinction. In his philosophy, *Verstand* becomes the faculty of concepts and judgments, and *Vernunft* is the faculty of inference. But *Vernunft* also has

> a higher role: it is the faculty of ideas and the source of metaphysical concepts; it reflects on the knowledge acquired by the understanding and attempts to make it a self-enclosed whole, an attempt which leads it to transgress the limits of experience which reason itself imposes on the understanding.[36]

As Onora O'Neil points out, when Kant drew a parallel between understanding and reason he meant that both are 'faculties of unity', but 'the unity the two achieve contrast sharply'.[37] Kant in 'Transcendental Dialectic' of *Critique of Pure Reason* wrote:

> If understanding may be a faculty of unity of appearance by means of rules, then reason is the faculty of unity of the rules of understanding under principles. Thus it never applies directly to experience or to any object, but instead applies to the understanding, in order to give unity *a*

priori through concepts to the understanding's manifold cognitions, which may be called "the unity of reason," and is of an altogether different kind than any unity that can be achieved by the understanding.[38]

O'Neill notes that Kant

> rejects the rationalist claim that the principles of reason can provide a unique and integrated answer to all possible questions. [...] A main objective of the Transcendental Dialectic is to show how any view of the principles of reason as divinely inscribed axioms or rules of thought, that corresponds to reality, leads to contradictions—to paralogism, antimonies, and impossibilities.[39]

We can now come to Descartes and the question of foundationalism. I should in passing point out that Descartes believed that 'vindication of reason' is the first task of philosophy, which later turned into excessive belief in 'power of reason' by rationalists, which Kant would expose and undermine. We must initially recognize that in the rationalist tradition, foundationalism had to be *known* with *certainty*. Knowledge had to be apodictic, it had to yield an incorrigible knowledge. The appearance of *Critique of Pure Reason* and Kant's critique of Descartes's 'I think' radically required that foundationalism be restated. In post-Kantian German idealism up to Hegel and the entire romantic generation, the *systematic* knowledge discussed under the term came to be known as *antifoundationalism*, or a critique of foundationalism, undercutting the rationalist discourse by bringing forth the 'circular epistemology' as opposed to linearity in the conception of a system of knowledge leading to philosophy being conceived as a 'scientific system'.[40] With critical philosophy and for the entire post-Kantian German philosophy, the question was this: how to account for knowledge in the absence of a foundation. German idealism had to complete the philosophical revolution inaugurated by Kant. Antifoundationalism can be interpreted as the result of the romantic attack on the Enlightenment and therefore must be criticized under the fundamental tenets of foundationalism. In principle, it must be treated and understood as a variation on the same *foundation theory*, a theory that, as Karatani reminds us, would not be necessary 'if not in response to a *crisis* of foundation itself' [my emphasis]. This is the crux of the matter. As soon as this *crisis* attains to the dignity of *concept*, it must be related to the 'mathematical foundation' that Karatani tackles under the Kantian 'Problematic of Synthetic Judgment'.[41]

To reiterate, with Kant systematic philosophy was viewed as system building which requires epistemological ground as its condition of possibility. In this view, philosophic discourse is replete with building analogy. If building and theory of knowledge both, as it is said, are constructed on a solid foundation, then nothing can shake the higher storeys. This idea of foundationalism reaches back to the Greek tradition and comes back to secular modernity in Descartes' writings which are taken to be the paradigm of foundationalism.[42] Descartes' theory 'exemplifies the foundationalist approach to knowledge as requiring an unshakable foundation as the necessary condition of claims to know in full, or the traditional sense, in Cartesian language of apodictic knowledge'.[43] What must be pointed out at this early stage of the argument is that it is on this firm foundation of knowledge which the Enlightenment faith in 'authority of reason' is rested. As Beiser states, 'The alternative to a firm foundation seemed to be the abyss of skepticism. The search for a foundation appears in both the empiricist and rationalist traditions of the Enlightenment'.[44] He further points out that

> While the empiricist tradition discovered that foundation in the simple ideas of experience, the rationalist tradition sought it in *self-evident first principles*. Despite their opposing ideas about where to place it, both shared a belief in the possibility, and indeed necessity, of some foundation.[45] [my emphasis]

What has come to be called 'antifoundationalism' is characterized by Tom Rockmore 'as any effort to validate knowledge claims without appealing to an absolute or ultimate basis known with certainty', and further, 'we understand antifoundationalism as the contrary to the Cartesian approach to knowledge, we can describe it simply as any effort to attain knowledge in the absence of secure foundation'.[46] It is to be noted here that by no means all foundationalism can be associated with forms of Cartesianism, as Rockmore explains, and by the same token, not all forms of antifoundationalism can be defined adequately as anti-Cartesianism. Rockmore writes:

> The complex nature of the debate concerning the reconstruction of the critical philosophy as system can be described as beginning with an attempt at foundationalism, which, in the course of the discussion, is transformed into an argument for antifoundationalism. More precisely, the initial argument for foundationalist system is altered during the debate, as a result of basic criticism directed against the concept of the foundationalist form of system, into an alternative, antifoundationalist form.[47]

He further points out that

> the key in this discussion, which leads from concern with founda-
> tionalist system to an interest in antifoundationalist system, is a basic
> change in the understanding of epistemological circularity. It is
> through this revised understanding of epistemological circularity
> that, in spite of decisive criticism advanced against the foundational-
> ist type of system, a way was found to argue for an antifoundationalist
> approach to knowledge.[48]

At this point we must pose this question: How did 'building analogy'
enter the philosophy of foundationalism? In Descartes—after Plato—we
find the most well-known case of it. It is pursued in his *Discourse on
Method*, where he writes:

> As for the other sciences, inasmuch as they borrow their first princi-
> ples from philosophy, I judged that no solid building could have been
> made on such shaky foundations; and neither the honour nor the
> profit that they promised was enough to induce me to learn them. For
> I did not feel myself obliged, thank heaven, to mend my fortune by
> making science my profession; and though I made no pretence of a
> Cynic contempt for fame, I yet made very slight account of fame that
> I could only hope to win by false pretences.[49]

In Part II of *Discourse on Method*, Descartes remarks:

> One of the first things I thought it well to consider was that as a rule
> there is not such great perfection in works composed of several parts,
> and proceeding from the hands of various artists, as in those on which
> one man has worked alone. Thus we see that buildings undertaken
> and carried out by a single architect are generally more seemly and
> better arranged than those that several hands have sought to adapt,
> making use of old walls that were built for other purposes.[50]

And further:

> True, we do not observe that all the houses of a city are pulled down
> merely with the design of rebuilding them in a different style and thus
> making the street more seemly; but we do see that many men have
> theirs pulled down in order to rebuild them, and that they are even
> sometimes obliged to, when the houses are in danger of falling in any

case, and the foundations are insecure. By this parallel I became convinced that it would not be sensible for a private citizen to plan the reform of a state by altering all its foundations and turning it upside down in order to set it on its own feet again, or again for him to reform the body of the sciences or the established order of teaching them in the schools […] I firmly believed that in this way I should much better succeed in the conduct of my life than if I build only upon old foundations, and leant upon principles which in my youth I had taken on trust without examining whether they were true.[51]

He continues with his building analogy in Part III:

Before beginning to rebuild the house in which one lives, one must not merely pull it down, and make provision for materials, and for architects (unless one does one's own architecture), and besides have ready a carefully drawn plan; one must also have provided oneself with another house where one may conveniently stay while the work goes on. In the same way, in order not to be in a state of indecision in action at a time when reason would oblige me to be so in thought, and not to fail to live thereafter as happily as I could, I formed a provisional code of morals consisting just of three or four axioms …[52]

Later, in his *Meditation on the First Philosophy*, Descartes comes back to his building analogy. In the 'First Meditation', after confessing that he had observed a 'multitude of errors' that he 'had accepted as rule' in his earlier years, and expressing 'the consequent need of making a clean sweep for once' in his life and 'beginning again from the very foundations' to establish 'some secure and lasting result in sciences', he finally comes to say that 'Today is my chance; I have banished all care from my mind, I have secured myself peace, I have retired by myself; at length I shall be at leisure to make a clean sweep, in all seriousness and with full freedom, of all my opinions'. To this end, he writes:

I shall not have to show they are all false, which very likely I could never manage; but reason already convinces me that I must withhold assent no less carefully from what is not plainly false; so the discovery of some reason for doubt as regards each opinion will justify the rejection of all. This will not mean going over each of them—an unending task; when the foundation is undermined, the superstructure will collapse of itself; so I will proceed at once to attack the very principles on which all my former beliefs rested.[53]

Descartes's employment of building metaphor to seek a secure foundation leads him to build on his meditations on *cogito*. In *Discourse on
Method* he expresses that his thoughts might be 'too metaphysical', and
therefore he feels 'obliged to speak of them so as to make it possible to
judge whether the foundation I have chosen is secure enough'.[54] 'Finally',
he writes,

> considering that the very same experiences (*pensées*) as we have in
> waking life may occur also while we sleep, I decided to feign that
> everything that had entered my mind hitherto was no more true than
> the illusions of dreams.

And from there he arrives at his famous declaration:

> But immediately upon this I noticed that while I was trying to think
> everything false, it must needs be that I, who was thinking this (*qui le
> pensais*), was something. And observing that this truth 'I am thinking
> (*je pense*), therefore I exist' was so solid and secure that the most
> extravagant suppositions of the sceptics could not overthrow it,
> I judged that I need not scruple to accept it as the first principle of
> philosophy that I was seeking.[55]

And then:

> Observing that there is nothing at all in the statement 'I am thinking,
> therefore I exist' which assures me that I speak the truth, except that I
> see very clearly that in order to think I must exist, I judged that I could
> take it as a general rule that whatever we conceive very clearly and
> very distinctly is true; only there is some difficulty in discerning what
> conceptions really are distinct.[56]

And in *Meditations on First Philosophy* he writes:

> What then am I? A conscious being (*res cogitans*), What is that? A
> being that doubts, understands, asserts, denies, is willing; further,
> that has sense and imagination. These are a good many properties—if
> only they all belong to me. But how can they fail to? Am *I* not the
> very person who is now 'doubting' almost everything; who 'under-
> stands' something and 'asserts' this one thing to be true, and 'denies'
> other things; who is 'willing' to know more, and 'is willing' to be
> deceived; who 'imagines' many things, even involuntarily, and per-
> ceives many things coming as it were from the senses'? Even if I am
> all the while asleep; even if my creator does all he can to deceive me;

how can any of these things be less of a fact than my existence? Is any of these something distinct from my consciousness (*cogitatione*)? Can any of them be called a separate thing from myself? It is so clear that it is I who doubt, understand, will, that I cannot think how to explain it more clearly. Further, it is I who make up my experience (*cogitationis*). Finally, it is I who have sensations, or who perceives corporeal objects as it were by the senses. Thus, I am now seeing light, hearing a noise, feeling heat. These objects are unreal, for I am asleep; but at least I seem to see, to hear, to be warmed. This cannot be unreal; further, sensation, precisely so regarded, is nothing but an act of consciousness (*cogitare*).[57]

Karatani in *Transcritique: On Kant and Marx*, where he discusses Descartes, comes to do two incisive things. First, he defends Descartes against Claude Lévi-Strauss, who 'passes off' Descartes 'as a villain', and second, takes Descartes to task by incisively bringing out Kant's critique of him. Karatani acknowledges that there is a 'confusion' in Descartes that warrants his criticism by his accusers. The problem though lies, as Karatani notes, in the discrimination between 'to doubt [*dubitare*]' and 'to think [*cogitare*]'. As we have seen, Descartes affirms the 'existence of doubting subject' but then he quickly goes on to conclude his 'I think, therefore, I am [*cogito ergo sum*]'—famously or infamously. 'Nonetheless', as Karatani notes, '"doubting" and "thinking"—or the "subject of doubt [*res dubitans*] and the "subject of thinking [*res cogitans*] must be different'.[58] Pointing out that Descartes 'posits "thinking" as the ground of actions', Karatani quotes what I cited previously: 'But, what, then, am I? A thing that thinks. What is a thing that thinks? That is to say, a thing that doubts, perceives, affirms, denies, wills, does not will, that imagines also, and which feels'.[59] It is here that Karatani cites Kant who called this 'thinking subject' a 'transcendental subject of thought = X'. To Kant, 'it is apperception that can never be represented, and for him Descartes' formulation that "it *is* (or I am) [*sum*]" is a fallacy'.[60] Karatani adds that 'Cartesian cogito is dogged by the ambiguity between "I doubt" and "I think"; furthermore, the ambiguity is inevitable as far as trying to speak of the transcendental ego is concerned'.[61] Karatani perceptively draws our attention as to how Descartes jumps from 'I doubt' to 'I think'. He writes:

In Descartes, 'I doubt' is a personal determination of will. And this 'I' is a singular existence—Descartes himself (1). In a sense, (1) is an empirical self, and is simultaneously a doubting subject (2), who doubts the empirical subject (1)—by way of which the transcendental ego (3) is discovered.

In Descartes's discourse, however, the relationship between these three phases of the *ego* is blurred. Karatani importantly explains that:

> When Descartes says, 'I am [*sum*] if he means that his 'transcendental ego exists,' it is a fallacy, as Kant said. For the transcendental ego is something that can only be thought, but cannot *be* or *exist*, that is, it cannot *be instituted*. On the other hand, Spinoza interpreted 'I think, therefore I am' as neither a syllogism nor a reasoning but as meaning simply, 'I am as I think' or 'I am thinking [*ego sum cogitans*]; or, even more simply and definitively, 'man thinks [*homo cogitant*]. But, speaking more realistically, the Cartesian, 'I think, therefore I am' means 'I am as I doubt [*ego sum dubitans*]'. The 'determination' to doubt the self-evidence of the psychological ego cannot simply originate from a psychological ego, but neither can it from the transcendental ego that is discovered by doubt. If this is so, however, what exists? Actually, [...] the correct way of formulating the question is not, 'what exists?' but '*who is it?*'[62]

After taking a long detour by way of discussing Husserl's phenomenology and his adoption of 'transcendental' not from Kant but from Descartes, which need not detain us here, Karatani comes back to draw certain important conclusions by way of Kant's *transcendental* idea, which inherently contains 'the other'. Karatani writes:

> To Descartes, however, the existence of the objective world had to be *founded* in the first place. Seen from this perspective, one recognizes that what Descartes called God was the very difference that compelled him to doubt, namely, the otherness that can never be internalized. In the final analysis, and from the very beginning, what is hidden under doubting is the alterity—the otherness of the other. Pascal accuses Descartes of wanting to do away with God, if possible. And if one really tries to do away with God, one should just restate 'God' as 'the other'—who is not transcendent and absolute, but relative. The crux of cartesian doubt = Cogito is that it was constantly dogged by the other. This crucial problem of transcriticism was effectively lost after Descartes' *Meditations*, which corresponded, in turn, to his loss of 'being as doubting' and its external mode of existence. And so it was that Lévi-Strauss, too, lost his 'anthropological Cogito' in his later years. Once he stated that his stance would be progressive towards his own culture and conservative toward the objective cultures; finally, he ended up being conservative towards his own culture as well.[63]

Here I want to briefly bring in Slavoj Žižek who, in the same fashion as Karatani, recognizes Descartes's epistemological break in the rationalist tradition but at the same time invokes Kant's challenge to it. Žižek offers his reflections in the context of his insightful analysis of the film *Blade Runner* with his usual Lacanian approach in his *Tarrying with the Negative*. Noting that Descartes was first 'to introduce a crack in the ontologically consistent universe' that contracts 'absolute certainty' to the 'punctum of "I think"', which

> opens up, for a brief moment, the hypothesis of Evil Genius (*le malin génie*) who, behind my back, dominates me and pulls the strings of what I experience as "reality"—the protype of the Scientific-Maker who creates as artificial man, from Dr. Frankenstein to Tyrell in *Blade Runner*.

Žižek reminds us that, nevertheless, 'by reducing his *cogito* to *res cogitans*, Descartes, as it were, patches up the wound he cut into the nature of reality'.[64] Žižek then continues to say that 'Only Kant fully articulated the inherent paradoxes of self-consciousness' in pointing out that Kant's 'transcendental turn' manifested the 'impossibility of locating the subject in the "great chain of being", into the Whole of the universe'.[65] In contrast, as he notes, the subject in a radical sense is 'out of joint', does not have a fixed place, which Lacan designated by the mathem $, or the 'barred' S. In Descartes, Žižek notes, this divided subject still remains concealed. He then goes on to pose this question: 'What, then marks the break between Descartes' *cogito* and Kant's "I" of transcendental apperception?' His answer is illuminating:

> The key to it is offered by Kant's Wittgensteinian remark, aimed at Descartes, that it is not legitimate to use 'I think' as a complete phrase, since it calls for a continuation—'I think that … (it will rain, you are right, we shall win …)'[66]

According to Kant, Žižek writes,

> Descartes falls prey to the 'subreption of the hypostasized consciousness': he wrongly concludes that, in the empty 'I think' which accompanies every representation of an object, we get hold of a positive phenomenal entity, *res cogitans* (a 'small piece of the World', as Husserl put it), which thinks and is transparent to itself in its capacity to think.[67]

'In other words', as Žižek puts it, 'self-consciousness renders self-transparent the "thing" in me which thinks', while noting that

> What is lost thereby is the topological discord between the form 'I think' and the substance which thinks, i.e., the distinction between the analytical proposition on the identity of the logical subject of thought, contained in 'I think' and the synthetical proposition on the identity of a *person* qua thing-substance.[68]

Žižek makes a crucial point that, according to this distinction, 'Kant logically *precedes* Descartes: he brings to light a kind of "vanishing meditator", a moment which has to disappear if the Cartesian *res cogitans* is to emerge'.[69]

Citing a paragraph from *Critique of Pure Reason* where Kant wrote, 'in the synthetic original unity of apperception, I am conscious of myself, not as I appear to myself, nor as I am in myself, but only that I am', Žižek comments that the first thing we should notice is

> the fundamental paradox of this formulation: I encounter *being* devoid of all determinations-of-thought at the very moment when, by way of the utmost abstraction, I confine myself to the empty form of thought which accompanies every representation of mine. Thus the empty form of thought coincides with being, which lacks any formal determination-of-thought.[70]

Žižek draws our attention to the fact that there is an infinite distance that separates Kant from Descartes: 'in Kant, this coincidence of thought and being in the act of self-consciousness no way implies access to myself qua thinking substance', and goes on to cite Kant from *Critique of Pure Reason*:

> Through this I or he or it (the thing) which thinks, nothing further is represented than a transcendental subject of thoughts=X. It is known only through the thoughts which are its predicates, and of it, apart from them, we cannot have any concept whatsoever.

Žižek concludes that

> In short: we can provide no possible answer to the question 'How is the Thing which thinks structured?" The paradox of self-consciousness is that *it is possible only against the background of its own impossibility*: I am conscious of myself only insofar as I am out of reach of myself qua the real kernel of my being.[71]

The exploration in this chapter into Descartes' *foundationalism*, which resorts to 'building metaphor' to support his *cogito ergo sum* and 'thinking being', later challenged by Kant, is aimed to confirm Karatani's insight that a foundational theory is only needed when there is a *crisis* in foundation. Later, in Chapter 3, we will come back to Kant to resume our discussion of 'foundationalism' under his concepts of 'architectonics' and 'reason' and explore his singular employment of 'building metaphor'.

Notes

1 See Frederick C. Beiser, *The Fate of Reason: German Philosophy from Kant to Fichte* (Cambridge: Harvard University Press, 1987). See especially his excellent Introduction to the book.
2 Frederick C. Beiser, *The Fate of Reason*, 1.
3 Frederick C. Beiser, *The Fate of Reason*, 3.
4 Frederick C. Beiser, *The Fate of Reason*, 2.
5 Immanuel Kant, *Critique of Pure Reason*, trans. and eds. Paul Guyer and Allen W. Wood (Cambridge: Cambridge University Press, 1998), A xi, Axii, 100–101.
6 Immanuel Kant, *Critique of Pure Reason*, Axi–Axii, 100–101.
7 See David Hume, *A Treatise of Human Nature*, ed. with into. Ernest C. Mossner (Penguin Books, 1969). Also see David Hume, *An Inquiry Concerning Human Understanding*, ed. Eric Steinberg, Second Edition (Indianapolis and Cambridge, Hackett, 1993).
8 Frederick C. Beiser, *The Fate of Reason*, 3.
9 Frederick C. Beiser, *The Fate of Reason*, 3.
10 In Kōjin Karatani, *Transcritique: On Kant and Marx*, 93.
11 David Hume, *A Treatise of Human Nature*, 315.
12 David Hume, *A Treatise of Human Nature*, 316.
13 Kōjin Karatani, *Transcritique: On Kant and Marx*, 94.
14 David Hume, *A Treatise of Human Nature*, 316.
15 David Hume, *A Treatise of Human Nature*, 316.
16 Frederick C. Beiser, *The Fate of Reason*, 3.
17 See Lucas Thorpe, *The Kant Dictionary* (London: Bloomsbury), 80.
18 Lucas Thorp, *The Kant Dictionary*, 189.
19 See Yirmiyahu Yovel, *Kant's Philosophical Revolution: A Short Guide to the Critique of Pure Reason* (Princeton and Oxford: Princeton University Press, 2018), 10–11. Yovel further explains that 'Historically, Kant associates dogmatism with Leibniz's rationalist school and skepticism with British empiricists'.
20 Yirmiyahu Yovel, *Kant's Philosophical Revolution*, 11.
21 Yirmiyahu Yovel, *Kant's Philosophical Revolution*, 11. Yovel notes that 'Among the dogmatists Kant counts all the rationalists since antiquity, including Plato, Aristotle, the scholastics of the late Middle Ages and the Renaissance, and recent generations—Leibniz, with his army of followers, and he himself, Kant, in his precritical period. In those years, Kant says, he had been submerged in "dogmatic slumber," until skeptical challenge drove him to discover a new road', 11–12.
22 Lucas Thorp, *The Kant Dictionary*, 189.
23 For more of this see Frederick C. Beiser, *The Fate of Reason*, chapter 1.
24 See Frederick Beiser, *Hegel* (New York and London: Routledge, 2005).
25 Here I am relying on the entry 'Reason and Understanding' in Michael Inwood's excellent *A Hegel Dictionary* (Oxford: Blackwell, 1992).

26 Michael Inwood, *A Hegel Dictionary*, 242.
27 Michael Inwood, *A Hegel Dictionary*, 242.
28 Michael Inwood, *A Hegel Dictionary*, 242.
29 Michael Inwood, *A Hegel Dictionary*, 242–243.
30 See Martin Jay, *Reason after its Eclipse: On Late Critical Theory* (Madison: The University of Wisconsin Press, 2016), 14–15.
31 Martin Jay, *Reason after Its Eclipse*, 15.
32 Martin Jay, *Reason after Its Eclipse*, 15. Jay attributes the coining of the word 'apperception' to Renée Descartes, but in fact it was Leibniz who coined the word that later came to Kant. For this see the entry 'Apperception' in Howard Caygill, *A Kant Dictionary* (Oxford: Blackwell, 1995).
33 Martin Jay, *Reason after Its Eclipse*, 15.
34 Martin Jay, *Reason after Its Eclipse*, 15. Jay further explains: 'Developed in Socrates's polemic with the Sophists, it emerged as the primary organon of thought in Aristotle, elaborated in the sixth book of his *Niicomachean Ethics*. Dianoetic reasoning can buttress scientific *episteme*, knowledge used for its sake; *techne*, knowledge used to produce something; or *phronesis*, knowledge used to guide conduct', 15.
35 Michael Inwood, *A Hegel Dictionary*, 243.
36 Michael Inwood, *A Hegel Dictionary*, 243. Inwood notes further that

> Hegel's (and Schelling's) conception of *Verstand* and *Vernunft* contains elements of all these views. The essence of *Verstand*, says Schelling, is clarity without depth. It fixes, and isolates from each other, concepts such as infinity and finitude. It produces clear analyses and argues deductively. It is thus associated with concepts in the traditional sense, not with the Hegelian concept that flows over into other concepts and generates its own instantiation. But it is an indispensable first stage of logic and science in general: we cannot, as Jacobi and, at times, Schelling supposed, proceed directly to the truth of reason without a preliminary abstract understanding of the subject-matter', 243–244. Inwood continues: 'The objectification of reason and understanding are essential to Hegel's idealism: The processes and ontological hierarchies of nature and spirit are conceived as governed by an immanent understanding and reason that is analogous, in its development, to the understanding and reason of the human mind. Genuine rationality consists in the submission and conformity of *our* reason to the reason inherent in things. In cognition we should follow the immanent dialectic of concepts, objects and processes. In practical life, we should conform to the intrinsic rationality of our society, of the actual. Apparently irrational features of the natural or social worlds are in reality essential elements in an overarching rationality, just as error is not only an essential step on the way to truth, but an essential ingredient to it.

(244)

37 See Onora O'Neill, 'Vindicating Reason' in *The Cambridge Companion to Kant*, ed. Paul Guyer (Cambridge: Cambridge University Press, 1992). I will come back to this seminal article extensively when I discuss architectonics in Kant in a later chapter.
38 Immanuel Kant, *Critique of Pure Reason*, A302, B359, 388.
39 Onora O'Neill, 'Vindicating Reason', 283.
40 For this see Tom Rockmore's 'Introduction' and 'Hegel, German Idealism, and Antifoundationalism', in Tom Rockmore and Beth J. Singer, eds. *Antifoundationalism, Old and New* (Philadelphia: Temple University Press, 1992).

41 In Kōjin Karatani, *Transcritique: On Kant and Marx*. I will come back to discuss this question of 'mathematical foundation' in a later chapter.
42 See Tom Rockmore's 'Introduction' and 'Hegel, German Idealism, and Antifoundationalism'.
43 Tom Rockmore, 'Introduction', 7–8.
44 Frederick Beiser, *Hegel*, 23–24.
45 See Frederick Beiser, *Hegel*, 24.
46 Tom Rockmore, 'Introduction', 8.
47 Tom Rockmore, 'Hegel, German Idealism, and Antifoundationalism', 112.
48 Tom Rockmore, 'Hegel, German Idealism, and Antifoundationalism', 112–113.
49 In Descartes, *Philosophical Writings: A Selection*, trans. and eds. Elizabeth Anscombe and Peter Thomas Geach, intro. Alexander Koyre (Upper Saddle River: Prentice Hall, 1971), 12.
50 *Descartes, Philosophical Writings*, 15.
51 Descartes, *Philosophical Writings*, 17.
52 Descartes, *Philosophical Writings*, 24.
53 Descartes, *Philosophical Writings*, 61.
54 Descartes, *Philosophical Writings*, 31.
55 Descartes, *Philosophical Writings*, 31–32.
56 Descartes, *Philosophical Writings*, 32.
57 Descartes, *Philosophical Writings*, 70–71.
58 Kōjin Karatani, *Transcritique: On Kant and Marx*, 86.
59 Quoted in Kōjin Karatani, *Transcritique: On Kant and Marx*, 86.
60 Kōjin Karatani, *Transcritique: On Kant and Marx*, 86.
61 Kōjin Karatani, *Transcritique: On Kant and Marx*, 86.
62 Kōjin Karatani, *Transcritique: On Kant and Marx*, 87.
63 Kōjin Karatani, *Transcritique: On Kant and Marx*, 92.
64 See Slavoj Žižek, *Tarrying with the Negative: Hegel, Kant, and Ideology Critique* (Durham: Durham University Press, 1993), 12.
65 Slavoj Žižek, *Tarrying with the Negative*, 12.
66 Slavoj Žižek, *Tarrying with the Negative*, 13.
67 Slavoj Žižek, *Tarrying with the Negative*, 13.
68 Slavoj Žižek, *Tarrying with the Negative*, 13.
69 Slavoj Žižek, *Tarrying with the Negative*, 13–14. Žižek expands on his Lacanian approach here by saying:

> This Kantian distinction is revived by Lacan in the guise of the distinction between the subject of the enunciation (sujet de l'énonciation) and the subject of the enunciated (*sujet de l'énoncé*): the Lacanian subject of the enunciation ($) is also an empty nonsubstantial logical variable (not function), whereas the subject of the enunciated (the "person") consists of the fantasmatic "stuff" which fills out the void $.
>
> (14)

Žižek goes further to point out that

> Kant's reasoning is here far more refined than it appears. In order to appreciate fully its finesse, one has to make use of Lacan's formula of fantasy ($ <> a$): 'I think' only insofar as I am inaccessible to myself qua noumenal Thing which thinks. The Thing is originally lost and the fantasy-object (a) fills out its void (in this precise Kantian sense Lacan remarks that a is 'the stuff of the I'. The act of 'I think' is trans-phenomenal, it is not an object of inner experience or institution; yet for all that, it is not a noumenal Thing,

but rather the void of its lack: it is sufficient to say about the I of pure apperception that of it, apart from them [the thoughts which are predicates], we cannot have any concept whatsoever. One has to add that *this lack of instituted content is constitutive of the I; the inaccessibility to the I of its own 'kernel of being' makes it an I.*

(14)

70 Slavoj Žižek, *Tarrying with the Negative*, 14–15. For the cited passage in Immanuel Kant see *Critique of Pure Reason*, trans. and eds. Paul Guyer and Allen W. Wood (Cambridge: Cambridge University Press, 1998), B157, 259. For more clarity, here I quote a longer part of the paragraph B157 in this translation with its continuation to B158, which goes as follows:

In the transcendental synthesis of the manifold of representation in general, on the contrary, hence in the synthetic original unity of apperception, I am conscious of myself not as I appear to myself, nor as I am in myself, but only **that** I am. This **representation** is a **thinking**, not an instituting. Now since for the cognition of ourselves, in addition to the action of thinking that brings the manifold of every possible intuition to the unity of apperception, a determinate sort of intuition, through which this manifold is given, is also required, my own existence is not indeed appearance (let alone mere illusion), but the determination of my existence can only occur in correspondence with the form of inner sense, according to the particular way in which the manifold that I combine is given in inner intuition, and I therefore have no **cognition** of myself **as I am**, but only as **I appear** to myself. The consciousness of oneself is therefore far from being cognition of oneself, regardless of all the categories that constitute the thinking of an **object in general** through combination of the manifold in an apperception.

(B157, B158, 259–260)

71 Slavoj Žižek, *Tarrying with the Negative*, 15. See also Immanuel Kant, *Critique of Pure Reason*, A 346.

2

THE THING-IN-ITSELF

Karatani and the Kantian Turn

In the 'Afterword' to his *Architecture as Metaphor*, Kōjin Karatani says that for Kant *Idee* is an 'imaginary representation of the "thing-in-itself"': it is that which can never be grasped and represented by any theoretical approach'.[1] However, the concept of 'thing-in-itself' that was proposed by Kant, Karatani states, 'is less an account of the true world, as with Plato's *Idea*, than as the basis upon which to criticize all the ideation as *Schein*'.[2] Karatani explains that Kant did not deny *Idee* but claimed that it is no more than *Schein* that functions 'regulatively', although it 'cannot be proven theoretically and must never be realized "constitutively"'.[3]

Karatani should be recognized as a philosophical thinker who has boldly retuned the much contested concept of the *thing-in-itself* in Kant by giving it a novel interpretation in his formidable reading of *Critique of Pure Reason*. The publication of *Architecture as Metaphor* marks his initial entry into Kant's *transcendental critique* that he treated more fully later in his *Transcritique: On Kant and Marx*. In the former book, he begins by taking up the distinction between 'phenomena' and the 'thing-in-itself'. This distinction is at the very foundation of transcendental idealism. As Karatani reminds us, Kant regarded any thought that might claims to grasp *theoretically* the thing-in-itself as an 'arrogation of reason', what he called *Schein* (an illusion). In 'The Kantian Turn', the first chapter of *Transcritique*, Karatani significantly returns to a much neglected precritical 'journalistic' essay Kant had penned in 1766 titled 'Dreams of a Visionary Explained by Dreams of Metaphysics'.[4] In reading this essay Karatani extracts the term 'pronounced parallax' that he will employ for his interpretation of the concept *thing-in-itself*. Here it must be pointed out that in *Architecture as Metaphor* Karatani had already presented a framework for an understanding of the 'thing-in-itself', which for some people is an 'antiquated' term. Karatani conceives of '*Schein*', 'phenomena', and 'thing-in-itself' as a triad structure that he relates to Jacques

DOI: 10.4324/9781032647616-3

Lacan's 'Borromean Knot', a structure in which if one of the three terms is discarded it will cause the collapse of the whole. In this way, Karatani goes further to ingeniously relate the Kantian triadic structure to Lacan's triadic 'Imaginary, Symbolic, Real', respectively.[5] Underlying this is the notion that Freudian metapsychology is in fact a 'transcendental psychology' which in post-Freudian psychoanalysis degenerated into *empirical* psychology. It was Lacan who as a 'transcendental' thinker revived psychoanalysis as 'transcendental critique'. Karatani reminds us that Lacan, however, became aware of Kant long after the 'invention of his own triadic formula'.[6] From this observation Karatani derives a crucial point:

> Many thinkers who appear to be antagonistic toward Kant—Marx and Nietzsche, for example—reprised, employing different terms, the same structure that Kant introduced. In other words, these thinkers attempted to revive the thing-in-itself on their own terms and in different contexts.[7]

In this respect, and in relation to Marx, Karatani observes that the subtitle of *Capital* as 'A Critique of Political Economy' 'is neither a denial nor an affirmation of classical economics or of Hegel, but a Kantian "critique" of them'.[8] An important lesson is drawn that if Kant's triadic concept is 'replaceable with different triads', it is an indication that it 'forms a kind of structure that can be grasped *transcendentally*'[9] [my emphasis]. It is precisely this 'transcendental structure' that Kant called 'architectonics' (discussed in the next chapter). In the following I take up Karatani's exposition of the 'thing-it-itself' in *Transcritique: On Kant and Marx*. I must state here that I have chosen to plunge into Kant's revolutionary *Critique of Pure Reason* to understand it, for my part, through Karatani's remarkable reading of it. In this regard, I begin first with Karatani's clarification of the essence of the 'Copernican Revolution', which is *sine qua non* for understanding Kant's 'Copernican turn'.

The standard, but simplistic, narrative about Nicolaus Copernicus and his cosmological reversal is that he made us see that the sun stands at the center while the earth revolves around it. It is more complex than this. The idea of heliocentrism, as Karatani reminds us, was known since the ancients and was not Copernicus's invention. Copernicus was an empirical astronomer who introduced his astronomical theory on a posteriority basis as a *mere hypothesis*, to be proven later by Newton. His real contribution was the

> proposition that the discrepancy among the revolutions of heavenly bodies, which had dogged geocentricism since Ptolemy, could be solved if and only if we see the globe as revolving around the sun.

This hypothesis does not offer positive proof of heliocentrism itself, however, and it took as long as a century for it to be fully accepted as a cosmological principle.[10]

In a well-known footnote to Preface B in *Critique of Pure Reason*, Kant wrote:

> In the same way, the central laws of motion of the heavenly bodies established with certainty what Copernicus assumed at the beginning only as a hypothesis, and at the same time they proved the invisible force (of Newtonian attraction), that binds the universe, which would have remained forever undiscovered if Copernicus had not ventured, in a manner contradictory to the senses yet true, to seek for the observed movement not in the objects of the heavens but in their observer.[11]

As Karatani states, 'In order to grasp the Kantian Copernican turn precisely, one first has to clarify the turn of Copernicus himself'.[12] Nonetheless, Karatani points out, 'even those who still believed in egocentrism had to rely on the Copernican system of calculation'. Karatani continues with his incisive remarks:

> Although they believed that the truth was that the sun revolves around the earth, for the sake of calculation they still could think '*as if*' the opposite were the case. After all, the true significance of the Copernican turn lay in the hypothetical stance itself. In other words, the significance lay not in forcing any choice between egocentrism or heliocentrism, but rather in grasping the solar system as a *relational structure*—using terms such as 'earth' and 'sun'—that is totally independent of empirically observed objects or event. And only this stance could render the turn toward heliocentrism.[13]

Thus we must say that, in fact, Copernicus 'rediscovered', as Karatani puts it, 'sun' and 'earth' as two terms in the solar system 'qua reciprocal structure'. This 'reciprocal structure' must guide our understanding of Kant's revolutionary reversal of the hierarchical relation between *subject* and *object*. It must also guide our understanding of Kant's 'Copernican turn' in confrontation with the main contradiction in the philosophy of his time, namely, *rationalism* and *empiricism*, dogmatism and skepticism. In Karatani's words, when Kant named his new project in *Critique of Pure Reason* the 'Copernican turn', he was 'alluding to his own inversion of the subject/object hierarchy', which means this: 'while pre-Kantian metaphysics had maintained that subject copies the external object, Kant proposed that objects are constituted by the form the subject *projects into* the external world'.[14] This might sound as though Kant's 'subject-centrism' is the opposite of what we know by the name Copernicus, but Karatani thinks otherwise. He writes: 'It is my contention that in his constellation of thought surrounding the "thing-in-itself" and/or "transcendental object," he was echoing this very essence of Copernican turn, especially in stressing the passivity of subject in relation with the external object world'. Here Karatani cites a key passage from *Critique of Pure Reason* to support his point:

> The sensible faculty of intuition is really only receptivity for being affected in a certain way with representations, whose relation to one another is a pure intuition of space and time (pure forms of our sensibility), which, insofar as they are connected and determinable in these relations (in space and time) according to laws of the unity of experience, are called object. The non-sensible cause of these representations is entirely unknown to us, and therefore we cannot intuit it as an object; for such an object would have to be represented neither in space nor in time (as mere conditions of our sensible representation), without which conditions we cannot think any intuition. Meanwhile we can call the merely intelligible cause of appearances in general the transcendental object, merely so that we may have something corresponding to sensibility as a receptivity. To this transcendental object we can ascribe the whole extent and connection of our possible perceptions, and say that it is given in itself prior to all experience. But appearances are, in accordance with it, given not in themselves but only in this experience, because they are merely representations, which signify a real object only as perceptions, namely when this perception connects up with all others in accordance with the rule of the unity of experience.[15]

But what does the term 'transcendental' mean? In the face of numerous definitions of this term in academic literature, Karatani does something exceptional. He grounds the *transcendental* in the structure of the *unconscious*. Simply put, he says: 'the transcendental approach seeks to cast light on the unconscious structure that precedes and shapes experience'.[16] Like Freud's 'id, ego, superego', Karatani tells us, Kant's 'sensibility, understanding, and reason' do not exist empirically. What constitutes Kant's Copernican turn in this approach is not that it is 'a turn toward the philosophy of subjectivity, but that toward the thing-in-itself by a detour of the scrutiny of subjectivity'.[17] What is important to note here is that the concept *thing-in-itself*, as Karatani emphasizes, has always been related to the 'problematic of ethics', or in other words, to the 'problematic of *the other*', which must be associated with the Freudian *unconscious*. In Lacanian psychoanalytical theory, the 'thing-in-itself' is associated with 'the Real'. As to the alleged 'duality' of phenomena and thing-in-itself, the subject of many contestations leveled against Kant, Karatani provides a novel answer, as will be discussed subsequently. We must consider it to be a thing inherent in rational human subject related to the distinction between *sensibility* and *understanding*, between intuition and intellect. In a familiar passage in *Critique of Pure Reason*, Kant wrote:

> If we call the **receptivity** of our mind to receive representations insofar as it is affected in some way **sensibility**, then on the contrary the faculty for bringing forth representations itself, or **spontaneity** of cognition, is the **understanding**. It comes along with our nature that **intuition** can never be other than **sensible**, i.e., that it contains only the way in which we are affected by objects. The faculty for **thinking** of objects of sensible intuition, on the contrary, is the **understanding**. Neither of these properties is to be preferred to the other. Without sensibility no object would be given to us, and without understanding none would be thought. Thoughts without content are empty, intuitions without concepts are blind. […] Further, these two faculties or capacities cannot exchange their functions. The understanding is not capable of intuiting anything, and the senses are not capable of thinking anything. Only from their unification can cognition arise. But on this account one must not mix up their roles, rather one has great cause to separate them carefully from each other and distinguish them.[18]

In defense of the idea of *duality* in Kant, Yirmiyahu Yovel in his concise *Kant's Philosophical Revolution* says that this radical heterogeneity between the two poles of spontaneity and receptivity is the 'foundation of the rigorous dualism that characterizes Kant in *all* parts of his system', and that

> Kant needs to sharply separate between the two in order to maintain critical purity in knowledge and in ethics, yet on the other hand he needs to link them reciprocally to ensure the possibility of knowing objects and performing moral action. Hence the problem of bringing the duality (known as "schematism" in the broad sense) that recurs in most parts of his system.[19]

As Yovel further points out, the *Critique of Pure Reason*, which presents the structure of the rational human subject that we are, 'must necessarily start from human duality as an unshakable fact'.[20] In the Preface to second edition of *Critique of Pure Reason*, Kant wrote:

> In the analytical part of the critique it is proved that space and time are only forms of sensible intuition, and therefore only conditions of the existence of the things as appearances, further that we have no concepts of the understanding and hence no element for the cognition of things except insofar as an intuition can be given corresponding to these concepts, consequently that we can have cognition of no object as a thing in itself, but only insofar as it is an object of sensible intuition, i.e., as an appearance; from which follows the limitation of all even possible speculative cognition of reason to mere object of **experience**. Yet, the reservation must also be well noted, that even if we cannot **cognize** these objects as things in themselves, we at least must be able to **think** them as things in themselves.[21]

Further, in the B edition, Kant wrote:

> Nevertheless, if we call certain objects, as appearances, beings of sense (*phenomena*), because we distinguish the way in which we intuit them from their constitution in itself, then it already follows from our concept that to these we as it were oppose, as objects thought merely through the understanding, either other objects conceived in accordance with the latter constitution, even though we do not intuit it in them, or else other possible things, which are not objects of our sense at all, and call these beings of understanding (*noumena*).[22]

In *Prolegomena* we read:

> If our intuition had to be of such a nature as to represent things as they are in themselves, there would not be any intuition *a priori*, but intuition would be always empirical. For I can only know what is contained in the object in itself if it is present and given to me. It is indeed even then inconceivable how the intuition of a present thing should make me know this thing as it is in itself, as its properties cannot migrate into faculty of representation.[23]

And further:

> Accordingly, it is only the form of sensuous intuition by which we can intuit things *a priori*, but by which we can know objects only as they *appear* to us (to our senses), not as they are in themselves; and this

assumption is absolutely necessary if synthetic proposition *a priori* be granted as possible or if, in case they actually occur, their possibility is to be conceived and determined beforehand.[24]

Based on these passages (and similar ones in both *Critique* and *Prolegomena*) directly related to the distinction between 'phenomena' (appearance) and 'thing in itself', Henry Allison, a perceptive defender of Kant's 'transcendental idealism', writes that

> the cognitive vacuity of a consideration of things as they are in themselves does not amount to incoherence. That would be the case only if the understanding could not even *think* things apart from the conditions of sensibility, which Kant repeatedly affirms that we can. As a result, there is nothing preventing a consideration of things as they are in themselves.[25]

The authors of the useful guide to *Kant's Critique of Pure Reason*, who comment on Allison's argument, point out that a 'thing in itself' is not a 'special type of thing (for example, a noumenal substance) that would really exist even if there were no sensible beings to cognize them; rather it means the ordinary objects of human experience but considered as they are in themselves'.[26] They further write that

> The distinction between the appearing thing and thing in itself (understood in this 'two-aspects' way) is simply a necessary procedure of transcendental reflection when we seek to avoid a transcendentally realist conception. The noumena, on the other hand, is the conceptually determined object of a *non-sensible* intuition.[27]

'What is new in Kant, what follows directly from the Copernican revolution, is the claim that it is impossible for us to stand outside of our presentations and compare them with some transcendental real thing.'[28] 'Instead', they add, 'philosophy is given the task of identifying and analyzing the role of the transcendental conditions of cognition; the transcendental object = x "points" us to this task'.[29] Here they are referring to what Allison wrote in this regard:

> In the preliminary portion of Deduction, in which the concept of the transcendental object is introduced, the issue concerns what might be termed 'immanentization' of cognition, which is a direct consequence of Kant's Copernican revolution. The basic problem is that we cannot, as it were, stand outside our representations in order to

compare them with some transcendentally real entity. Accordingly, such an object 'must be thought only as something in general = X', which is later identified with the transcendental object. In this context, then, the concept functions as a kind of transcendental pointer, which serves to define the philosophical task by indicating that the commonsensical and transcendentally realistic concern with the 'real' nature of objects must be replaced by a critical analysis of the conditions of representation of an object. So constructed, the term *transcendental object* obviously cannot be used in plural, which is why Kant there describes it as being in all our cognitions 'really always one and the same = X'. As he later puts it, this transcendental object can serve only as a 'correlate of the unity of apperception'.[30]

The foregoing passages in Kant and affirmative views of the distinction between phenomena and thing-in-itself, the so-called 'duality', or better, 'two-aspects' way, are meant to prepare the ground for Karatani's unique interpretation of the same distinction by taking a totally different route for its affirmation. For this reason, I call all the previous interpretations 'pre-Karatani'. What distinguishes Karatani's from all the others is his attempt to go back to Kant's essay 'Dreams of a Visionary Explained by Dreams of Metaphysics' from which he perceptively took the notion of 'pronounced parallax' for an extended analysis. In Karatani's reckoning, Kant's precritical essay is crucial for reading *Critique of Pure Reason*. Kant wrote the essay in the aftermath of the famous Lisbon earthquake on November 1, 1755, All Saints Day, which badly shook Europe to its core, giving rise to skepticism about the 'Grace of God', affecting the general publics, as well as the intellectuals. It also had certain philosophical consequences. As Karatani notes, 'It rent a deep crack between sensibility and understanding, as it were, which, right up to Leibniz, had maintained a relationship of remarkably seamless continuity. The Kantian critique cannot be separated from this profound and multilayered crisis'.[31]

In 'Dreams of a Visionary', Kant wrote the following:

Formerly, I viewed human common sense only from the standpoint of my own; now I put myself into the position of another's reason outside myself, and observe my judgments, together with their most secret causes, from the point of view of others. It is true that the comparison of both observations results in pronounced parallaxes, but it is the only means of preventing the optical delusion, and of putting the concept of the power of knowledge in human nature into its true place.[32]

Karatani takes up this passage for an extended analysis. He pointedly notes that

> Here Kant is not expressing the commonplace, that not only must one see things from one's own point of view, but also, simultaneously, from the point of view of others. If this is what he meant, it would be run-of-the-mill: the history of philosophy is filled with reflections on seeing oneself as others would see.[33]

Rather, this 'point of view', Karatani states, would show itself only by way of the 'pronounced parallax'. Now to understand this term, Karatani perspicuously brings up the question of 'reflection' and a technology which did not of course exist in Kant's time, that is, *photography*. This technology is in contrast to the notion of the 'mirror image' which is identified with 'image seen by the other'. Seeing one's own image in mirror, in water, or in one's painted portrait is too subjective:

> Although the mirror image can be identified with the image seen by the other, there is still a certain complicity with regard to one's own point of view. After all, we can see our own image in the mirror 'any way we like'; and the mirror image is not fully fixed (not to mention the fact that it is left/right inverted or inside out).

Here I should parenthetically recall that Kant once made a reference to 'mirror image' in his *Prolegomena* in the context of the remarks he made on space and time where he tries to make clear the differences between 'sensible intuition' and 'understanding', on the one hand, and 'appearance' and 'thing in itself' on the other. He wrote:

> What can be more similar in every respect and in every part more alike to my hand and to my ear than their images in the mirror? And yet I cannot put such hand as is seen in the mirror in the place of its original, for if this is a right hand, that in the mirror is a left one, and the image or reflection of the right ear is a left one, which never can serve as a substitute for the other. There are in this case no internal differences which our understanding could determine by thinking alone. Yet the differences are internal as the senses teach, for, notwithstanding their complete equality and similarity, the left hand cannot be enclosed in the same bounds as the right one (they are not congruent) …What is the solution? These objects are not representations of things as they are in themselves, and as some pure understanding

would cognize them, but sensuous intuitions, that is appearance, whose possibility rests upon the relation of certain things unknown in themselves to something else, viz., to our sensibility.[34]

Now, by contrast to the mirror image and its *subjectivity*, photography 'sustains a different, much more severe, *objectivity*', as Karatani points out. 'Even though there is always a photographer, his or her subjectivity is less influential than the painter's for there is an ineradicable, mechanical distance in the photographic image'.[35] These remarks lead Karatani to his most important theoretical insight by which he puts the whole distinction between phenomena and thing-in-itself in a new light, thus overcoming the so-called 'duality'. He writes:

> Strange as it may be, we cannot see our faces (read the thing-in-itself), except as an image reflected in the mirror (read phenomena). And only thanks to the advent of photography, did we learn that fact. But, again, photography is also an image, and of course, people eventually get used to the mechanical image, so much so that they eventually come to feel that the image is themselves. But the crux here is the "pronounced parallax"—that which people presumably experience when they "first" see their photographic image.[36]

The effects of 'parallax' are the result of the viewpoint of the *other*, the 'displacement and derangement' that one experiences as the result of the intervention of the other point of view causing 'hideousness or uncanniness' as when one sees one's own image or hears one's own voice for the first time. One has eventually to get used to it. Literally, 'parallax' can be defined—and here I follow Slavoj Žižek who once adopted Karatani's terms for his *The Parallax View*—as 'the apparent displacement of an object (the shift of its position against the background), caused by a change in observational position that provides a new line of sight'.[37] Karatani draws a broader view for philosophy that always begins with 'introspection'. He says: 'The philosophy that begins with introspection-mirror remains snared within the specular abyss of introspection. No matter how it seeks to introduce the other's stance, this situation never alters'.[38] If it is said that philosophy began with Socrates's dialogue, Karatani says that the dialogue itself is 'trapped within the mirror'.

Many have criticized Kant for having remained in a subjectivist self-scrutiny, and suggest that he sought an escape in *Critique of Judgment* when he introduced plural subjects. But the truly revolutionary event in philosophy had already occurred in *Critique of Pure*

Reason, where Kant attempted to implode the complicity inherent in introspection precisely by *confining* himself to the introspective framework.

due to the fact of introducing 'an objectivity (qua otherness) that is totally alien to the conventional space of introspection-mirror'.[39] Karatani draws a broader implication that 'pronounced parallax' entailed for Kant's critical position within the philosophical conflict in his time. He notes that 'pursuing rationalist philosophy on the line of Leibniz/Wolff, there was no other choice but to accept Hume's empiricist skepticism, yet he [Kant] was not at all satisfied by either'.[40] And further:

> The stance that he called *transcendentalism* came into existence sometime during this period. Kant's approach in *Critique of Pure Reason* is different not only from subjective introspection, but also from objective scrutiny. [...] The transcendental stance, however, could not have appeared if not for the pronounced parallax. *Critique of Pure Reason* is not written in the mode of self-criticism as is 'Dreams of a Visionary,' but the pronounced parallax is present, functioning therein, it came to take the form of 'antinomy,' the device to reveal both thesis and antithesis as optical illusion.[41]

Concerning 'antinomy' in relation to the distinction between phenomena and thing-in-itself, Karatani mentions that Kant had in fact realized that (after the publication of the first version of *Critique of Pure Reason*) it would have been better if he had dealt with it after 'The Antinomy of Pure Reason' in the section of 'Transcendental Dialectic'.[42] The fact that Kant first started with the distinction of phenomena and thing-in-itself became the cause of the misunderstanding of his 'total design' (his architectonic system) leading to regression to the (in)famous 'duality', to 'phenomena and essence', or 'surface and depth'. This led to both impressions, as Karatani points out, to those who affirm or deny the concept of the 'thing-in-itself'. As Karatani writes:

> Those who reject it as mystical understand it only *within* the dichotomy, and even those who retain it, like Heidegger, interpret it only in the sense of the ontological depth or "abyss" [*Abgrund*]. In truth, however, there are no mystical implications in the properly Kantian thing-in-itself.[43]

Going back to the previous discussion of technology of photography and the 'face', we must come to understand it as 'something like one's own face in the sense that it undoubtedly exists but cannot be seen except as an image (read *phenomena*)'.[44]

Kant in a passage in *Prolegomena* warned against the mystical understanding of 'thing-in-itself':

> Idealism consists in the assertion that there are none but thinking beings; all other things which we believe are perceived in intuitions are nothing but representations in thinking beings, to which no object external to them in fact corresponds. On the contrary, I say that things as objects of our senses existing outside us are given, but we know nothing of what they may be in themselves, knowing only their appearances, i.e., the representations which they cause in us by affecting our sense. Consequently, I grant by all means that there are bodies without us, that is, things which, though quite unknown to us as to what they are in themselves, we yet know by representations which their influence on our sensibility procures us, and which we call bodies. This word merely means the appearance of the thing, which is, unknown to us but is not therefore less real. Can this be termed idealism? It is the very contrary.[45]

Karatani comments that here Kant

> actually acknowledges that both the world and other selves are not our products; they exist and become, irrespective of our being; in other terms, we are beings-in-the world. He uses the thing-in-itself in order to stress the passivity of the subject.[46]

Karatani concludes the chapter on 'The Kantian Turn' in *Transcritique: On Kant and Marx* with these remarks: 'The rigorous consistency of the Kantian critique, which informs all his work, derives directly from this radical point of departure: the problematic of universality in the judgement of taste, which is also to say, criticism in a journalistic sense'.[47] The Part I on Kant in *Transcritique*, before it continues to the Part II on Marx, includes the chapters entitled respectively as 'The Problematic of Synthetic Judgment' and 'Transcritique'. The latter ends with an excellent section titled 'Nature and Freedom'. In this section, which is about Kant's moral philosophy, Karatani comes back to the 'thing-in-itself' to discuss it in conjunction with the notion of '*others*', as Kant did. Kantian ethics that sees 'the others as the thing-in-itself, takes hold of *the others who have been and who will be*'.[48] Karatani points out that

> This sense of responsibility is different from the residue of duty's call to community that has endured since the primitive stage of human

history. It appears only in correspondence to the imperative 'be free', and 'treat others as free agent!'.[49]

He writes: 'Notwithstanding that Kant called this the *inner* moral law, it does not exist *internally*. It exists vis-à-vis the others who cannot be internalized'.[50] One must note, he continues, that

> Kantian others are always posited in asymmetric relationships, and they are distinct from Hegel's and Sartre's 'another self-consciousness', namely those who share the same set of rules and desires. The others are rather uninterested in me. When speaking of 'the others', people call to mind only those others living today. But the otherness of the other appears most strikingly in the dead'.[51]

Here he cites Kierkegaard:

> the most frightful of all is that one dead gives no hint at all. Beware, therefore, of the dead! Beware of cunning; beware of his definiteness, beware of his strength; beware of his pride! But if you love him, then remember him lovingly, and learn from him, precisely as one who is dead, learn the kindness in thought, the definiteness in expression, the strength in unchangeableness, the pride in life which would not be able to learn as well from any human being, even the most gifted.
>   One who is dead does not change; there is not the slightest possibility of excuse by putting the blame on him; he is faithful. Yes, it is true. But he is nothing actual, and therefore he does nothing, nothing at all, to hold on to you, except that he is unchanged. If, then, a change takes place between one living and one dead, it is very clear that it must be the one living who has changed.[52]

On which Karatani reflects:

> One cannot project one's empathy onto the dead. Neither can one represent their will. They never talk; they never show their interest. Those who speak for the sake of the dead are just speaking for themselves. Those who mourn for the dead do it in order to forget them. By not changing at all. By mourning, the dead won't change; it is we who change. By not changing at all, they reveal our changes. Thus they are cunning. They are the others in this very sense. Seeing the others as the thing-in-itself, as Kant did, is equal to seeing the others as someone from whom one can never evoke mutual consent, onto whom one can never project a representation, and of whom one can never speak as representative. They are, however, different from Levinas's

"absolute other." They are the relative others who are around one everyday. What is absolute is not the others themselves but our relationship with the relative others.[53]

Karatani tells us that 'the inclination toward universality in Kant's epistemology and aesthetics premises the future other', and

> In the same way, in order for moral law to be universal, not only does it have to be formal, but it also has to presume the future other. And in the final analysis, the future other implies the past other—the dead—because for the future other, one is dead. One must not forget one's destined position in history.[54]

It is important that we understand that

> In this precise sense, the Kantian critique essentially involves the problematic of history. At the end of his career, Kant began to tackle the problem of history head-on. Yet this was not as a change of attitude, because his stance, both *theoretical and practical*, persisted. Theoretically speaking, history has no end; it has only a complex of causality. […] But, from the beginning, the meaning and end of history do not exist in the same dimension as theoretical scrutiny; they are practical problems par excellence.[55]

I end my discussion of Karatani's extraordinary investigation into the Kantian 'thing-in-itself' here. What was examined previously by no means exhausts Karatani's project on Kant's transcendental philosophy, which must be discussed in connection to Marx under his notion of *transcritique*. I take this up elsewhere.[56] This brief examination of Karatani's reflections on 'The Kantian Turn' is mainly aimed to prepare a background for my further investigation in the following chapters in which I take up the central thesis of the '*Will to Architecture*' that will be conceptually framed in the structure of the concept of *architectonics* in Kant.

Notes

1 Kōjin Karatani, *Architecture as Metaphor*, trans. Sabu Kohso, ed. Michael Speaks (Cambridge: The MIT Press, 1995), 185.
2 Kōjin Karatani, *Architecture as Metaphor*, 185.
3 Kōjin Karatani, *Architecture as Metaphor*, 185–186.
4 See Immanuel Kant, 'Dreams of a Visionary Explained by Dreams of Metaphysics' in *The Philosophy of Kant, Immanuel Kant's Moral and Political Writings*, ed. and intro. Carl J. Friedrich (New York: The Modern Library, 1993).

5 See Kōjin Karatani's 'Introduction to the English Edition' in *Architecture as Metaphor*.
6 Kōjin Karatani's 'Introduction to the English Edition', xlii.
7 Kōjin Karatani's 'Introduction to the English Edition', xlii.
8 Kōjin Karatani's 'Introduction to the English Edition', xliii.
9 Kōjin Karatani's 'Introduction to the English Edition', xliii.
10 Kōjin Karatani, *Transcritique: On Kant and Marx*, trans. Sabu Kohso (Cambridge: The MIT Press, 2005 [2003]), 30–31. Karatani mentions that

> According to Thomas Kuhn, Copernicus basically followed the Ptolemaic cosmology even in *De Revolutionibus*, which was published in 1543, the year he died; it was only the addendum to the book, the part that only astronomers could decipher, that became influential for the coming age.
> (30)

11 Immanuel Kant, *Critique of Pure Reason*, trans. and ed. Paul Guyer and Allen W. Wood (Cambridge: Cambridge University Press, 1998), B xxii, 113.
12 Kōjin Karatani, *Transcritique*, 30.
13 Kōjin Karatani, *Transcritique*, 31.
14 Kōjin Karatani, *Transcritique*, 29.
15 In Immanuel Kant, *Critique of Pure Reason*, A 494/ B 523, 512–513; also see Kōjin Karatani, *Transcritique*, 29–30.
16 Kōjin Karatani, *Transcritique*, 1.
17 Kōjin Karatani, *Transcritique*, 34.
18 Immanuel Kant, *Critique of Pure Reason*, A 51–52, B 75–76, 193–194.
19 See Yirmiyahu Yovel, *Kant's Philosophical Revolution: A Short Guide to the Critique of Pure Reason* (Princeton and Oxford: Princeton University Press, 2018), 10. He further remarks that

> what is it that enables the two poles to come together despite their heterogeneity? Some Kant followers suggested that both the intellect and senses branch off from secret and unknowable common root, but Kant adamantly rejected this solution. The unknowable sources can only be intellectual intuition, and whoever affirms the existence of such source is already claiming to know and to use it.
> (10)

20 Yirmiyahu Yovel, *Kant's Philosophical Revolution*, 10.
21 Immanuel Kant, *Critique of Pure Reason*, B xxvi–B xxvii, 115.
22 Immanuel Kant, *Critique of Pure Reason*, B 306, 360.
23 Immanuel Kant, *Prolegomena to any Future Metaphysics, Second Edition*, trans. and intro. James W. Ellington (Indianapolis and Cambridge: Hackett, 1977), 24.
24 Immanuel Kant, *Prolegomena*, 25.
25 See Henry E. Allison, *Kant's Transcendental Idealism: An Introduction and Defence* (New Haven and London: Yale University Press, 2004), 56.
26 See Douglas Burnham with Harvey Young, *Kant's Critique of Pure Reason* (Bloomington and Indianapolis: Indiana University Press, 2007), 136.
27 Douglas Burnham with Harvey Young, *Kant's Critique of Pure Reason*, 136.
28 Douglas Burnham with Harvey Young, *Kant's Critique of Pure Reason*, 136.
29 Douglas Burnham with Harvey Young, *Kant's Critique of Pure Reason*, 136–137. They add that

> For other philosophers, this notion of a 'task' would suggest that philosophy requires a specifically *historical* study of the nature of its presentations, including the a priori. Just such a study is undertaken, though in

very different ways, by Hegel (*Phenomenology of Spirit*), Nietzsche (in, for example, the *Genealogy of Morality*), Heidegger (in *Being and Time*), Gadamer (in *Truth and Method*) or Foucault (*The Order of Things*).
(137)

30 See Henry E. Allison, *Kant's Transcendental Idealism*, 60–61.
31 Kōjin Karatani, *Transcritique*, 45. Karatani further remarks that

> Several years later, Voltaire wrote *Candide*, deriding Leibnizian predestined harmony, and Rousseau insisted that the earthquake was punishment for human society's having lost touch with nature. By distinct contrast, Kant (who wrote as many as three analyses of the problem) asserted that the earthquake of 1755 had no religious meaning whatsoever, attributable as it was to natural causes alone. He also advanced scientific hypotheses about the cause of the quake, as well as possible countermeasures to avert the future occurrences. It is noteworthy that while even empiricists could not help searching for 'meanings' to attribute to the event, Kant did no such thing.
> (45)

32 In Immanuel Kant, 'Dreams of a Visionary Explained by Dreams of Metaphysics', 15.
33 Kōjin Karatani, *Transcritique*, 47.
34 Immanuel Kant, *Prolegomena*, 27–28.
35 Kōjin Karatani, *Transcritique*, 48.
36 Kōjin Karatani, *Transcritique*, 48.
37 For this definition see Slavoj Žižek, *The Parallax View* (Cambridge: The MIT Press, 2006), 17. Žižek adopts Karatani's term for his own purpose reflecting on Hegel and Lacan. Žižek remarks that

> The philosophical twist to be added, of course, is that the observed difference is not simply "subjective," due to the fact that the same object which exists "out there" is seen from two different stances, or points of view. It is rather that, as Hegel would have put it, subject and object are inherently "mediated," so that an "epistemological" shift in the subject's point of view always reflects an "ontological" shift in the object itself.
> (17)

Obviously, Žižek bypasses Karatani's novel exposition of the term of 'objectivity' obtained in relation to the technology of photography.
38 Kōjin Karatani, *Transcritique*, 49.
39 Kōjin Karatani, *Transcritique*, 49.
40 Kōjin Karatani, *Transcritique*, 49.
41 Kōjin Karatani, *Transcritique*, 49.
42 Karatani mentions that in the letter of May 11, 1781,

> right before the publication of the first edition of *Critique of Judgment*, Kant confessed that he had an alternative plan in mind. That is, he should have started with "The Antinomy of Pure Reason," "which could have been done in colorful essays and would have given the reader a desire to get at the sources of the thing-in-itself." In Kant's published version, the thing-in-itself is explicated as if were ontologically premised, whereas in fact it would more properly intervene *skeptically* by way of the antinomy or dialectic in Kantian sense. The same is true of transcendental subjectivity.
> (Kōjin Karatani, *Transcritique*, n. 32, 310)

43 Kōjin Karatani, *Transcritique*, 50.
44 Kōjin Karatani, *Transcritique*, 50.
45 Immanuel Kant, *Prolegomena*, 30.
46 Kōjin Karatani, *Transcritique*, n. 33, 311. Going back to 'phenomena', Karatani insists on understanding 'antinomy as pronounced parallax' as the 'sole thing that reveals what is more than an image (phenomena)', 50. In fact, he writes, Kant

> poses antinomy not only in the section on the transcendental dialectic but almost everywhere. For instance, as one of the crucial examples, he draws out transcendental subjectivity X from the antimony between Cartesian thesis, 'There is an identical ego,' and the Humian antithesis, 'There is no identical ego'.
>
> (50)

47 Kōjin Karatani, *Transcritique*, 53.
48 Kōjin Karatani, *Transcritique*, 125.
49 Kōjin Karatani, *Transcritique*, 126.
50 Kōjin Karatani, *Transcritique*, 126.
51 Kōjin Karatani, *Transcritique*, 126.
52 Quoted in Kōjin Karatani, *Transcritique*, 126; see also Søren Kierkegaard, *Works of Love*, trans. Howard and Edna Hong (New York: Harper and Row, 1962), 328.
53 Kōjin Karatani, *Transcritique*, 126.
54 Kōjin Karatani, *Transcritique*, 127.
55 Kōjin Karatani, *Transcritique*, 127.
56 I discuss this connection extensively in my forthcoming book tentatively titled *Marx and the Science of Spirit: On Kōjin Karatani*.

3

KANT ON THE TOWER OF BABEL AND THE ARCHITECTONIC OF PURE REASON

> Human reason is by nature architectonic.[1]
>
> —Kant, *Critique of Pure Reason*

In Kant's philosophy the 'critical project' is *analogous* to a 'building project'. A distinct 'building metaphor' governs over this project which goes beyond Cartesian foundationalism as grounded in rationalism. Building the 'critical project' is equal to *building reason*. The latter is the central concept I will discuss later. Here it suffices to state that this 'reason' is 'by nature' a *human reason*, which in Kantian terms is *architectonic*. This architectonic is the subject of examination in this chapter. It is first useful to outline Kant's 'architectonic structure' that underlies his entire transcendental system. It can be defined as 'sensibility, understanding, and reason; thing-in-itself, phenomenon, and idea (transcendental illusion)'.[2] Underlying this structure is 'the faculty of judgment' forming the matrix of Kant's entire philosophy in the three *Critiques*, respectively, the 'theoretical judgment', the 'practical judgment', and the 'aesthetic and teleological judgment'.[3] In general terms, judgment can be defined as 'the name given to the act of synthesis by means of which the unity of consciousness across a manifold is realized and, in the same act, coherent and meaningful experience of object is achieved'.[4] But how are the three judgments related to one another? Kōjin Karatani concisely explains this:

> When we confront the world, we have at least three kinds of judgments at the same time: cognitive judgment of true or false, ethical judgment of good or bad, and aesthetic judgment of pleasure or displeasure. In real life, they are intermixed and hard to distinguish.[5]

DOI: 10.4324/9781032647616-4

Karatani insightfully suggests the notion of 'bracketing' as a way to sort out these intermixes:

> Scientists make observations by bracketing ethical and aesthetic judgments: only by this act can the objects of cognition come into existence. In aesthetic judgment, the aspects of true and false and good and bad are bracketed, only at the precise moment that artistic objects come into existence. These operations are emphatically not done naturally. Rather one is always *ordered* to bracket by the external situation.[6]

This brief summary of 'architectonic structure' sufficiently lays the ground for my examination of 'building reason'. I begin with the last part of *Critique of Pure Reason* titled 'Transcendental Doctrine of Method', which is composed of four elements, respectively, 'The discipline of pure reason', 'The canon of pure reason', 'The architectonic of pure reason', and 'The history of pure reason'. In his introductory remarks to this last part, Kant wrote the following:

> If I regard the sum total of all cognition of pure and speculative reasons as an edifice for which we have in ourselves at least the idea, then I can say that in the Transcendental Doctrine of Elements we have made an estimate of the building materials and determined for what sort of edifice, with what height and strength, they would suffice. It turned out, of course, that although we had in mind a tower that would reach the heavens, the supply of materials sufficed only for a dwelling that was just roomy enough for our business on the plane of experience and high enough to survey it; however, that bold undertaking had to fail from lack of material, not to mention the confusion of languages that unavoidably divided the workers over the plan and dispersed them throughout the world, leaving each to build on his own according to his own design. Now we are concerned not so much with the materials as with the *plan*, and having been warned not to venture some arbitrary and blind project that might entirely exceed our entire capacity, yet not being able to abstain from the erection of a sturdy dwelling, we have to aim at an edifice in relation to the supplies given to us that is at the same time suited to our needs.[7]

While this paragraph might be taken to be yet another exposition of the 'building metaphor', it is in fact unique. It contains a *critique* of all other so-called 'architecture metaphors' in the long tradition of rationalism from Plato to Descartes. In this paragraph we should notice the veiled reference to the famous Tower of Babel and its *hubris* against which Kant raises his objection. More significant is Kant's invocation of the term *plan*. I will come to this subsequently in relation to the 'vindication of reason' that underpins Kant's 'building project'. Various writers have taken up Kant's architectonic philosophy in relation to the 'building metaphor' and, in one notable case, in relation to the story of the Tower of Babel, including Daniel Purdy in his excellent *On the Ruins of Babel*.[8] For my purposes, the most insightful is the sustained analysis by Onora O'Neill. In her perceptive essay entitled 'Vindicating Reason', O'Neill reads the two Prefaces A and B in *Critique of Pure Reason* in conjunction with the last part, 'Transcendental Doctrine of Method', and brings out Kant's use of building metaphor for her analysis.[9] In addressing the concept of 'reason' in Kant, O'Neill is mainly concerned with the first two component elements, namely, 'discipline' and 'canon', leaving aside 'architectonic' and 'history'. In her book on Kant's practical philosophy entitled *Constructions of Reason*, published prior to her essay, O'Neill had discussed the 'building metaphor' under 'politics of reason' in the context of Kant's moral philosophy.[10] Her reflections provide a helpful background for the examination of the 'architectonic of pure reason' that she left out.

In 'Vindicating Reason', O'Neill traces three main points in the Kant paragraph quoted previously. The first is the long tradition of analogy between building and philosophy which, of course, goes back to Plato and was extended to Descartes and other rationalists as discussed earlier. The second is the 'darker story of the building of the Tower of Babel, whose builders aspired to a splendid tower' but failed in their enterprise as it exceeded their capacities and resources. Before I get to the third point, it is useful to mention here the role that the myth of the Tower of Babel plays in Western philosophy as a metaphorical feature that Kant invoked. As Purdy writes,

> Babel becomes an attractive metaphor with which to critique both metaphysics and absolutist power. The eighteenth century establishes the modern correspondences between epistemological critique and earlier Protestant understanding of the tale as a moral/political lesson about the hubris of oversized state planning.[11]

The Tower of Babel does not just represent 'metaphysical speculation'; rather it 'seeks to literally place the human at the same level as the divine'.[12] In terms of Kant's idea of *'plan'* it is necessary to stress the specific point O'Neill brings out:

> The chastened builders of the tower of Babel, who cannot wholly turn their backs on building projects, are not forced to settle on some specific new building. Rather they are advised to settle on *some* feasible plan that *all* of them can share. The condition that they must meet if they are to avoid the fate of "nomads"—isolation, dispersal, noncommunication— is to adopt *some* plan, that neither posits unavailable resources nor is unsharable with others. [...] Unlike Descartes, Kant does not think there is a unique edifice of reason, or that it could be created by any solitary builder. On Kant's account we think and act reasonably provided we neither invoke illusory capacities or authorities—that is what it is to take account of our actual resources and starting point—nor base our thinking or acting on nonlawlike, hence unsharable, principles.[13]

O'Neill notes that Kant came to Part II, 'Transcendental Doctrine of Method', after some 700 difficult pages of the *Doctrine of Elements*. This is why for her purpose, after taking up the two Prefaces in the first and second edition of *Critique of Pure Reason*, she directly goes to the 'Transcendental Doctrine of Method', in which she finally finds the 'vindication of reason' in Kant. Noting that from the very first pages of *Critique of Pure Reason* 'human thinking and doing are depicted as undisciplined striving that leads into tangles of contradiction', O'Neill remarks that 'Kant's critique of rationalism shows that this striving cannot be disciplined by conforming to some given (outside, "alien") reality. Striving for such conformity would be analogous to the hubris of the builders of Babel: Both projects must collapse'.[14] However, if rationalism or foundationalism are not the way to go in this striving, the unfortunate fate of the builders of Babel, abandoning the project of building, should not lead us in the direction of 'postmodern' *un*reasoned ways of thinking and doing. By no means are we in a 'position to live without reason', as O'Neill properly claims. She writes: 'Neither foundationalism nor postmodernism are genuine options for us. In terms of humble vocabulary of building trades, our only feasible option is to ask, What can be built with the materials and labor force available to us?'[15] She goes on to suggest that at this point

> an objection might be that metaphors of building or construction cannot shed light on a reflexive task. Buildings, it might be said need foundations, hence metaphors of construction are only appropriate if

we accept a foundationalist conception of the vindication of reason—for example, that of Descartes.[16]

'However', she problematically asserts that 'this objection overlooks the possibility of constructions without foundations, such as kites or space satellites, whose components are mutually supporting, although no part of the structure forms a foundation for the rest'.[17] Unfortunately, this statement misses the point that 'building' in the discourse of architecture is building only and only because of the fact that it is under the force of *gravity* in Newtonian science, with which Kant was quite familiar. This is different from using 'building' metaphorically for any other 'construction in mind' that has nothing to do with gravity. Building is a 'shelter' into which I walk because I am an *upright body* under the same force of gravity walking on the surface of the earth. If tomorrow I am walking on the surface of the moon and 'build' a shelter which is not subject to gravity, I cannot describe that 'building' by the term 'architecture'; it will need to be called something else. It is the fact that as long as we live on the surface of the earth, our construction of shelter, the 'art of building', has always to deal with the notion of foundation. In this regard, a more accurate way of considering the quandary of foundationalism, and its critique, in the discourse of rationalism is exactly the way Karatani puts the problem, that foundational theory or its opposite, antifoundational-ism, comes into view only when there is crisis in the foundation itself, and this is the crux of Karatani saying that philosophy is another name for the '*Will to Architecture*'.

Now we must understand that 'critique of reason' is a *task*, as Kant tells us. It is because we are 'unavoidably committed to thinking and acting', as O'Neill asserts. And let us never forget that we are '*reasoning beings*'. Building *hubris*, causing the failure of the builders of Babel, has its source in 'metaphysical hubris', in the Kantian sense. In her *Constructions of Reason*, O'Neill asserts that a 'Categorical Imperative is the supreme prin-ciple of reason'[18] and states that 'Reason betrayal constitutes a crisis in the foundation of European Sciences—in the rationalist enterprise—that threatens our thinking with complete disorientation'.[19] In this respect, she cites in part a passage from the Preface to the first edition of *Critique of Pure Reason* that I quote in its entirety:

Human reason has the peculiar fate in one species of its cognition that it is burdened with questions which it cannot dismiss, since they are given to it as problems by the nature of reason itself, but which it also cannot answer, since they transcend every capacity of human reason. Reason falls into this perplexity through no fault of its own. It begins from the principles whose use is unavoidable in the course of experience and at the same time sufficiently warranted by it. With these principles it rises (as its nature also requires) ever higher, to more remote conditions. But since it becomes aware in this way that its business must always remain incomplete because the questions never ease, reason sees itself necessitated to take refuge in principles that overstep all possible use in experience, and yet seem so unsuspicious that even ordinary common sense agrees with them. But it thereby falls into obscurity and contradictions, from which it can surmise that it must somewhere be proceeding on the ground of hidden errors; but it cannot discover them, for the principles on which it is proceeding, since they surpass the bounds of all experiences, no longer recognize any touchstone of experience. The battlefield of these endless controversies is called **metaphysics**.[20]

Kant in the same First Preface brings out the famous notion of the tribunal of reason:

This is evidently the effect of the thoughtlessness of our age, but of its ripened **Power of judgment**, which will no longer be put off with illusory knowledge, and which demands that reason should take on anew the most difficult of all its tasks, namely, that of self-knowledge, and to institute a court of justice, by which reason may secure its rightful claims while dismissing all its groundless pretensions, and this not by mere decree but according to its own central and unchangeable laws; and this court is none other than the **critique of pure reason** itself.[21]

Based on the *reflexive* and *political* task of the critique of reason, O'Neill goes back to the same introductory remarks of 'Transcendental Doctrine of Method' to comment that 'Like Descartes, Kant uses metaphor of construction to explain his view of philosophical method; but he states with a more down-to-earth view of building projects. The result is a quite different vision of philosophical procedures.'[22] However, she remarks:

Rationalism failed because it took no account either of the paucity of materials or the disagreements about the plan among the fellow workers. It relied on the fiction of a unitary and authoritative architect, whose innate ideas correspond to their real archetypes, to construct the edifice of human knowledge. All that could be built by relying on such a fiction was disagreement, strife and mutual noncomprehension. Like the tower of Babel, the edifice of rationalism was doomed to collapse. The disputes of metaphysics are ample evidence that the lofty structure of our metaphysical dreams cannot be built.[23]

'On the other hand', she continues,

> Kant acknowledges that we cannot turn our backs on the task of construction: 'we cannot well refrain from building a secure home'. Skepticism would condemn us to 'nomadic' existence that does not meet our deepest needs, including the needs of reason.[24]

She cites the First Preface I quoted previously to say that 'the insatiable needs of human reason are at the heart of our predicament'.[25] O'Neill puts the matter nicely: '*Even if we do not need a lofty tower, we need a shelter*'[emphasis mine], and continues,

> Even on "the plain of experience" we have tasks, and we need to be able to form a view of our immediate surroundings. We may not need a lofty tower that reaches the heavens, but we do need at least a modest cottage. Instinct provides an inadequate basis for human life, and we must guide our actions by adopting certain practical principles as our maxims.

She goes on to make the important point that

> To approach this task responsibly we must begin by recognizing that "Our problem is not just to do with materials, but even more to do with the plan." The plan must be one that can be followed by a plurality of "fellow workers" whose coordination is guaranteed neither by instinct nor by preestablished harmony.[26]

In 'Vindicating Reason', O'Neill returns to the same point:

> The chastened builders of the tower of Babel, who cannot wholly turn their backs on building projects, are forced to settle in some specific new building. Rather they are advised to settle on *some* feasible plan that *all* of them can share. The condition that they must meet if they are to avoid the fate of "nomads"—Isolation, dispersal, noncommunication—is to adopt *some* plan, that neither posits unavailable resources nor is unsharable with others.[27]

Unlike Descartes, as was already noted, she reminds us that 'Kant does not think that there is a unique edifice of reason, or that it could be created by any solitary builder'.[28]

Taking into account the foregoing commentaries on 'building reason' in Kant, we can now turn to the question of Kantian *architectonics*. First I must point out that in building reason, Kant knew well that the practice of laying a *foundation* is not an act *once and for all*. I cite subsequently the important passage where Kant comes to invoke the building metaphor directly related to the question of 'foundation'. There he lays down the foundation of *reason*, at the same time affirming that the *foundation* itself needs to be examined over and over again as it is never built on stable ground. It is a famous passage in the Preface to his *Prolegomenon to Any Future Metaphysics*, the book he published in 1783 to make the difficult *Critique of Pure Reason* more accessible to readers and to clear some misunderstandings of his philosophy of some critics. There he wrote the following:

> After all, it is nothing extraordinary in the elaboration of a science, when men begin to wonder how far it has advanced, that the question should at last occur as to whether and how in general such a science is possible? Human reason so delights in construction that it has several times built up a tower and then razed it to examine the nature of the foundation. It is never too late to become reasonable and wise; but if the insight comes late, there is always more difficulty in starting the change.[29]

Now this 'human reason' which 'so delights in construction' is named *architectonic*. In 'Transcendental Dialectic', the second division of the 'Transcendental Doctrine of the Elements' in *Critique of Pure Reason*, Kant wrote:

> Human reason is by nature architectonic, i.e. it considers all cognition as belonging to a possible system, and hence it permits only such principles as at least do not render an intended cognition incapable of standing together with others in some system or other. But the propositions of an antithesis are of a kind that they do render the completion of an edifice of cognitions entirely possible. [...] Hence the architectonic interest of reason (which is demanded not by empirical unity but pure rational unity) carries with it a natural recommendation for the assertion of the thesis.[30]

It is in the third chapter of 'Transcendental Doctrine of Method', entitled 'The Architectonic of Pure Reason', that Kant finally comes to have an extended definition of the word 'architectonic'. He writes:

> By an **architectonic** I understand the art of systems. Since systematic unity is that which first makes ordinary cognition into science, i.e.,

makes a system out of a mere aggregate of it, architectonic is the doctrine of that which is scientific in our cognition in general, and therefore necessarily belongs to the doctrine of method.[31]

This is then followed by an essential paragraph, in which he again brings up the building analogy at the same time that he 'vindicates reason' in accordance with *architectonic*. It goes as follows:

It is too bad that it is first possible for us to glimpse the idea in a clearer light and to outline a whole architectonically, in accordance with the ends of reason, only after we have long collected relevant cognitions haphazardly like building materials and worked through them technically with only a hint from an idea lying hidden within us. The systems seem to have been formed, like maggots, by a *generatio aequivoca* [spontaneous generation] from the mere confluence of aggregated concepts, garbled at first but complete in time, although they all had their schema, as the original seed, in the mere self-development of reason, and on that account are not merely each articulated for themselves in accordance with an idea but are rather all in turn purposively united with each other as members of a whole in a system of human cognition, and allow an architectonic to all human knowledge, which at the present time, since so much material has already been collected or can be taken from the ruins of collapsed older edifices, would not merely be possible but would not even be very difficult. We shall content ourselves here with the completion of our task, namely merely outlining the **architectonic** of all cognition from **pure reason**, and begin only at the point where the general root of our cognitive power divides and branches out into two stems, one of which is **reason**. By "reason" I here understand, however, the entire higher faculty of cognition, and I therefore contrast the rational to the empirical.[32]

Here it is proper to say a few words on the origins of the term 'architectonic' itself. The term might have originated in Leibniz. Kant partially adopted the term, roughly meaning 'the art of constructing a system of science', from Alexander Baumgarten's *Metaphysics*, published in 1739. Kant had taught Baumgarten's book for twenty-five years to his students. Baumgarten begins by saying that metaphysics is 'the science of the first principles in human knowledge', to which belong 'ontology, cosmology, psychology, and natural theology'.[33] And he then inserts 'architectonics' in 'Part I: Ontology, Prolegomena', where he writes: 'ONTOLOGY (ontosophia, metaphysics … universal metaphysics, architectonics, first philosophy) is the science of the more general predicates of a being'.[34]

When the system is characterized as an 'organized unity' to which 'the parts of science are related to each other', the architectonic *end* should not be conceived as 'technical' but must be unveiled as *philosophy*: 'Not philosophy as it exists, but philosophy as a "general delineation or outline" of the system of human reason'.[35] The 'ideal philosopher practicing this architectonic' is the one who does not 'simply reflect on the product of human reason—which would be "technical" and thus the work of an artifice'.[36] In this respect Kant wrote:

> Until now, however, the concept of philosophy has been only **a scholastic concept**, namely that of a system of cognition that is sought only as a science without having as its end anything more than the systematic unity of this knowledge, thus the **logical** perfection of cognition. But there is also a cosmopolitan concept (*conceptus cosmicus*) that has always grounded this term, especially when it is, as it were, personified and represented as an archetype in the ideal of the **philosopher**. From this point of view philosophy is the science of the relation of all cognition to the essential ends of human reason (*teleologia rationis humanae*) [teleology of human reason] and the philosopher is not an artist of reason but the legislator of human reason. It would be very boastful to call oneself a philosopher in this sense and to pretend to have equaled the archetype, which lies only in the idea.[37]

For Kant the architectonic of human reason would have two objects: nature and freedom. He writes:

> Now the legislation of human reason (philosophy) has two objects, nature and freedom, and thus contains the natural law as well as the moral law, initially in two separate systems but ultimately in a single philosophical system. The philosophy of nature pertains to everything that **is**; that of morals only to that which **should be**. All philosophy, however, is either cognition from pure reason or rational cognition from empirical principles. The former is called pure philosophy, the latter empirical.[38]

It is within the two objectives, the '*is*' and the '*ought*', respectively pertaining to the law of 'nature' and the moral law of 'freedom', that we must understand Kantian architectonics. As I pointed out before, in relation to the 'structure of Kant's architectonic', Karatani reflects on the fundamental elements constituting Kant's critical philosophy, that is, sensibility, understanding, and reason underpinned by 'thing-in-itself', 'phenomenon', and *Schein* or 'transcendental illusion'. It is this structure that Kant called 'architectonics'.[39]

I can now go back to Kant's distinct use of the 'building metaphor' as contained in the block quotation at the beginning of this chapter, the first paragraph at the beginning of 'Transcendental Doctrine of Method'. Karatani in *Architecture as Metaphor* argued that, as was noted previously in the Introduction, for Kant 'architectonics as metaphor is indispensable to the critique of architecture as metaphor'.[40] Karatani informs us that Kant employed architectonics as a metaphor and cites the following passage from Kant's *Critique of the Power of Judgment* where, in the 'Preface to the first edition, 1790', Kant wrote:

> For if such a system, under the general name of metaphysics, is ever to come into being (the complete production of which is entirely possible and highly important for the use of reason in all respects), then the critique must previously have probed the ground for this structure down to the depth of the first foundations of the faculty of principles independent of experience, so that it should not sink in any part, which would inevitably lead to the collapse of the whole.[41]

Karatani warns us, as noted before, that the foregoing paragraph should not be understood as Platonic but rather the opposite. Kant claimed that his investigation is not a doctrine but rather a 'transcendental critique'; in Karatani's words, 'Kant's critiques were intended not to construct a system but to reveal that any system "inevitably bring[s] with it the ruin of all" inasmuch as it is upheld under the aegis of the "arrogation of reason"', and 'Since "arrogation" is a juridical term, Kant's architectonics might also be substituted by a set of juridical metaphors'.[42] And, therefore, as I cited previously, 'What is crucial to note is that architectonics as metaphor is indispensable to the critique of architecture as metaphor', in so far as 'architecture as metaphor' is employed in order to give the idea of a system built on a solid *foundation* immune to future destruction and reconstruction. In other words, a system without its *critique*. But, in order to properly understand and appreciate the force of this argument, and in order to reflect on Kant's use of the 'building analogy' in his *Critique of Pure Reason*, one has to delve deeper into the concept of *architectonics* related to the notion of *reason* in Kant. Its affirmation is in the following concise paragraph in *Critique of Pure Reason*, A13/ B27, where Kant wrote:

> Transcendental philosophy is here the idea of a science, for which the critique of pure reason is to outline the entire plan architectonically, i.e., from principles, with a full guarantee for completeness and certainty of all the components that comprise this edifice.[43]

Kant is the 'modern philosopher of reason' who radically breaks from all the 'philosophers of reason'—from Plato to Descartes, from Spinoza to Leibniz, and 'from the thinkers of the pre-Critical enlightenment'. As Yirmiyahu Yovel aptly puts it, Kant stands in 'dual opposition to them'. That is,

> first, in ascribing to human reason an extraordinary power within its legitimate domain, and second, in radically shrinking and limiting this domain. Hence, as much as Kant is the modern philosopher of reason in its world-shaping role, he is also the genuine philosopher of 'reason's *finitude* and the finitude of the human reason'.[44]

In the second section of 'The Canon of Pure Reason' of 'Transcendental Doctrine of Method', Kant wrote that

All intertest of my reason (the speculative as well as the practical) is united in the following three questions':

1 **What can I know?**
2 **What should I do?**
3 **What may I hope?**[45]

The first question, Kant says, is 'merely speculative'. The second is 'merely practical', that 'It can belong to pure reason, but it is not transcendental but moral, and thus it cannot be in itself a subject of our critique', and the third question,

> namely 'if I do what I should do, what may I then hope?' is simultaneously practical and theoretical, so that the practical leads like a clue to a reply to the theoretical question and, in its highest form, the speculative question. For all **hope** concerns happiness, and with respect to the practical and moral law it is the very same as what knowledge and the natural law is with regard to theoretical cognition of things.[46]

For O'Neill, these three questions are related to the 'vindication of reason', which for Kant is 'fundamentally a modest affair'. She expands on it with the following remarks:

> It does not disclose any hidden route back to the Principle of Sufficient Reason. The heroic challenges of rationalist demands to ground reason are rejected, as are their difficulties. All that is vindicated is a precept of thinking and doing without relying on any fundamental principle which either presupposes some arbitrary "authority," or cannot be followed by others. Minimal indeed, but far from empty. Any

form of relativism that "submits" to some arbitrary power (state, churches, majority, tradition, or dictator) as the source of reason is rejected. So is any form of rationalism that "submits" to supposed divine or other "necessities." So is any form of skepticism or postmodernism that equates "reason" with momentarily available ways of thought. Within these constraints we may be able to work out how far Kantian conception of reason guides and constrains what we can know, what we ought to do, and what we may hope'.[47]

With these remarks I bring this chapter to an end by reiterating what Karatani said about Kant's triadic concept, that is, thing-in-itself, phenomena, and *Schein*, that can be grasped only *transcendentally*, forming what Kant called 'architectonics'. It is only within this triadic structure that the omnipresence of 'metaphor', and for that matter, the 'building metaphor' grounded in the imperative of '*building reason*', must be understood.

Notes

1 Emmanuel Kant, *Critique of Pure Reason*, trans. and ed. Paul Guyer and Allen W. Wood (Cambridge: Cambridge University Press, 1998), A 474, B 502, 502.
2 In Kōjin Karatani, *Transcritique: On Kant and Marx*, trans. Sabu Kohso (Cambridge: The MIT Press, 2005), 90.
3 See Howard Caygill, *A Kant Dictionary* (Malden: Blackwell, 1995), the entry 'Judgment'. Caygill explains that Kant in the *Critique of the Power of Judgment* shifted his focus of his account of judgment,

> moving from an emphasis on completed judgments to one directed towards the faculty of judgment (*Urteilskraft*). From this perspective judgment is viewed less in terms of subsumption than in those of "thinking the particular as contained under universal" ... When the universal is given, and the particular subsumed under it by the faculty of judgment, then the judgment is determinant; when only the particular is given and the universal has to be sought by the faculty of judgment, then its judgment is reflective.
>
> (269)

4 See Douglas Burnham with Harvey Young, *Kant's Critique of Pure Reason* (Bloomington and Indianapolis: Indiana University Press, 2007), 186.
5 Kōjin Karatani, *Transcritique: On Kant and Marx*, 114.
6 Kōjin Karatani, *Transcritique: On Kant and Marx*, 114.
7 Immanuel Kant, *Critique of Pure Reason*, A 707/B 735, 627. 'Therefore', Kant says, 'by the transcendental doctrine of method' he understands 'the determination of the formal conditions of a complex system of pure reason', and that

> we shall have to concern ourselves with a **discipline**, a **canon**, an **architectonic**, and finally a **history** of pure reason, and will accomplish, in a transcendental respect, that which, under the name of a **practical logic**, with regard to the use of the understanding in general...
>
> (A 708/ B 736, 627)

8 Here I should mention the significant study by Daniel Purdy in his *On the Ruins of Babel: Architectural Metaphor in German Thought* (Ithaca and New York: Cornell University Press, 2011), in which he brings up the notion of the Tower of Babel and takes up the 'metaphor of architecture' in Kant for an extensive analysis. Purdy presents us with fine scholarship and demonstrates a sound knowledge of architectural theory and history, but he nevertheless goes too far in reading *too* much 'architecture' into Kant's *Critique of Pure Reason*, which gives the reader a wrong impression that it is an 'architectural treatise' like the one by the Renaissance architect Leon Batistta Alberti, *The Art of Building in Ten Books*, or Vitruvius's *Ten Books on Architecture*! One gets the impression that Kant wrote *Critique of Pure Reason* as an 'architect' and makes us to think that he had read Vitruvius's and Alberti's treatises closely! For example, in a section of his book entitled 'Kant's Debt to Renaissance Architecture Theory', Purdy draws an analogy between Kant and Alberti and writes that 'Kant adapts Alberti's architecture of the mind for his own epistemology. Alberti's rich discussion of the proper selection, compartition, distribution, and outline of buildings reappears in *Critique of Pure Reason*', 101. Or 'Kant acknowledges the parallel between his own epistemology and classical architecture theory, the beginnings of which lie in Vitruvius and Alberti', 103. Purdy's book is replete with these kind of analogies; He indulges in his stretched analogy of Kant's 'system of building' with that of the writers of architectural treatises in history. Kant's cursory knowledge of architecture treatises, as Purdy himself mentions, must have come from his reading of Christian Wolff's extensive writings in this area. Aside from these indulgences, Purdy is quite perceptive in many points he raises, in particular in chapter 3, when he takes Mark Wigley to task in his *The Architecture of Deconstruction* for his misguided reading of Kant through Heidegger's *Kant and the Problem of Metaphysics*. I should mention that in Purdy's vast scholarship and extensive references in his book it is curious that there is no mention of Kōjin Karatani's *Architecture as Metaphor*, which was published long before Purdy's book.

 Among other notable books that treat the architectonic in Kant, more on philosophical ground than exclusively on the 'architecture metaphor', I should mention Diane Morgan's *Kant Trouble: The Obscurities of the Enlightenment* (London and New York: Routledge, 2000); Leslie Jaye Kavanaugh, *The Architectonic of Philosophy: Plato, Aristotle, Leibniz* (Amsterdam: Amsterdam University Press, 2007); Edward Wilatt, *Kant, Deleuze and Architectonics* (London: Continuum, 2010); and Claudia Brodsky Lacour, *Lines of Thought: Discourse, Architectonics, and the Origin of Modern Philosophy* (Durham and London: Duke University Press, 1996), which is more about Descartes than Kant.

9 Onora O'Neill, 'Vindicating Reason', in *The Cambridge Companion to Kant*, ed. Paul Guyer (Cambridge: Cambridge University Press, 1992).

10 See Onora O'Neill, *Constructions of Reason: Explorations of Kant's Practical Philosophy* (Cambridge: Cambridge University Press, 1989).

11 Daniel Purdy, *On the Ruins of Babel*, 53.

12 Daniel Purdy, *On the Ruins of Babel*, 55.

13 Onora O'Neill, 'Vindicating Reason', 297.

14 Onora O'Neill, 'Vindicating Reason', 297.

15 Onora O'Neill, 'Vindicating Reason', 291.

16 Onora O'Neill, 'Vindicating Reason', 291.

17 Onora O'Neill, 'Vindicating Reason', 291.

18 Onora O'Neill, *Constructions of Reason*, 3.

19 Onora O'Neill, *Constructions of Reason*, 8.
20 Immanuel Kant, *Critique of Pure Reason*, A viii, 99.
21 Immanuel Kant, *Critique of Pure Reason*, A xi–xiii, 100–101.
22 Onora O'Neill, *Constructions of Reason*, 11.
23 Onora O'Neill, *Constructions of Reason*, 12.
24 Onora O'Neill, *Constructions of Reason*, 12.
25 Onora O'Neill, *Constructions of Reason*, 12.
26 Onora O'Neill, *Constructions of Reason*, 12.
27 Onora O'Neill, 'Vindicating Reason', 297.
28 Onora O'Neill, 'Vindicating Reason', 297.
29 Immanuel Kant, *Prolegomena to Any Future Metaphysics, Second Edition, and the Letter to Marcus Herz, February 1772*, trans. with intro. and notes, James W. Ellington (Indianapolis and Cambridge: Hackett, 2001), 1–2.
30 Immanuel Kant, *Critique of Pure Reason*, A475/ B 503, 502.
31 Immanuel Kant, *Critique of Pure Reason*, A 833/ B 861, 691.
32 Immanuel Kant, *Critique of Pure Reason*, A 835/ B 863, 692–693.
33 See Alexander Baumgarten, *Metaphysics, A Critical Translation with Kant's Elucidations, Selected Notes, and Related Materials*, trans. and edited by Courtney D. Fugate and John Hymers (London, Bloomsbury, 2013), 99.
34 Alexander Baumgarten, *Metaphysics*, 100.
35 See Howard Caygill's *A Kant Dictionary*, under the entry 'architectonic' (Malden: Blackwell, 1995), 85.
36 Howard Caygill's *A Kant Dictionary*, 85.
37 Immanuel Kant, *Critique of Pure Reason*, A 839/ B 867, 694–695.
38 Immanuel Kant, *Critique of Pure Reason*, A 840/ B868, 695. Caygill on his commentary in the entry 'architectonic' makes the point that

> With this concern for the philosophical system Kan inherited the Wolffian project of encyclopedic philosophy or *philosophia generalis*. This Project was the form of in which German Philosophy defended its claims against the discrete sciences (and faculties) of law, theology and medicine as well as the emergent natural sciences. The view of philosophy as an architectonic system flourished after Kant in the system of Fichte (1794), Schelling (1800) and Hegel (1830), but was abandoned by the middle of the nineteenth century.
>
> (*A Kant Dictionary*, 84–85)

39 See Kōjin Karatani, *Architecture as Metaphor: Language, Number, Money*, trans. Sabu Kohso (Cambridge: The MIT Press, 1995), xliii.
40 Kōjin Karatani, *Architecture as Metaphor*, xliv.
41 Immanuel Kant, *Critique of the Power of Judgment*, ed. Paul Guyer, trans. Paul Guyer and Eric Mathews (Cambridge: Cambridge University Press, 2000), 56. Karatani uses an old translation with a slight difference which goes as follows:

> For if such a system is some day worked out under the general name metaphysic—and its full and complete execution is both possible and of the utmost importance for the employment of reason in all departments of its activity—the critical examination of the ground for this edifice must have been previously carried down to the very depths of the foundations of the faculty of principles independent of experience, lest in some quarter it might give way, and, sinking, inevitably bring with it the ruins of all.
>
> (*Architecture as Metaphor*, xliii)

Also see Immanuel Kant, *Critique of Aesthetic Judgement*, trans. James Creed Meredith (Oxford: Clarendon Press, 1911), 5.

42 Kōjin Karatani, *Architecture as Metaphor*, xliv.
43 Immanuel Kant, *Critique of Pure Reason*, trans. and eds. Paul Guyer and Allen W. Wood (Cambridge: Cambridge University Press, 1998), A13/ B27, 150.
44 See Yirmiyahu Yovel, *Kant's Philosophical Revolution: A Short Guide to the Critique of Pure Reason* (Princeton and Oxford: Princeton University Press, 2018), 4.
45 Immanuel Kant, *Critique of Pure Reason*, A 805/ B833, 677. A
46 Immanuel Kant, *Critique of Pure Reason*, A 805/ B833, 677.
47 Onora O'Neill, 'Vindicating Reason', 305.

4

ARCHITECTONICS AND MATHEMATICAL FOUNDATIONS

Reason rules the world.[1]

—Anaxagoras

Kōjin Karatani put forward the thesis that architecture as metaphor dominated mathematics until 1931 when Kurt Gödel's *incomplete theorem* 'invalidated mathematics as the ground for the architectonic'.[2] This inaugurated the 'crisis of foundation' in mathematics. Karatani made his statement in *Architecture as Metaphor* and followed it up by his extensive examination of Gödel's proof. Later, in his *Transcritique: On Kant and Marx*, Karatani returned to Gödel to shed more light on the presence of 'non-Euclidean' geometry in Kant's mathematical thinking. In this chapter I examine Karatani's argument while exploring Gödel's proof and the idea of 'mathematical foundations' in relation to non-Euclidean geometry. This is aimed at a better understanding of the 'architectonic metaphor' in Kant as Karatani has brought out. In his early attempt to arrive at Kant's transcendental critique in *Architecture as Metaphor*, that he will fully take up in his *Transcritique*, Karatani had reminded us that it was Gödel who introduced 'undecidability' into mathematics.[3] He makes the following incisive statement: 'Gödel's proof presents us with a case wherein the attempt to *architectonize* mathematics results not in a mathematical foundation but in the impossibility of mathematical foundations'.[4] To comprehend the import of this remark, and for a full examination of Karatani's thesis, we need first to revisit non-Euclidean geometry and Gödel's proof, for which we have to reflect on the notions of *formal systems* and *formalization*, and the mathematical relation between *axiom* and *theorem*.[5]

The Greeks, unlike other early civilizations, sought the truths about human beings and attempted to solve their mystery not in religion but with the power of *reason*. It was the Greeks of the classical period (the

DOI: 10.4324/9781032647616-5

years 600 to 300 BCE), as Morris Kline tells us, 'who recognized that man has an intellect, a mind which, aided occasionally by observation of experimentation, can discover truths'.[6] They had a unique intellectual attitude to nature which was 'rational, critical and secular'. It can be summarized by what the Ionian philosopher Anaxagoras said: 'Reason rules the world'.[7] Nature for the Greeks had a 'mathematical design'. After the Pythagoreans, Platonists, led by Plato, took over and disseminated the doctrine of the mathematical design of nature. It is well-known that Platonists distinguished sharply between the 'world of things and the world of ideas': 'Objects, and relationships in the material world were subject to imperfections, change, and decay and hence did not represent the ultimate truth, but rather was an ideal world in which there were absolute and unchanging truths'.[8] In their thoughts, 'Infallible knowledge can be obtained only about pure ideal forms. These ideas are in fact constant and invariable, and knowledge concerning them is firm and indestructible'.[9] As Rebecca Goldstein in her *Incompleteness: The Proof and Paradoxes of Kurt Gödel* writes, for the ancient Greeks, mathematical knowledge was the least problematic and 'in fact the very model toward which all knowledge ought to aspire: certain and unassailable, in short *proved*'.[10] Therefore for Plato onward, the 'standards and methods of mathematics ought to be applied, insofar as is possible, to *all* our attempts to know'.[11] 'So the question is: Where is certainty? What is our *source* for mathematical certainty?'; Goldstein poses this question in order to bring out the persistent 'tricky' problem of 'intuition' in the discourse on mathematics. She writes that 'The bedrock of empirical knowledge consists of sense perceptions: what I am directly given to know—or at least to think—of the external world through my senses of sight and hearing and touch and taste and smell'. 'Sense perception', she goes on to say,

> allows us to make contact with what's out there in physical reality. What is the bedrock of mathematical knowledge? Is there something like sense perception in mathematics? Do mathematical *intuitions* constitute this bedrock? Is our faculty for intuition the means for making contact with what's out there in mathematical reality?[12]

She makes the important point that 'Mathematical intuition is often thought of as the a priori analogue to sensory perception'.[13] 'All *genuine* intuitions', she asserts, 'are (tautologously) true (tautologously because we would not call them "genuine" unless they were true)'.[14]

Now mathematics is considered to be unique because it 'alone' seems to 'offer a method for truth-purification: the axiomatic system. [...]

The desire to universalize the truth-purifying rigor of the mathematical method is precisely what the epistemological movement known as rationalism is all about'.[15] But what is an axiomatic system exactly, and how is it rigorous? Goldstein writes that the idea behind the axiomatic, or axiomatized, system is that 'the manifold truths of some particular branch of mathematics, say geometry or arithmetic, can be organized into axioms, rules of inference, and theorems. The axioms are the basic truths of the system, intuitively obvious.'[16] 'The theorems of an axiomatic system', Goldstein importantly states, 'are *only* accepted as true once they are proved, derived from the axioms or derived from other theorems, using truth-preserving rules of inference'.[17] Goldstein explains that 'The motive behind the axiomatic system is to maximize certainty by minimizing appeals to intuitions, restricting them to the few ineliminable axioms', adding that 'For much of the history of Western thought, at least since the time of Euclid, the axiomatized system was generally deemed to represent mathematics—and thus knowledge itself—in its most perfect form'.[18] This relates to the way for limiting intuitions aimed at eliminating it altogether: 'This aim is what bring us, at long last, to the notion of a *formal system*. A formal system is an axiomatic system divested of all appeals to intuition.'[19] In this respect, the nineteenth century is the century which 'subverted our confidence in those intuitively obvious givens of our axiomatic systems', and 'the most dramatic of these undermining events was the discovery of non-Euclidean geometry'.[20] To explain non-Euclidean geometry, we must first recall Euclid's fifth postulate. As Kline states, 'one axiom of Euclidean geometry had bothered mathematicians somewhat, not because there was in their minds any doubt of its truth but because of its wording',[21] well known as the 'parallel axiom', or the fifth postulate. In the simple Playfair's axiom (that we learn in high school) it goes as follows: 'Given a line *l* and a point *p* not on that line, there exists in the plane of *p* and *l* and through *p* one and only one line *m*, which does not meet the given *l*'. Kline puts it in its original terms in the following:

> If a straight line falling on two straight lines makes the interior angles on the same side less than two right angles, then the two straight lines if extended will meet on that side of the straight line on which the angles are less than two right angles.[22]

Goldstein points out that 'Euclid himself wasn't all that happy with this last postulate, sensing how different it was from the others, with its covert reference to infinity, and had avoided using it in his derivations whenever he could'.[23] And 'why does the parallel postulate invokes infinity?' The answer is:

> Two lines are parallel if and only if they'll never intersect. But if you take a finite region of space then you can draw more than one line through a point that will be parallel (i.e., won't intersect) the line. So the parallel postulate makes implicit reference to infinity, and we are always rightly suspicious of our intuitions about infinity.[24]

We now come to the nineteenth century and 'non-Euclidean' geometry. Three mathematicians must be named who independently are credited for non-Euclidean geometry: Carl Friedrich Gauss (1777–1855), Nicolai Ivanovich Lobachevsky (1729–1856), and the young János Bolyai (1802–1860). Gauss proceeded with the 'logical implication of a system of axioms which included the assumption that *more than one* parallel line passed through a given point, and thus created non-Euclidean geometry'.[25] The main idea, conceived by the three men, asserts that one was 'logically free to adopt a parallel axiom which differs fundamentally from Euclid's, and that one could construct a new geometry which would be as valid as Euclid's and which might even be a good description of physical space'.[26] Gauss, Lobachevsky, and Bolyai, as Kline points out, had realized that the

> Euclidean parallel axiom could not be proved on the basis of the other nine axioms and that some additional axiom about parallel lines was needed to found Euclidean geometry. Since this last was an independent fact it was then at least logically possible to adopt a contradictory statement and develop the consequences of the new set of axioms.[27]

Kline writes:

> The most significant fact about non-Euclidean geometry is that *it can be used to describe the properties of physical space as accurately as Euclidean geometry does*. Euclidean geometry is not the necessary geometry of physical space; its physical truth cannot be guaranteed on any a priori grounds. This realization, which did not call for any technical mathematical development, because this had already been done, was first attained by Gauss.[28]

Gauss believed that we cannot be sure of the *truth* of Euclidean geometry. Kline writes

That Gauss was influenced directly by the writing of Hume cannot be ascertained. Kant's rebuttal of Hume he disdained. Nevertheless he lived at a time when the truth of mathematical laws was being challenged, and he must have absorbed the intellectual atmosphere as surely as all of us breathe the air about us. New intellectual outlooks take hold even if imperceptibly.[29]

Along with non-Euclidean geometry, the 'set theory' also set back the 'putative intuition'. It led to the formation of 'such paradox-infected sets as the sets of all sets that are not members of themselves'.[30] The foundation seemed to be not that solid. If possible, all the 'axiomatic systems of appeals to intuition' was the way to go. Goldstein writes:

> The elimination of intuition is accomplished by draining the axiomatic system of all meanings, except those that can be defined in terms of the stipulated rules of the system. The rules, in terms of which everything else is defined, make no claim to being anything other than stipulated. […] A formal system is precisely what we are left with after this meaning-draining.[31]

Therefore:

> A formal system, then, is an axiomatic system—with its primitive given (the axioms), its rules of inference, and its proved theorems— except that instead of being constructed of meaningful symbols— such as terms referring to the number 0 or to the successor function—it is constructed entirely of meaningless signs, marks on paper whose only significance is defined in terms of *the relations of each to one another as set forth by the rules*. While pre-purged axiomatic systems were understood as being about, say, numbers (arithmetic) or sets (set theory) or space (geometry), a formal system is an axiomatic system that is not, in itself, *about anything*. We don't have to appeal to our intuitions about numbers or sets or space in laying down the given of the formal system.[32]

A formal system is nothing but rules, and to follow it one engages in a '*combinatorial* activity that, consisting purely of *recursive* functions' that

> could be programmed into a computer, that is, that is *computable*. This activity amounts to figuring things out by using an *algorithm*, a sequence of operations that tells you what to do at each step, depending on what the outcome of the previous step was.[33]

Intuition cannot get a foothold in formal systems. If intuition is useful to tell us what to think about actual things such as space, numbers, or sets, we do not need it for meaningless symbols. If it can be shown that 'logically consistent formal systems are adequate for proving all the truths of mathematics, then we would have successfully banished intuition from mathematics', and then importantly, 'The assertion of the possibility and desirability of banishing intuitions by showing formal systems to be entirely adequate to the business of mathematics is the metamathematical view known as *formalism*'.[34] And based on analogy with the formalism of chess with its 'stipulated rules', mathematics is raised to a 'higher order of intricacy', in which according to formalism,

> the stipulated rules constitute the whole truth of mathematics. We win in mathematics by proving theorems—that is, by showing some uninterpreted string of symbols to follow from other uninterpreted strings of symbols, using the agreed-upon rules of inference. There is no external truth against which mathematics has to measure itself.[35]

Based on the foregoing remarks regarding intuition, we come to Gödel's incompleteness on which Goldstein says the following:

> Gödel's first incompleteness theorem states the incompleteness of any *formal system* rich enough to express arithmetic. So Gödel's conclusion, you might suspect, has something to say about the feasibility (or lack thereof) of eliminating all intuitions from mathematics. The most straightforward way of understanding intuitions is that they are given to us by the nature of things; again intuition is seen as the a priori analogue to sense perception, a direct form of apprehension. So Gödel's conclusion, in having something to say about the feasibility (or lack thereof) of eliminating all appeals to intuitions from mathematics might also have a thing or two to say about the actual existence of mathematical objects, like numbers and sets. In other words, the adequacy of formal systems—their consistency and completeness—is linked with the question of ultimate eliminability of intuitions, which is linked with the question of the ultimate eliminability of a mathematical reality, which is the defining question of mathematical realism, or Platonism. It is because of these linkages that Gödel's conclusion about the limits of formal systems have so *much* to say. [...] The young students had found a proof for a theorem, the first incompleteness theorem, that had the rigor of mathematics and the reach of philosophy.[36]

At this point Goldstein in her exploration of Gödel examines the works of the mathematicians David Hilbert and Georg Cantor, which we do not need to get into. Suffice it to mention that Goldstein points out that

> The leading advocate of formalism was David Hilbert, who was the most important mathematician of his day. 'Mathematics,' wrote Hilbert, 'is a game played according to certain simple rules with meaningless marks on paper.' His proposal to formalize one branch of mathematics after the other, starting with the most basic branch of all, arithmetic, came to be called the Hilbert program.[37]

Before I return to Karatani's discussion of Gödel's *incompleteness* theorem in relation to the 'crisis' in mathematical foundation and non-Euclidean geometry in Kant, as stated at the beginning of this chapter, it is useful to briefly summarize the trajectory of mathematical thoughts from the ancient Greeks to our time. Morris Kline in a later chapter of his *Mathematics: The Loss of Certainty*, titled 'Whither Mathematics?', expresses the same crisis of the mathematical thoughts and offers us a summary of the long trajectory of mathematics to its 'present plight', as he names it, by wonderfully employing 'building analogy' and 'foundation' to demonstrate it. He starts with the Egyptians and Babylonians and says that

> The Egyptian and Babylonian mathematicians, who first began building mathematics, were not at all able to foresee what kind of structure they would erect. Hence they did not lay a deep foundation. Rather they built directly on the surface of the earth. At that time the earth seemed to offer a secure base, and the material with which they commenced construction, facts about numbers and geometrical figures, was taken from simple earthly experiences. This historical origin of mathematics is signalized by our continuing use of the word geometry, the measurement of land.[38]

The structure began to rise above the ground but proved to be shaky if more was added to the construction. We then come to the Greeks. Kline writes:

> The Greeks of the classical period not only saw the danger but supplied the necessary rebuilding. They adopted two measures. The first was to select firm strips of ground along with which one could run the walls. These strips were the self-evident truths about space and the whole numbers. The second was to put steel into the framework. The steel was deductive proof of each addition to the structure.[39]

Although the foundation of the Greek mathematics was based on the stable ground of Euclidean geometry, as Kline says, one fault showed itself, namely, that 'certain line segment—such as the diagonal of an isosceles right angle whose arms are 1 unit long—would have to have a length of √2 units', that is an irrational number. And since the Greeks recognized only the ordinary whole numbers, they would not accept such an irrational number. Therefore,

> they resolved the dilemma by ostracizing these irrational 'numbers,' and abandoning the idea of assigning numerical lengths to line segments, areas, and volume. Hence, they built no additions to arithmetic and algebra beyond the whole numbers and what could be incorporated into the structure of geometry. It is true that some Alexandrian Greeks, notably Archimedes, did operate with irrational numbers, but these were incorporated into the logical structure of mathematics.[40]

Kline continues with his building analogy and remarks:

> By expanding the mathematics of number, the Hindus, Arabs, and Europeans added floor to floor: complex numbers, more algebra, calculus, differential equations, differential geometry and many more subjects. However, in place of steel they used wooden columns and beams composed of intuitive and physical arguments. But these supports proved unequal to their load and cracks began to show in the walls. By 1800, the structure was once again in peril and mathematicians hastened to replace the wood with steel. While the superstructure was being strengthened, the ground—the axioms chosen by the Greeks—caved in under the walls. The creation of non-Euclidean geometry revealed that the axioms of Euclidean geometry were not truly solid strips of earth but only seemed so on superficial inspection. Nor were the axioms of non-Euclidean geometries a firm ground.[41]

'Thus', the story continues, 'the entire structure of mathematics, geometry, and arithmetic with its extensions to algebra and analysis, was in grave peril. The by now lofty building was in danger of collapsing and sinking into a quagmire', as Kline puts it.[42] Thus the conceived 'firm ground' of earth was not solid enough to build the fountain of mathematics, the seeming solid earth proved to be deceptive. But apparently 'mathematicians rose to the challenge'. Another structure could be built on a more solid foundation. And this would consist of sharply worded definitions, complete sets of axioms, and explicit proof of all results no matter how obvious they might seem to intuition. Moreover, in place of truth there was to be logical consistency. The theorems were to be carefully interwoven, so that the entire structure would be solid. Through the axiomatic of activity of the late 19th century, the mathematicians seemingly achieved the solidity of structure.

and although a crisis in the history of mathematics was resolved, mathematics 'lost its grounding in reality'.[43]

Kline continues to detect more troubles and like a capable architect-engineer diagnoses that,

> Unfortunately, the cement used in the foundation of the new structure did not harden properly. Its consistency had not been guaranteed by the builder, and when the contradictions of set theory appeared, mathematicians realized that an even graver crisis threatened their handiwork. Of course, they were not going to sit by and see centuries of efforts crumble into ruins. Since consistency was dependent on the bases chosen for the reasoning, it seemed clear that only a reconstruction of the entire foundation of mathematics would suffice.[44]

After pointing out that mathematics had reached the stage where the mathematicians held conflicting views, that is, logicism, intuitionism, formalism, and set theory, with diverging superstructures on the construction, Kline comes finally to Gödel and writes:

> Under the limitation imposed by Hilbert, Gödel showed that any significant formal system contains undecidable propositions, propositions that are independent of the axioms. One could then take either such a proposition or its denial as an additional axiom. However, after this choice, the enlarged system must, according to Gödel's result, also contain undecidable propositions and so a choice again became possible. The process is in fact unending. The logicists, formalists, and set theorists rely on axiomatic foundations. [...] But Gödel's theorem showed that that no one system of axioms embraces all of the truths that belong to any one structure ...'[45]

As a tentative conclusion to his 'building analogy' in his surveying more than two thousand years of history of mathematics, Kline, stating that mathematics is a 'human construction and any attempt to find an absolute basis for it is probably doomed to failure', writes that

Several of the schools have tried to enclose mathematics within the confines of men's logic. But intuition defies encapsulating in logic. The concept of a safe, indubitable, and infallible body of mathematics built upon a sound foundation stems of course from the dream of the classical Greeks, embodied in the work of Euclid. This ideal guided the thinking of mathematicians for more than twenty centuries. But apparently mathematicians were misled by the 'evil genius' Euclid.[46]

On this note I now return to Karatani's argument.

By his incisive inquiry into the importance of *formalism* that had emerged in different fields of study in the twentieth century, with its origin going back to the Platonic problem of *form*, Karatani in *Architecture as Metaphor* informs us that it was Gödel, himself a Platonist, who 'developed an internal critique of formalism that had repercussions in formalist practices in all disciplinary fields'.[47] The Platonists contemporary to Nietzsche, who had followed his prototypical critique of Platonism, had missed the 'paradoxical fact' that, as Karatani puts it, the 'will to construct a solid edifice' would not 'achieve a foundation, but reveals instead the very absence of its own foundation'.[48] As to the place of mathematics in Plato, Karatani makes the following remarks:

> Plato consistently embraced mathematics as a norm, though not because it provided an architectonic; the mathematics that had been developed in Babylonia and other places was not, for Plato, rigorous, because it was practical and empirical. Plato introduced the proof as *reductio ad absurdum*: if a proposition is agreed upon and established, anything contradictory to it must be avoided as unsound. Euclid developed his framework into an axiomatic system and determined as true only that which is deductible from it. None of these efforts was a sine qua non for mathematical development; on the contrary, they inhibit the algebraic developments that had begun in Babylonia. Mathematics developed, and continues to develop, indifferent to the Platonic desire for architectonicity. What is important to point out here is that Plato fabricated an edifice using as his materials mathematical practices that were not in the least architectonic.[49]

The upshot is that 'it is in mathematics that the Platonic will to architecture is most often encountered, and, accordingly, it is through mathematics that the critique of Plato must be focused'.[50] Later, in a chapter of *Architecture as Metaphor* entitled 'Natural Numbers', Karatani returns to Gödel's proof and non-Euclidean geometry to examine them in depth.

He begins first with the 'deconstructive' movement and mentions Paul de Man's reading of John Locke to remark that 'constructive' or 'architectural will' would 'reveal its inversion' exactly the way that the 'Euclidean principle that sought architectonic precision disclosed non-Euclidean geometry'.[51] 'First and foremost', Karatani says, 'a deconstruction of the architectonic must be focused on the very realm in which the architectonic or construction seems to be most unassailably constituted, that is mathematics'. This means that we must better understand the 'problematics of mathematical formalization' that date to the late nineteenth century. Karatani incisively makes the same observation about the Euclidean postulate discussed previously:

> Within the field of nineteenth-century geometry it was understood that the Platonic and Euclidean attempt to turn mathematics into axiomatic architecture was inconsistent with respect to "the fifth postulate" (of parallel lines). While developing the postulate, Euclid had relied on apperceptual self-evidence. But according to Euclid's principle, a postulate must be constituted independent of apperceptual self-evidence; otherwise it cannot serve as the foundation of a solid edifice. Euclid defined a point as devoid of spatial expansion; and it is precisely because it is not a perceptible object with spatial dimension that it can be a foundation for mathematical edifice. Conversely, since the parallel postulate does not provide a solid foundation, mathematicians have long questioned its status, repeating the futile attempt to deduce it as a theorem from the other Euclidean postulate.[52]

Karatani crucially remarks that

> Since it was discovered that non-Euclidean geometry could be established by introducing the postulate 'parallel lines intersect,' faith in mathematical architectonicity has been fundamentally shaken. The flaw in Euclid's work lies in his reliance on perception, or natural language, and in his inference of the straight line and point and on the other hand, non-Euclidean geometry made it clear that mathematics could exist independent from reality of perception; in one sense, this constituted a move toward a more rigorous formalization of mathematics.[53]

Karatani points out that, connected to the challenge of non-Euclidean geometry, the early twentieth century 'crisis in mathematics began with the development of the theory of sets', and goes on to observe that

From the moment Descartes defined points as geometry of numbers, the point and line segment in geometry became an issue of numbers. For a line segment to be continuous, no matter how short it may be, there must exist an infinite number of infinitely minute points along the lines; the numbers corresponding to these points are called real numbers, though in essence they are *imaginary*.[54]

Here Karatani brings up Gorge Cantor's theory of sets which was formulated in order to deal with the problem of infinity:

Cantor saw infinity not as limitless but as a number. With this, paradox of set theory emerged, which can be described as follows: if we grant the theorem 'Given any set, finite or infinite, a set with more elements can always be obtained,' then the moment one considers 'the set of all the possible elements,' a contradiction arises.[55]

We must be clear that, as Karatani advises us, 'aporia' resulting from the theory of set and geometry are essentially the same. And in this connection we must also know that 'real numbers' are described by 'natural numbers'. For an example,

that a real number, 0.24910370 ..., is described by the natural numbers 0, 2, 4, 9 ... proves that natural numbers are fundamental. However, since Cantor, set theory has attempted to formalize natural numbers according to sets. [...] It was Gödel's proof that exposed the impossibility of giving a foundation to natural numbers by such a procedure. The problematic of perception and form in geometry was thus replaced by that of natural numbers and their formalization, equating the founding of Euclidean geometry with the founding of natural numbers.[56]

We have seen before the difference between the 'intuitionists' and 'logicists'. Bertrand Russell, who belonged to the latter, rendered mathematics as a 'subgenre of logic'. Intuitionists tried to restrict mathematics and focus only on the ways it is 'affected and made operable by "intuition"'. But a different approach was introduced by David Hilbert, as mentioned before. In this regard, Karatani remarks that

Hilbert's formalist approach sought to render mathematics genuinely independent of perception. By depleting the axiom of all intuitive meanings, Hilbert formalized mathematics as a nonsensical collection of symbols or formulas and their transformational rules of inferences. For Hilbert, the meaning of the axiom is not questioned; it no longer requires intuitive self-evidence. Rather, what matters is the qualification of the propositions that form an axiom and, upon acceptance of such propositions, what type of axiomatic system is constituted.[57]

What is important is that in order to establish a

consistent mathematical system based purely upon logical concepts, logicists had to take as a premise the not necessarily logical axiom of infinity. For Hilbert, however, to the extent that axiomatic system is free of consistency, any system—including even the axiom of infinity—can be taken as premise.[58]

According to Karatani, Hilbert

discovered the solid foundation of mathematics in the consistency of its formal system: mathematics does not have to be 'true' as long as it is 'consistent,' and as long as this is the case, there is no further need for further foundation. As a consequence, proof of consistency in the formalized axiomatic system becomes crucial.[59]

Following the proposition that 'As long as Euclidean geometry is consistent, non-Euclidean geometry should also be consistent', and yet, 'because it relies on "intuition", the consistency of Euclidean geometry cannot be proven internally', Karatani observes that

The crux of Hilbert's formalist approach lies in his decision to give up such a method altogether. He distinguished the system of axioms from the logic that proves its consistency, and called the latter 'meta-mathematics.' To avoid mathematical contradiction, and in order to satisfy even the intuitionists, Hilbert designed his approach to be finite and compositional. *Yet just as Hilbert's method seemed to be emerging as a success, Gödel's incompleteness theorem arrived to deal it a fatal blow.*[60] [my emphasis]

As Karatani explains:

The incompleteness theorem can be outlined as follows: insofar as the axiomatic system achieved by formalizing the theory of natural numbers is consistent, it can be understood as neither provable nor disprovable with regard to the system. Hence, an undecidable formula always exists. In addition, the theorem includes the following thesis: "Even if a theory T, that includes the natural number theory, is consistent, its proof cannot be achieved within T; a theory stronger than T is required".[61]

Simply put, as Karatani further explains,

> by arthimetizing meta-mathematics (which he accomplished by translating the symbols of meta-mathematics into natural numbers, called Gödel's numbers) Gödel discovered a cyclical and seemingly self-enclosed movement. By means of this calculation he ingeniously set up a self-referential paradox wherein meta-mathematics, understood as a class, gets mixed into a formal system as a number of that class. Gödel's theorem has many implications

including the 'reconfirmation of the paradox that Cantor revealed'. Importantly, 'Gödel's demonstration in the incompleteness theorem was developed along the lines of Whitehead and Russell's *Principia Mathematica*'.[62] Mentioning Morris Kline, whose work we discussed before, Karatani asks: 'Is Gödel's proof, as Morris Kline stated, so desperate for mathematical foundations?' 'I think not',[63] Karatani says, going on to make the following crucial remarks:

> The real developments in mathematics have been made by applied mathematicians, who remain indifferent to foundations as such; indeed, mathematical development has proceeded *irrationally*, as it were. It is thus inaccurate to say that Gödel's proof pushed mathematics to the point of uncertainty. What is more accurate is that it emancipated mathematics from the too heavy burden of certainty that had unfairly been placed upon its shoulder. More to the point, *Gödel's proof released mathematics from the illusion of architectonic and showed that, under the guise of accepting mathematics as normative, the architectonic had always concealed the absence of its foundation.* Despite its solid, if tautological, appearance, mathematics continues even today to develop in manifold ways precisely because it is not an edifice. Mathematics, we can say, is essentially historical.[64] [emphasis mine]

I now come to the central point in this chapter, which is about Karatani's remarkable contention that non-Euclidean geometry was already present in Kant's mathematical thinking, underpinning his architectonic system. Karatani tackles this in his *Transcritique: On Kant and Marx*, where he returns to Gödel's proof once again. Karatani begins by addressing

'Mathematical Foundation' in the chapter entitled 'The Problematic of Synthetic Judgment', in which he exclaims that Kant's mathematical theory has often been misunderstood if not 'consistently disdained'. The crux is Kant's radical position to have considered *even* mathematics to be a domain belonging to synthetic *a priori* judgment, which had previously been thought to belong to analytical judgment. Referring to Freidrich Gauss and the so-called crisis of mathematics in the late nineteenth century with the two innovations of 'non-Euclidean geometry' and 'set theory', Karatani, relying on Gottfried Marti's work, argues that in fact by the mid eighteenth century, the idea of non-Euclidean geometry was already known.[65] Mentioning first that Kant's awareness of the new mathematics is evident in his papers on physics, Karatani then makes these astute remarks:

> What Kant sought to ground philosophically was certainly not the mathematics and physics that had already been solidly established in the eighteenth century. *A foundational theory would never have to be constructed in the first place if not in response to a crisis of foundation itself.* What drives philosophers toward rigorous theoretical grounding is always critical consciousness—as it is precisely exemplified also in Marx's "critique of political economy," which would not have come into existence in the absence of actual financial crises. For his part, what drove Kant toward his own foundational theory was a radical sense of crisis, which, however, was far too progressive to be shared or accepted by his contemporaries. And, to a certain degree, it could be said that Kant, like Gauss later, avoided publicly declaring the crisis (so as to avoid the legendary fate of Hippasos).[66] [emphasis mine]

As Karatani reminds us, one of the most important aspects of Euclid's *The Elements* is the thesis that 'a theorem can be deduced from an axiom without contradiction'.[67] But this does not hold for all mathematics that have developed in its long history. As Karatani states, 'The development of mathematics has been driven more by applied mathematics, or by games, than by any principle. This is because the crux of mathematics has been always located in the practice of grasping the *relation* of things', and that,

> As an effect of the Euclidean principle, however, it has been assumed that all mathematical procedure could and should follow the *proof* as a formal (and analytical) deduction from an axiom. And this is the reason why mathematics has become established as the fountainhead of analytical judgment.[68]

Karatani continues,

> Nevertheless, prioritizing analytical judgment was not the specific prop-
> erty of mathematics itself. It is metaphysics that has taken mathematics
> as the norm because of the presupposition that mathematics is analyti-
> cal. In other words, it is Plato's dogma that only analytical thinking is
> true that made Euclidean geometry possible. Therefore, to undermine
> Plato's position, mathematics must be the primary field of critique.[69]

In the eighteenth century, the so-called 'parallel postulate' in Euclidean
geometry, as we have seen, goes as follows: '*Through a point P outside a
line L there is one and only one line parallel to L*'.[70] This postulate, as
Karatani puts it,

> was thrown into doubt by the following question: Isn't this theorem
> deducible from other postulates and axioms? What non-Euclidean
> geometry made clear was that Euclid's fifth postulate is *independent*
> of the other Euclidean axioms; and further, not only that this is not
> *intuitively self-evident* but also that contradiction will not occur even
> if other postulates are adopted.[71]

And the crux is that 'Kant had already thought of the possibility of
non-Euclidean geometry. In fact, when Kant considered mathematics as
an "a priori synthetic judgment," he already had explicitly in mind the
very nature of axioms'.[72] As Karatani affirms,

> Empirically speaking, for example, since parallel lines do not inter-
> sect, it follows that the axiom, *parallel lines intersect*, is independent
> of empirical reality. Viewed from the Leibnizian standpoint, within
> the concept of the triangle (read the subject) what is already included
> is the predicate: *The sum total of the three internal angles of a triangle
> is equal to that of two right angles*. Therefore, non-Euclidean geome-
> try is just a *reductio ad absurdum*. From the Leibnizian standpoint,
> axioms *as such* had been obstacles, so he had sought to do away with
> them—in vain.[73]

Here, Karatani instructively informs us about the difference between
'analytic judgment' and 'synthetic judgment' in Kant that has important
implications for the mathematical thoughts that came after Kant:

> Kant thought of the problematic of axioms in a much more sophisti-
> cated manner. He explained the difference between analytic and
> synthetic judgment in two ways: analytic judgment is where the

concept 'predicate' is included in the concept 'subject', and it can be proven only by the law of contradiction. In contrast, synthetic judgment requires *something other than* the law of contradiction. Which is to say that Kant's consideration of mathematics as being an a priori synthetic judgment derives rigorously from his consideration of the status of axioms. Thus Kant opposed the reduction of mathematics to logic. Kant notwithstanding, however, the concept that mathematics is an analytic judgment proved itself not to be easily shaken. A notable example is the later nineteenth-century logicism of Frege/Russell, which expressed the clearest conviction that mathematics be logical. Russell, in particular, was this delusion's prime proponent. On the one hand, he was an empiricist like Hume; on the other, he insisted that mathematics was analytical.[74]

Here Karatani cites Russell as having said:

> The proof that all mathematics, including Geometry, is nothing but formal logic, is a fatal blow to the Kantian philosophy. Kant, rightly perceiving that Euclid's propositions could not be deduced from Euclid's axioms without the help of figures, invented a theory of knowledge to account for this fact; and it accounted so successfully that, when the fact is shown to be a mere defect in Euclid, and not a result of the nature of geometric reasoning, Kant's theory also has to be abandoned. The whole doctrine of a priori intuitions, by which Kant explained the possibility of pure mathematics, is wholly inapplicable to mathematics in its present form.[75]

Karatani takes Russell to task for his misconception:

> Russell's seminal account is deeply biased by the erroneous belief that Kant pursued mathematics in the context of pre-non-Euclidean geometry. But Kant's mathematics was already far beyond the assertion that it was 'wholly inapplicable to mathematics in its present form.' At the end of the day, it was sooner Russell's twentieth-century logicism—'all pure mathematics are nothing but formal logic'—that had been proleptically ruptured by possibilities conceived in the eighteenth century by Kant.'[76]

As we saw before, during the twentieth century, as Karatani emphasizes, the foundational theory of mathematics oscillated between three divergent sets: logicism, formalism, and intuitionism. In the same chapter in *Transcritique* under discussion here he expands extensively and cogently on what he had already argued in *Architecture as Metaphor* in dealing with the twentieth-century mathematicians up to Gödel and later Wittgenstein, which we do not need to discuss any further here. We only have to arrive at the important conclusion that Karatani draws between Gödel's proof and Kant's mathematical thinking, by which I conclude this chapter. His remarks go as follows:

> The dream of achieving a solid foundation by way of a formalist axiomatic system was never inherent in mathematics itself; this dream was informed by metaphysics, for which only analytic judgment is sound. And it was metaphysics, in this precise sense, that Kant sought to undermine. But inasmuch as metaphysics relies on mathematics, this critique first had to be executed in the mathematics—before throwing the result back into philosophy. Gödel's *meta-mathematical* critique had such a function in the history of mathematics. In this sense, Gödelian 'deconstruction' can be connected to Kant's transcendental critique. In any case, what I want to stress is that, from today's standpoint, Kant was entirely correct when he deemed mathematics a synthetic judgment. As Kant maintained, synthetic judgment is an expansive judgment [*Erweiterungsurteil*]. And so it is that mathematics has developed in the past and will continue to do so in the future.[77]

Notes

1 In Morris Kline, *Mathematics: The Loss of Certainty* (Oxford and New York: Oxford University Press, 1980), 11.

2 Kōjin Karatani, 'Introduction to the English Edition', in *Architecture as Metaphor: Language, Number, Money*, trans. Sabu Kohso, ed. Michael Speaks (Cambridge: The MIT Press, 1995), xxxii.

3 In this respect, Karatani informs us that

> Looking back at my previous work, I am beginning to understand two things, First, I might have been unwittingly engaging in a kind of Kantian critique all along. My works have been interventions that critically examine architecture as metaphor in order to expose its limits. The target I had in mind at the outset of the present work was the dominant ideology of modernism, understood as the "grand narrative" that insists on "constructing" human society. I became aware of Kant only as 'architecture as metaphor' collapsed; at that point it became evident to me that far from creating a total disappearance of the grand narrative, this collapse produced instead a set of alternative narratives or ideologies, namely the 'end of history' debate (the ultimate assertion of the superiority of Western reason) and cynicism. 'Architecture as metaphor' cannot be dissolved by denial. Today it is the Kantian transcendental critique that is called for. And it is in the light of these considerations that I have begun to reevaluate my previous work

Kōjin Karatani, 'Introduction to the English Edition', in *Architecture as Metaphor*, xl–xli.

4 Kōjin Karatani, 'Introduction to the English Edition', in *Architecture as Metaphor*, xxxiv.

5 In what follows I rely on Rebecca Goldstein's excellent *Incompleteness: The Proof and Paradoxes of Kurt Gödel* (New York and London: W. W. Norton, 2005), which follows the celebrated work by Ernest Nagel and James R. Newman, *Gödel's Proof*, ed. with a new foreword, Douglas R. Hofstadter, Revised Edition (New York and London: New York University Press, 2001) and Jaakko Hintikka's *On Gödel* (Belmont: Wadsworth Thomson Learning, 2000). For my general understanding of mathematical thoughts, I have benefitted from Morris Kline's *Mathematics for the Nonmathematician* (New York: Dover, 1967). For the original Gödel's incompleteness theorem paper I have consulted Hal Prince's *The Annotated Gödel: A Reader's Guide to his Classic Paper on Logic and Incompleteness* (Homebred Press, 2022). For my general understanding of mathematical thinking I have benefited from Morris Kline's exhaustive *Mathematics: The Loss of Certainty* (Oxford and New York: Oxford University Press, 1980), and also his earlier *Mathematics for the Nonmathematician*.

6 Morris Kline, *Mathematics: The Loss of Certainty*, 9.

7 Morris Kline, *Mathematics: The Loss of Certainty*, 11.

8 Morris Kline, *Mathematics: The Loss of Certainty*, 16.

9 Morris Kline, *Mathematics: The Loss of Certainty*, 16.

10 See Rebecca Goldstein, *Incompleteness: The Proof and Paradoxes of Kurt Gödel*, 121. For much of what follows I heavily rely on this fine book.

11 Rebecca Goldstein, *Incompleteness*, 121. Goldstein immediately adds that:

> yet, on the other hand, mathematical knowledge has seemed, to darker-souled epistemologists, highly problematic, its very certainty, which emboldens the utopians, making it suspect in warier eyes. How *can* any knowledge be certain and unassailable, in short: proved? Perhaps, some epistemologists of the darker cast argue, it is because mathematical knowledge is not really knowledge at all; perhaps it is simply a game, played by stipulated rules, telling us nothing about anything.
>
> (121–122)

12 Rebecca Goldstein, *Incompleteness*, 122.

13 Rebecca Goldstein, *Incompleteness*, 122. She continues:

> Intuitions. They are a tricky business, and not only in mathematics. An intuition is supposed to be something that we just know, in and of itself, not on the basis of knowing something else. (Sometimes, of course, the word is used in a wider way, conveying the sense of having a vague feeling, lacking in any certainty. But it is in the stronger sense that it functions in epistemological debates).
>
> (122)

14 Rebecca Goldstein, *Incompleteness*, 123.

15 Rebecca Goldstein, *Incompleteness*, 126.

16 Rebecca Goldstein, *Incompleteness*, 126. Goldstein explains further that

> We understand what they mean and that appears sufficient for knowing that they are true. They do not require any proof beyond this. We then use truth-preserving rules of inference to obtain other, nonobvious truths, the theorems, which flow from these givens. For example, consider arithmetic, the simplest branch of all mathematics. Arithmetic concerns the

structure of the natural numbers—again, the regular old counting numbers together with 0—and the relationships between them as given by the operations of addition, multiplication, and the successor relation, which takes you from any number n to the number immediately following it in the natural order (i.e., $n + 1$). All other arithmetical operations, such as subtraction and division, can be defined in terms of these three.

(126–127)

17 Rebecca Goldstein, *Incompleteness*, 127.
18 Rebecca Goldstein, *Incompleteness*, 128. In this regard, Goldstein mentions that

> Gottlob Frege said that "In mathematics we must always strive after a system that is complete in itself". It is this system-building that accounts, Frege said, for the unique certainty of mathematics and 'no science can be so enveloped in obscurity as mathematics, if it fails to construct a system.'
>
> (129)

19 Rebecca Goldstein, *Incompleteness*, 129.
20 Rebecca Goldstein, *Incompleteness*, 129.
21 Morris Kline, *Mathematics: The Loss of Certainty*, 78.
22 Morris Kline, *Mathematics: The Loss of Certainty*, 78.
23 Rebecca Goldstein, *Incompleteness*, 130.
24 Rebecca Goldstein, *Incompleteness*, 130. Goldstein further explains that 'Euclid's suspicion about this one element of his system … was duplicated down through the ages, with various mathematicians attempting to convert the problematic axiom into a theorem by deriving it from the other four axioms', 130.
25 See Morris Kline, *Mathematics for the Nonmathematician*, 456.
26 Morris Kline, *Mathematics for the Nonmathematician*, 456.
27 Morris Kline, *Mathematics: The Loss of Certainty*, 83.
28 Morris Kline, *Mathematics: The Loss of Certainty*, 84–85. Kline informs us that

> The problem of which geometry fits physical space, raised primarily in the work of Gauss, stimulated another creation, a new geometry that gave the mathematical world further inducement to believe that the geometry of physical space could be non-Euclidean. The creator was George Bernhard Riemann (1826–1866), a student of Gauss and later professor of mathematics at Göttingen. Though the details of Lobachevsky's and Bolyai's work were unknown to Riemann, they were known to Gauss, and Riemann certainly knew Gauss's doubt as to the necessary applicability of Euclidean geometry.
>
> (85)

29 Morris Kline, *Mathematics: The Loss of Certainty*, 87. Kline further writes,

> That Euclidean geometry is the geometry of physical space, that it is the truth about space, was so ingrained in people's minds that for many years any contrary thoughts such as Gauss's were rejected. The mathematician George Cantor spoke of a law of conservation of ignorance. A false conclusion once arrived at and widely accepted is not easily dislodged and the less it is understood the more tenaciously it is held. For thirty or so years after the publication of Lobachevsky's and Bolyai's works all but a few mathematicians ignored the non-Euclidean geometries. They were regarded as curiosity. Some mathematicians did not deny their logical coherence. Others believed that they must contain contradictions and so

> were worthless. Almost all mathematicians maintained that the geometry
> of physical space, *the* geometry, must be Euclidean.
>
> (88)

30 Rebecca Goldstein, *Incompleteness*, 130.
31 Rebecca Goldstein, *Incompleteness*, 131.
32 Rebecca Goldstein, *Incompleteness*, 131. Goldstein further points out that

> A formal system is constituted of stipulated rules: that specify the symbols
> ("alphabet") of the system; that tell us how we may combine the symbols
> with one another to produce grammatical configurations (wffs); and that
> tell us how we may proceed to deduce wffs from other wffs (the rules of
> inference). The formalization of the axiomatic systems was meant to offer
> the highest standard of certainty so that we don't have to depend on our
> intuitions as to what is mathematically obvious and what is not. It was
> meant to obviate our reliance on mathematical intuition altogether, to
> turn our mathematical activity into processes so completely determined
> by clearly specified rules as to be purely *mechanical*, requiring no imagi-
> nation or ingenuity, not even a grasp as to what the symbols mean.
>
> (131–132)

33 Rebecca Goldstein, *Incompleteness*, 132. In the footnote Goldstein usefully
    informs us that the word 'algorithm' comes from the ninth-century Persian
    mathematician by the name of Abu Ja'far Mohammad ibn Mûsâ al-Khowâ-
    sizm, 'who wrote an important mathematical book in about AD 825 that was
    called *Kitab al jabar w'al-muqabala*. We also derive our word "algebra" from
    the title of this book', 132, n. 4.
34 Rebecca Goldstein, *Incompleteness*, 133 and 134.
35 Rebecca Goldstein, *Incompleteness*, 134.
36 Rebecca Goldstein, *Incompleteness*, 134–135.
37 Rebecca Goldstein, *Incompleteness*, 136. For more see David Hilbert's major
    work, *The Foundation of Geometry* (La Salle: The Open Court, 1950).
38 Morris Kline, *Mathematics: The Loss of Certainty*, 307.
39 Morris Kline, *Mathematics: The Loss of Certainty*, 307.
40 Morris Kline, *Mathematics: The Loss of Certainty*, 308.
41 Morris Kline, *Mathematics: The Loss of Certainty*, 308.
42 Morris Kline, *Mathematics: The Loss of Certainty*, 308–309.
43 Morris Kline, *Mathematics: The Loss of Certainty*, 309.
44 Morris Kline, *Mathematics: The Loss of Certainty*, 309. Kline adds that

> The base on which the reconstructed mathematics rested, the logical and
> mathematical axioms, had to be strengthened, and so the workers decided
> to dig more deeply. Unfortunately, they disagreed about how and where
> to strengthen the foundations and so, while each maintained that he
> would ensure solidity, each set about rebuilding in his own way. The
> resulting structure was not tall and firmly grounded but sprawling and
> insecure, with each wing claiming to be the sole temple of mathematics
> and each housing what it regarded as the gems of mathematical thought.
>
> (309)

45 Morris Kline, *Mathematics: The Loss of Certainty*, 310.
46 Morris Kline, *Mathematics: The Loss of Certainty*, 313.
47 Kōjin Karatani, 'Introduction to the English Edition', in *Architecture as
    Metaphor*, xxxv.
48 Kōjin Karatani, *Architecture as Metaphor*, 8.

49 Kōjin Karatani, *Architecture as Metaphor*, 9.
50 Kōjin Karatani, *Architecture as Metaphor*, 9. Karatani remarks that

> It is admittedly facile to criticize the *idea* of a horse; to criticize the *idea* of a point is a more serious endeavour because in mathematics something genuinely *ideal* is inevitably exposed. For Nietzsche, mathematics was concerned only with number and quantity, while concepts was nothing but worn-out metaphor. Yet as Marx and others speculated, concept is relation. As a mode of inquiry that scrutinizes the relations of matter, mathematics studies relations that are immutable, relations that never change, regardless of how matter itself changes. Mathematics thus continues to be regarded as the norm it was for Plato.
>
> (9–10)

51 Kōjin Karatani, *Architecture as Metaphor*, 48. Karatani notes that 'The paradox exposed by de Man's reading of Locke is constituted only where the will to architecture is explicitly engaged', 48.
52 Kōjin Karatani, *Architecture as Metaphor*, 51.
53 Kōjin Karatani, *Architecture as Metaphor*, 51.
54 Kōjin Karatani, *Architecture as Metaphor*, 51–52.
55 Kōjin Karatani, *Architecture as Metaphor*, 52. Karatani explains that

> Bertrand Russell transformed this paradox into the simple form of the well-known paradox of Epimenides: '"All Cretans are Liars," said a Cretan.' Simplified further it becomes 'I am lying' or 'This sentence is false.' In all cases it is equally indeterminable whether the statement if true or false. In this way, various forms of paradox were discovered and named; yet they invariably occurred in sentences with self-referential structure. Russell therefore insisted that paradoxes were caused by a state of confusion wherein 'class' itself becomes its own 'number.' Paradoxes could be avoided if this mix-up were prohibited. Russell subsequently established the order of logical types and prohibited confusing them.
>
> (52)

56 Kōjin Karatani, *Architecture as Metaphor*, 53.
57 Kōjin Karatani, *Architecture as Metaphor*, 54.
58 Kōjin Karatani, *Architecture as Metaphor*, 54.
59 Kōjin Karatani, *Architecture as Metaphor*, 54. Karatani brings in the mathematician Bernhard Reimann, who writes that

> One way to insure consistency is to resort to an intuitive model, as in the case of Riemannian geometry: if one regards the plane as a sphere in Euclidean geometry, the point as a point on the sphere, and the straight line as a great circle are in its system of axioms, the sphere of Euclidean geometry becomes the primordial model. By so doing, every axiom of Riemannian geometry can be translated into theorem in Euclidean geometry.
>
> (54)

60 Kōjin Karatani, *Architecture as Metaphor*, 54–55.
61 Kōjin Karatani, *Architecture as Metaphor*, 55.
62 Kōjin Karatani, *Architecture as Metaphor*, 55. Karatani adds further that 'by showing that even typing would collapse when exposed to the incompleteness theorem, Gödel issued a kin challenge to Russell, who had attempted to evade the paradox by logical typing', 55–56.

63 Kōjin Karatani, *Architecture as Metaphor*, 56.

64 Kōjin Karatani, *Architecture as Metaphor*, 56.

65 See Kōjin Karatani, *Transcritique: On Kant and Marx*, trans. Sabou Kohso (Cambridge: The MIT Press, 2005), 57. Karatani explains that

> For instance, it had already been demonstrated that from the axiom, 'the sum total of the three internal angles of a triangle is smaller than that of two right angles', a system of theorems could be constructed without contradiction. Furthermore, non-Euclidean geometry in the context of the problem of sphere had also already been conceptualized. As Gottfried Martin points out, Johannes Heinrich Lambert (1728–1777), one of the founders of this tendency, was a friend of Kant's.
>
> (57)

See also Gottfried Martin, *Kant's Metaphysics and Theory of Science*, trans. P. G. Luca (Westport: Greenwood, 1974).

66 Kōjin Karatani, *Transcritique*, 57. It is interesting that Karatani mentions the name of Hippasos. Hippasos Metapontum was a Greek philosopher, 530–450 BCE, a follower of Pythagoras, who is said to be credited with the discovery of the irrational numbers. That discovery was so shocking to Pythagoreans for which it is said that Hippasos was supposed to be drowned in the sea for punishment from gods for having divulged it. Thus, regarding 'prudence' to avoid the fate of Hippsos, Karatani says that 'If Kant's texts are so still suggestive today, it is ultimately because pioneering sense of the crisis, but also because of his discursive prudence with regard to stating more publicly the depth and implication of the crisis', 58.

67 Kōjin Karatani, *Transcritique*, 58.

68 Kōjin Karatani, *Transcritique*, 58.

69 Kōjin Karatani, *Transcritique*, 58. Karatani further points out:

> And the truth of the matter is that the question of whether or not the Euclidean 'elements' are truly analytical has been asked more or less from the inception of mathematics. *The Element* consists of definitions, axioms, and postulates, and among these, it is the fifth postulate that has been controversial: *If a straight line crosses two other straight lines so that the sum of the two inferior angles on one side of it is less than two right angles, then two straight lines, if extended far enough, cross on that same side.*
>
> (58)

70 Cited in Kōjin Karatani, *Transcritique*, 59.

71 Kōjin Karatani, *Transcritique*, 59. As we have seen and Karatani restates here, Lobachevsky's geometry

> was driven from the proposition *The sum total of the three internal angles of a triangle is smaller than that of two right angles*, while Reimann's geometry came from the proposition *The sum total of the three internal angles of a triangle is larger than that of two right angles*. In other words, Lobachevsky adopted the postulate *In a plane, through a point outside a line L, there are an infinite number of lines which do not intersect*, while Riemann chose *Through a point P outside a line L there is no line parallel to it; that is, every pair of lines in a plane must intersect.*
>
> (59)

72 Kōjin Karatani, *Transcritique*, 59.

73 Kōjin Karatani, *Transcritique*, 59.

74 Kōjin Karatani, *Transcritique*, 60.

75 Quoted in Kōjin Karatani, *Transcritique*, 60.

76 Kōjin Karatani, *Transcritique*, 60.

77 Kōjin Karatani, *Transcritique*, 64–65. Karatani adds: 'In his later years, Wittgenstein spoke of mathematics as a motley bundle of inventions. In this expression, he, too, affirmed with Kant that mathematics is a synthetic judgment', 65.

5

ARCHITECTURE AND CONFLICT OF THE FACULTIES

In *The Conflict of the Faculties* Kant named philosophy a '*lower* faculty' and discussed its conflict with three '*higher* faculties', namely, theology, law, and medicine. His contention was grounded in the idea of the university whose institution in his time was under state control and censorship—complex political and intellectual circumstances, to which we will come later. In reading Kant's text I aim to advance a thesis that goes as follows: If 'philosophy is another name for the *will to architecture*', as Karatani has told us, and if philosophy, as the *lower* faculty, is in conflict with the *higher* faculties, as Kant informed us, then it goes that architecture embodies a *conflict* that encompasses *in itself* the lower and higher faculties that are inherent in its concept under the principles of *reason*. As a corollary to this, I contend that if Kant redefined the place of philosophy in the university, we must attempt to redefine the place of architecture in the same institution, grounded as it must be on the principles of *reason*. This conflict is to be understood as the conflict between *power* and *knowledge*. By bringing the *faculty* of architecture into Kant's *The Conflict of the Faculties*, I aim to demonstrate that the *philosophical* theory in architecture, suppressed in the university, can occupy an exceptional place in the hierarchical scheme in Kantian category between the *lower* faculty of philosophy and other *higher* faculties—yet to be identified anew beyond the three *higher* faculties specific to Kant's time. This will bring out a new dimension in Karatani's novel exposition explored so far in this work. At this point one might ask: What specifically does the term 'faculty' mean in architecture? To answer this question we must first understand what Kant meant by the word 'faculty' underlying the architectonic of his entire critical philosophy.

In general, the word 'faculty' in English carries two distinct meanings: (1) as a 'part', or a 'department', or a 'school', in a university, and (2) the power of the mind to reach an end. The second sense of faculty derives from the Latin *facultus* and the Greek *dynamis*, the meaning of which, as

DOI: 10.4324/9781032647616-6

we are informed, was established by Aristotle in the *Metaphysics* where he 'broadly attributed two senses to the term: the first referred to an ability or power to achieve an end, and the other to a potential for change which would be actualized through *energeia*'.[1] Now, Kant in his *Critique of the Power of Judgment* systematically reflected on the term 'faculty'. In the 'First Introduction' to the *Critique*, in Section III, entitled 'On the system of all faculties of the human mind', Kant says that 'We can trace all faculties of the human mind without exception back to these three: the **faculty of cognition**, the **feeling of pleasure and displeasure**, and the **faculty of desire**'.[2] Here Kant complained that 'philosophers who otherwise deserve nothing but praise' have sought to explain 'this distinction as merely illusory and to reduce all faculties to the mere faculty of cognition'.[3] Kant further explains that the *faculty of cognition*

> in accordance with concepts has its *a priori* principles in pure understanding (in its concept of nature), the *faculty of desire*, in pure reason (in its concept of freedom), and there remains among the properties of mind in general an intermediate faculty of receptivity, namely the **feeling of pleasure and displeasure**, just as there remains among the higher faculties of cognition an intermediate one, the power of judgment.[4]

Further on in Section XI, in the same First Introduction, entitled 'Encyclopedic introduction of the critique of the power of judgment into the system of the critique of pure reason', Kant reiterates that the faculties of the mind can all be reduced to the three, 'Faculty of cognition, feeling of pleasure and displeasure, faculty of desire', adding that the 'exercise' of all of them is always 'grounded in the faculty of cognition'. He then goes on to reflect that in relation to the faculty of cognition in accordance to principles, the 'higher powers take their place beside the powers of the mind', thus connecting the '**faculty of cognition** to **Understanding, feeling of pleasure and displeasure** to **Power of judgment** and **faculty of desire** to **Reason**'.[5] He explains that

> these formal principles ground a necessity which is partly objective, partly subjective, but partly also, just because it is subjective, at the same time of objective validity, in accordance with which, by means of higher faculties that stand beside them, they determine these corresponding powers of the mind: **Faculty of cognition—Understanding— to Lawfulness, Feeling of pleasure and displeasure—Power of judgment—to Purposiveness, and the Faculty of desire—Reason—**to purposiveness that is at the same time law (**Obligation**).[6]

Finally, Kant states that the foregoing divisions 'are associated with the adduced *a priori* grounds of the possibility of forms, as their products' that he categorizes in a systematic table reproduced as follows:

Faculty of the mind	Higher cognitive faculties	*A priori* principles	Products
Faculty of Cognition	Understanding	Lawfulness	Nature
Faculty of Pleasure	Power of Judgment	Purposiveness	Art and displeasure
Faculty of Desire	Reason	Purposiveness that is at the same time law (Obligation)	Morals

Note: Immanuel Kant, *Critique of the Power of Judgment*, 45.

In clarification, Kant says that 'The judgments that arise in this way from *a priori* principles peculiar to each of the fundamental faculties of the mind are **theoretical**, **aesthetics** and **practical** judgments', and then offers the following illuminating remarks:

> There is thus revealed a system of the powers of the mind, in their relation to nature and freedom, both of which have their own special, **determining** principles a priori and therefore constitute the two parts of philosophy (the theoretical and the practical) as a doctrinal system, and at the same time a transition by means of the power of judgment, which connects the two parts through its own special principle, namely the **sensible** substratum of the first part of philosophy to the **intelligible** substratum of the second, through the critique of a faculty (the power of judgment) which serves only for connecting and which hence cannot provide any cognition of its own nor make any contribution to doctrine, whose judgments, however, under the name of **aesthetic** (whose principles are merely subjective), insofar as they differ from all those, under the name of **logical**, whose fundamental principles must be objective (whether they are theoretical or practical), are of such a special sort that they relate sensible intuitions to the idea of nature, whose lawfulness cannot be understood without their relation to a supersensible substratum—the proof of which will be provided in the treatise itself.[7]

The foregoing brief reflection serves to clarify the senses of the term 'faculty' in Kant, as grounded in the cognitive power of the mind that itself is divided between the lower faculties of sensibility and the higher faculties of reason, judgment, and understanding, which together constitute the entire architectonic of Kant's critical philosophy. Next is the main task set for this chapter: To examine how this division of faculties of the mind enters in a different way into Kant's *The Conflict of the Faculties*, that is concerned with *scholars* in the institution of the University and *free speech*, in the center of which, as Kant argues, is the *lower* faculty of philosophy. This examination will provide the necessary background for my purpose, which is mainly concerned with the nature of the 'faculty' of architecture and its *constitutive conflict*.

The *Conflict of the Faculties* was the last book of Kant's to be published in 1798.[8] It has had a rocky history. The three parts that were included in the final version were in fact written at different times for different occasions (as Kant himself mentions in the Preface to the book); the first two parts were meant to be published separately but had to be postponed due to the censorship and repressive measure by Frederick Williams II.[9] At dispute was an earlier book Kant had written in 1793 with the title, *Religion Within the Limits of Reason Alone*, the second edition of which came out in 1794.[10] As Mary Gregor in her introduction to *The Conflict of the Faculties* writes,

> the precarious position into which the philosophical faculty was being forced made it imperative for Kant to define more clearly his faculty's rights in its inevitable conflict with the theological faculty [...] He must, therefore, make it clear to both parties that the philosophical faculty has the right and the duty to keep the conflict going, to accept no such settlement but rather press for a verdict on the part of reason.[11]

In the Preface to *The Conflict of the Faculties*, Kant revealed the threatening 'royal edict' issued to him in 1794, mentioning the purpose behind the title he chose for his book on religion aimed 'to prevent a misunderstanding to the effect that the treatise deals with religion *from* mere reason (without revelation)'.[12] It is the same principle of *reason* that will underlie his argument in *The Conflict of the Faculties*. Kant concluded the Preface by informing the reader that the three parts of the book

> form a systematic unity and combine in one work, though it was only later that I realized I could avoid scattering them by bringing them together in one volume, as the conflict of the *lower* faculty with the three *higher* faculties.[13]

It is mainly in the first part of *The Conflict of the Faculties*, 'The Conflict of the Philosophy Faculty with the Theology Faculty', that the distinction between the lower and higher faculties is discussed most extensively. In the 'Introduction', Kant begins with this distinction and defines the 'learned community' as a *university*. The university he says, would have a certain autonomy (since only scholars can pass judgment on schools as such), and accordingly it would be authorized to perform certain functions through its *faculties'*.[14] He goes on to say that we must distinguish between 'scholars proper' and 'those members of the *intelligentsia*' who graduate from the university to become functionaries, serving as an instrument of the state by filling positions in civil offices. It is enough for them to be equipped with empirical knowledge relevant to their office at the practical levels. 'Accordingly', Kant states, 'they can be called the businessmen or technicians of learning'.[15] They are 'tools of the government', as clergymen, magistrates, and physicians, who have 'legal influence on the public and form a special class of intelligentsia, who are not free to make public use of their learning as they see fit, but are subject to censorship of the faculties'.[16] In the next section Kant then goes on to spell out the 'general division of the faculties' that traditionally are divided into two ranks: '*three higher* faculties and one *lower* faculty'.

> For a faculty is considered higher only if its teachings—both as to their content and the way they are expounded to the public—interest the government itself, while the faculty whose function is only to look after the interests of science is called lower because it may use its own judgment about what it teaches.[17]

The higher faculties teach to keep the influence of the state over the public, and therefore the state reserves the right to '*sanction*' the teaching of the higher faculties, to command it, as Kant puts it. Now it is 'absolutely essential', Kant says, that the 'learned community at the university also contain a faculty that is independent of the government's command with regard to its teaching; one that, having no commands to give, is free to evaluate everything, and concerns itself with the interests of the sciences, that is, with *truth*: one in which *reason* is authorized to speak out publicly'[18] [my emphasis]. Here we have the elaboration of the theme that Kant had introduced in his earlier essays entitled 'An Answer to the Question: What Is Enlightenment' that he published in 1784, to which I come back later. Kant thus concludes the 'Introduction' to the first part with the following remarks:

> For without a faculty of this kind, the truth would not come to light (and this would be to the government's own detriment); but reason is by its nature free and admits of no command to hold something as true

(no imperative 'believe!' but only a free 'I believe'). The reason why this faculty, despite its great prerogatives (freedom), is called the lower faculty lies in human nature; for a man who can give commands, even though he is someone else's humble servant, is considered more distinguished than a free man who has no one under his command.[19]

As Gregor points out,

> The theme in question is Kant's methodological principles that the philosopher's first task is to separate out the a priori elements in experience and examine them in isolation from the empirical. Whether in metaphysics, in moral philosophy (ethics and philosophy of law), or in philosophy of religion, only confusion results from a failure to distinguish the a priori from the empirical.[20]

And further,

> the function of the philosophy faculty, in its 'department of pure rational knowledge,' is precisely to set forth the a priori principles involved in knowledge and action. The faculties of theology and law, on the other hand, take as their authority something empirically given: the historical document that we call Bible, and the law of the land.[21]

After the introductory remarks to the First Part concerning 'The Philosophy Faculty versus the Theology Faculty', Kant explains more extensively the distinction between the lower faculty and the higher faculties based on the principles of reason. He writes:

> So the biblical theologian (as a member of higher faculty) draws his teaching not from reason but from the *Bible*; the professor of law gets his, not from natural law, but from the *law of the land*; and the professor of medicine does not draw his *method of therapy as practiced on the public* from the physiology of the human body but from *medical regulations*. As soon as one of these faculties presumes to mix with its teachings something it treats as derived from reason, it offends against the authority of the government that issues orders through it and encroaches on the territory of the philosophy faculty, which mercilessly strips from it all the shining plumes that were protected by the government and deals with it on a footing of equality and freedom.[22]

Further down, in the section entitled 'The Concept and Division of the Lower Faculty', Kant says that the lower faculty is the rank in the university that 'occupies itself with teachings which are not adopted as directives by order of a superior, or in so far as they are not so adopted'.[23] He continues in making the following crucial point:

> Now the power to judge autonomously—that is, freely (according to principles of thought in general)—is called reason. So the philosophy faculty, because it must answer for the truth of the teachings it is to adopt or even to allow, must be conceived as free and subject only to laws given by reason, not only by the government.[24]

He points out that such a department must be established at a university:

> In other words, a university must have a faculty of philosophy. Its function in relation to the three higher faculties is to control them and, in this way, be useful to them, since *truth* (the essential and first condition of learning in general) is the main thing, whereas the *utility* the higher faculties promise the government is of secondary importance.[25]

The philosophy faculty, Kant tells us, consists of two departments: a 'department of historical knowledge', which includes history, geography, philology, and humanities, and all the empirical knowledge in natural sciences, and a 'department of *pure rational knowledge*', including mathematics, pure philosophy, the metaphysics of nature, and morals. Thus it includes the teaching of the higher faculties with an objective of examining and criticizing them for the sake of the science. The philosophy faculty can, therefore, 'lay claim to any teaching, in order to test its truth'. It goes that only the

> businessmen of higher faculties (clergymen, legal officials, and doctors) can be prevented from contradicting in public the teaching that the government has entrusted to them to expound in fulfilling their respective offices, and from venturing to play the philosopher's role.[26]

In the 'Third Section' titled 'On the Illegal Conflict of the Higher Faculties with the Lower Faculty', Kant writes:

> A public conflict of views, hence a scholarly debate, can be illegal by reason of its matter or its form. It would be illegal by reason of its *matter* if it were not permissible to *debate*, in this way, about a public proposition because it was not permissible to *judge* publicly this proposition and its opposite. It would be illegal by reason of its *form*, or the way in which the debate is carried on, if one of the parties

relied, not on objective grounds directed to his adversary's reason, but on the *inclinations* and so to gain his assent by fraud (including brib- ery) or force (threats). Now the faculties engage in public conflict in order to influence the people, and each can acquire this influence only by convincing the people that it knows best how to promote their welfare. But as for the way they propose to accomplish this, the lower faculty is diametrically opposed to the higher faculties.[27]

And further:

The people conceive of their welfare, not primarily as freedom, but as [the realization of] their natural ends and so as these three things: being happy after death, having their *possessions* guaranteed by pub- lic laws during their life in society, and finally, looking forward to the physical enjoyment of *life* itself (that is, health and long life).

But the philosophy faculty can deal with all these wishes only by precepts it derives from reason. It depends, accordingly, on the prin- ciples of freedom and limits itself to saying what man himself can and should do toward fulfilling these wishes—live *righteously*, commit no *injustice*, and, by being *moderate* in his pleasure and patient in his illness, rely primarily on the self-help of nature. None of these, indeed, requires great learning; but in these matters we can, for the most part, dispense with learning if we would only restrain our incli- nations and be ruled by our reason. But since this requires self-exer- tion, it does not suit the people.[28]

Considering that the teaching of the lower faculty of philosophy, as Kant says, is diametrically opposed to the teaching of the higher faculties when it comes to the basic *welfare* of the public, he goes on to analogi- cally compare the institution of learning with a parliament, writing that the 'rank of higher faculties',

as the right side of the parliament of learning, supports the govern- ment's statutes; but in as free a system of government as must exist when it is a question of truth, there must be also an opposition party (the left side), and this is the philosophy faculty's bench.[29]

The '*businessmen*' of the higher faculties sitting on the 'right' side of the virtual parliament by necessity have to obey the government statutes by virtue of the 'private reason' as opposed to the 'left' wing of the lower faculty who follow the principles of the 'public reason'. This distinction between the 'private' and 'public' reason brings us to Kant's 1784 essay

'An Answer to the Question: What Is Enlightenment?' that I mentioned previously.[30] This essay was written during the reign of Frederick the Great, in a different political atmosphere from the repressive regime of Frederick William II when he published his *Religion Within the Limits of Reason Alone*. In 'What Is Enlightenment', Kant radically changed the received meaning of the terms 'private' and 'public' contrary to common sense. Kant wrote that *'Enlightenment is man's emergence from his self-imposed immaturity'*.[31] This *immaturity* prevents the ability to use one's own reason, allowing the guardians and authorities to do the thinking, advising them to obey and not to argue. *'Sapere Aude*! "have courage to use your own understanding!"—that is the motto of enlightenment'.[32] Kant writes:

> Nothing is required for this enlightenment, however, except *freedom*; and the freedom in question is the last harmful of all, namely the freedom to use reason *publicly* in all matters. But on all sides I hear: *"Do not argue*!" The officer says, "Do not argue, drill!" The taxman says, "Do not argue, pay!" The pastor says, "Do not argue, believe!"[33] (only one ruler in the world says, *"Argue* as much as you want and about what you want, but obey!").

That 'one ruler' was, of course, Fredrick II (the Great). Which restriction on freedom hinders and which does not, Kant asks. 'The *public* use of one's reason must always be free, and it alone can bring about enlightenment among mankind', he replies, and goes on to say: 'By the public use of one's own reason I understand the use that anyone as a *scholar* makes of reason before the entire *literate world*'.[34] This 'scholar', coming back to *The Conflict of the Faculty*, belongs to the *lower* faculty of philosophy. The 'private' reason that one uses in a civic post by obeying the state rules belongs to the 'businessmen' of the *higher* faculties. In the latter case one does not argue but obeys. As Mladen Dolar has perceptively put it, 'private obedience is the inner condition of the public freedom of reasoning'.[35] For this division between private and public, read *power* as private and *knowledge* as public. Coming back to the *university* discussed by Kant in *The Conflict of the Faculty*, we can now say that this division of power/knowledge is drawn inside the very institution responsible for the universality of knowledge: the university. Dolar reminds us how Kant, like Althusser *avant la lettre*, identified the institution of the university as the fundamental 'ideological' apparatus in the modern age. 'The University in fact duplicates the internal division power/knowledge.' In it 'Reason is not master in its own house'.[36] Putting Kant's argument in our terms, the higher faculties serve the power and its ideological state apparatuses by training functionaries not grounded in reason. The lower faculty of philosophy, by contrast, peruses knowledge and truth. Grounded in the autonomy of reason, it does not need to obey any authority. But it pays a price: It gives up power to take care of knowledge. As Dolar nicely puts it, 'the whole edifice of knowledge is thus constructed on the basis of an underlying supposition that reason is powerless and power is not based on reason. The law is valid but true.'[37]

The foregoing brief discussion should be sufficient to let us return to the thesis I put forward at the beginning concerning the place of architecture in this Kantian 'conflict of the faculties'. It must be put in relation to the statement made before about the nature of the institution of learning called the university. In this respect, I must make reference to an influential reading of *The Conflict of the Faculties* by Jacques Derrida entitled 'Mochlos; or, The Conflict of the Faculties'. Derrida delivered a paper under this title at a conference held at the University of Alabama in 1987, later published as the lead essay in a book of collected essays entitled *Logomachia: The Conflict of the Faculties*.[38] At the center of Derrida's essay is his argument concerning the institution of the university. He wrote:

> The western university is a very recent *constructum* or artifact, and we already sense that its model is *finished*: marked by finitude, just as, at the instauration of its current model, between *The Conflict of the Faculties* (1798) and the foundation of the university of Berlin (10 October 1810, at the close of the mission entrusted to Humboldt), it was thought to be ruled by an idea of reason, by a certain link, in other words, with infinity.[39]

He further elaborates that

> When regions of knowledge can no longer give rise to the training and evaluation properly belonging to a university, then the whole architectonics of *The Conflict of the Faculties* finds itself menaced, and with a model regulated by the happy concord between royal power and pure reason.[40]

Derrida acknowledges that 'The pure concept of university is constructed by Kant on the possibility and necessity of a language purely theoretical, inspired solely by an interest in truth, with a structure that one today would call purely constative.'[41] Derrida recognizes that Kant wanted to make a 'line of demarcation pass between thinkers in the university and businessmen of knowledge or agents of government power, between the inside and outside closest to the university enclosure'.[42] He confirms that Kant's argument is that the faculties of theology, law, and medicine are called 'higher' faculties because they are closer to the government power; 'and a traditional hierarchy holds that power should be higher than non-power', confirming that Kant's 'political ideal tends to favor a certain reversal of this hierarchy', and goes on to cite Kant as saying, 'Thus we may indeed eventually see the last becoming first (the lower faculty becoming the higher faculty), not in the exercise of power, but in giving counsel...'.[43] 'This freedom of judgment', Derrida remind us,

> Kant takes to be the unconditioned condition of university autonomy, and that unconditioned condition is nothing other than philosophy. Autonomy is philosophical reason insofar as it grants itself its own law, namely the truth. Which is why the lower faculty is called the philosophical faculty.[44]

Now Derrida makes a categorical statement that must be taken seriously: '*without a philosophy department in a university, there is no university*' [my emphasis]. He properly remarks that: 'The concept of *universitas* is more than the philosophical concept of a research and teaching institution; it is the concept of philosophy itself, and its Reason, or rather the principle of reason *as an institution*'.[45]

If Derrida is right to say that without a philosophy department in a university there cannot be a university, which I endorse, and if we link Derrida's statement to Kōjin Karatani's proposition that 'philosophy is another name for the *will to architecture*', I am prompted to make this categorical statement: *There cannot be a university without a faculty of architecture*. This is intended to mean that the conflicted concept of architecture coincides with the *architecture* of the university, by reflecting back on the *conflict* inherent in its institution. And since this faculty of architecture *in itself* is a *conflicted* faculty, as I have claimed, it exemplifies and reflects the *conflictual* nature of the University on the principles of Reason, insofar as the University, as said before, duplicates the internal division between power/knowledge, that is, 'Reason is not a master in its house'. Or, again, as was stated, 'reason is powerless and power is not based on reason'.

The teaching faculty, the *businessmen* of the faculty of architecture, constituting the *higher* faculties bolstered by the 'private reason', submit to the state regulations—they do not argue. Put in Gramscian or Althusserian terms, they are under the *hegemony* of the ideological state apparatus—they *obey* but do not argue. In our time, they are the ones who have submitted to the neoliberal order of postmodern capitalism which is in the process of complete *commodification* of knowledge within the institution of the university. If there is no Fredrick William II in our time to censor the *scholars* in the lower faculty, that does not mean that the institution of the university is not under the state hegemony which is under the 'absolute monarchy of capital' in our neoliberal order. Contrary to the misconception of some, the state directly intervenes into this neoliberal order. But, again, this faculty of architecture is a *conflicted* faculty. Which means that the *lower* faculty of philosophy comes into conflict with the *higher* faculties not grounded in the 'public reason' in the Kantian sense. The lower faculty is in a weakened position and powerless. This is why a reading of Kant's *The Conflict of the Faculties*, supposedly written when Kant was rather ill in his old age, dwindling in his power of the mind, must once more be read with a renewed urgency. Thus, the faculty of architecture (with 'faculty' in both senses of the term discussed before) as located in the university must be thought as being constitutionally a *conflicted* faculty. The *lower* philosophy faculty must come to *control* the *higher* faculties as part of an ongoing struggle against the hegemony of state power with its repressive ideological apparatuses.

Notes

1 See the entry 'Faculty' in Howard Caygill's *A Kant Dictionary* (Malden: Blackwell, 1995), 190.
2 Immanuel Kant, *Critique of the Power of Judgment*, ed. Paul Guyer, trans. Paul Guyer and Eric Matthews (Cambridge: Cambridge University Press, 2000), 11. The editor explains that Kant basically referred to Wolff's famous doctrine that 'all powers of the soul reduce to different manifestations of a single cognitive power of representation', 358.
3 Immanuel Kant, *Critique of the Power of Judgment*, 11.
4 Immanuel Kant, *Critique of the Power of Judgment*, 12. Kant continues to say that

> a certain suitability of the power of judgment to serve as the determining ground for the feeling of pleasure, or to find one in it, is already **unmistakable, insofar as, while in the division of faculties of cognition through concepts understanding and reason** relate their representations to objects, in order to acquire concepts of them, the power of judgment is related solely to the subject and does not produce any concepts of objects for itself alone. Likewise, if in the general **division of the power of the mind** overall the faculty of cognition as well as the faculty of desire contain an **objective** relation of representation, so by contrast the feeling of pleasure and displeasure is only the receptivity of a determination of the object, so that if the power of judgment is to determine anything for itself alone, it could not be anything other than the feeling of pleasure, and, conversely, if the latter is to have *a priori* principle at all, it will be found only in the power of judgment.
>
> (12–13)

5 Immanuel Kant, *Critique of the Power of Judgment*, 45.

6 Immanuel Kant, *Critique of the Power of Judgment*, 45. I have followed the divisions in Kant's table.
7 Immanuel Kant, *Critique of the Power of Judgment*, 46.
8 Immanuel Kant, *The Conflict of the Faculties*, trans. and intro. Mary J. Gregor (Lincoln and London: University of Nebraska Press, 1992).
9 For more see the informative 'Translator's Introduction' to the book by Mary Gregor.
10 See Immanuel Kant, *Religion Within the Limits of Reason Alone*, trans. and intro. Theodore M. Greene and Hoyt Hudson, with an essay by John R. Silber (New York: Harper and Brothers, 1960).
11 See 'Translator's Introduction' to *The Conflict of the Faculties*, viii.
12 Immanuel Kant, *The Conflict of the Faculties*, 9.
13 Immanuel Kant, *The Conflict of the Faculties*, 21.
14 Immanuel Kant, *The Conflict of the Faculties*, 23. In the footnote Kant informs us that each faculty has its 'Dean, who is the head of faculty' and interestingly explains that

> This title, taken from astrology, originally meant one of the three astral spirits that preside over a sign of the Zodiac (of 30 degrees), each governing 10 degrees. From the stars it was transferred to the military … and finally to the university, where, however, the number 10 (of professors) was not taken into account.
>
> (23)

15 Immanuel Kant, *The Conflict of the Faculties*, 25.
16 Immanuel Kant, *The Conflict of the Faculties*, 25.
17 Immanuel Kant, *The Conflict of the Faculties*, 26–27.
18 Immanuel Kant, *The Conflict of the Faculties*, 28–29.
19 Immanuel Kant, *The Conflict of the Faculties*, 29.
20 See 'Translator's Introduction' to *The Conflict of the Faculties*, xxvi–xxvii.
21 'Translator's Introduction' to *The Conflict of the Faculties*, xxvii.
22 Immanuel Kant, *The Conflict of the Faculties*, 35.
23 Immanuel Kant, *The Conflict of the Faculties*, 43. Kant explains that

> Now we may well comply with a practical teaching out of obedience, but we can never accept it as true simply because we are ordered to (*de par le Roi*). This is not only objectively impossible (a judgment that *ought not* to be made), but also subjectively quite impossible (a judgment that no one *can* make). For the man who, as he says, wants to err does not really err and, in fact, accepts the false judgment as true; he merely declares, falsely, an assent that is not to be found in him. So when it is a question of the *truth* of a certain teaching to be expounded in public, the teacher cannot appeal to a supreme command nor the pupil pretend that he believed it by order. This can happen only when it is a question of *action*, and even then the pupil must recognize by a *free* judgment that such a command was really issued and that he is obligated or at least entitled to obey it; otherwise, his acceptance of it would be an empty pretense and a lie.
>
> (43)

24 Immanuel Kant, *The Conflict of the Faculties*, 43.
25 Immanuel Kant, *The Conflict of the Faculties*, 45. Here Kant says that

> We can also grant the theology faculty's proud claim that the philosophy faculty is its handmaid (though the question remains, whether the servant is mistress's *torchbearer*, or *trainbearer*), provided it is not driven away or

silenced. For the very *modesty* [of its claim]—merely to be free, as it leaves others free, to discover the truth for the benefit of all sciences and set it before the higher faculties to use as they will—must commend it to the government as above suspicion and, indeed, indispensable.

(45)

26 Immanuel Kant, *The Conflict of the Faculties*, 45–47.
27 Immanuel Kant, *The Conflict of the Faculties*, 47–49.
28 Immanuel Kant, *The Conflict of the Faculties*, 49.
29 Immanuel Kant, *The Conflict of the Faculties*, 57–59.
30 See 'An Answer to the Question: What Is Enlightenment (1784)', in Immanuel Kant, *Perpetual Peace and Other Essays*, trans. Ted Humphry (Indianapolis and Cambridge: Hackett, 1983).
31 Immanuel Kant, 'An Answer to the Question: What Is Enlightenment?', 41.
32 Immanuel Kant, 'An Answer to the Question: What Is Enlightenment?', 41.
33 Immanuel Kant, 'An Answer to the Question: What Is Enlightenment?', 42.
34 Immanuel Kant, 'An Answer to the Question: What Is Enlightenment?', 42.
35 See Mladon Dolar, 'The Legacy of the Enlightenment: Foucault and Lacan', in *New Formations*, 14 (Summer 1991). I have discussed Dolar's great discussion on this point more extensively in my *An Architecture Manifesto: Critical Reason and Theories of a Failed Practice* (Milton Park: Routledge, 2019).
36 Mladon Dolar, 'The Legacy of the Enlightenment: Foucault and Lacan', 49.
37 Mladon Dolar, 'The Legacy of the Enlightenment: Foucault and Lacan', 49. For more on this see my *An Architecture Manifesto: Critical Reason and Theories of a Failed Practice*.
38 See *Logomachia: The Conflict of Faculties*, ed. Ricard Rand (Lincoln and London: University of Nebraska Press, 1992).
39 Jacques Derrida, 'Mochlos; or, The Conflict of the Faculties', in *Logomachia: The Conflict of the Faculties*, ed. Richard Rand (Lincoln and London: University of Nebraska Press, 1992), 10. Derrida further asks:

Will it suffice today to speak contradiction in the university? Is it not the first interest of the Kantian text to recognize a conflict at the university's very interior? Kant foresees its inevitable recurrence, a necessity somehow transcendental and constitutive. He classes the different types and places of contradiction, the rules of their return, the forms of their legality or illegality.

(13)

40 Jacques Derrida, 'Mochlos; or, The Conflict of the Faculties', 14. He continues by saying that 'The *representation* of this model remains almost identical throughout the West, but the link to power, and to the investigations it programs in research academies and institutes, differ widely between states, regimes and national traditions', 14.
41 Jacques Derrida, 'Mochlos; or, The Conflict of the Faculties', 19–20.
42 Jacques Derrida, 'Mochlos; or, The Conflict of the Faculties', 25.
43 Jacques Derrida, 'Mochlos; or, The Conflict of the Faculties', 25.
44 Jacques Derrida, 'Mochlos; or, The Conflict of the Faculties', 25–26.
45 Jacques Derrida, 'Mochlos; or, The Conflict of the Faculties', 25–26.

6

CONSTRUCTIVISM

From Parmenides to Kant

Marx in *Capital* wrote:

> A spider conducts operations which resemble those of the weaver, and a bee would put many a human architect to shame by the construction of its honeycomb cells. But what distinguishes the worst architect from the best of bees is that the architect builds the cell in his mind before he constructs it in wax. At the end of every labour process, a result emerges which had already been conceived by the worker at the beginning, hence already existed ideally. Man not only effects change of form in the material of nature; he also realizes [*verwirklicht*] his own purpose in those materials.[1]

The *construction* in mind, or in *imagination*, in Marx's preceding building analogy is in essence the *condition of possibility of knowing* the object in relation to the knowing subject who constructs the object. That is to say, it is the question of epistemology, or theory of knowledge, and foundationalism, the sources of which go back to Kant and to what is known as 'constructivism'.[2] Here I want to recall what Nietzsche wrote, as if he were responding to Marx's remarks quoted previously. He says 'man'—by which he means the philosopher—is a 'mighty genius of construction' who constructs upon precariously shifting foundations, hence 'constructing' his architectonic of philosophy. This is what he said in 'On the Truth and Lies in a Nonmoral Sense' that I have previously cited in the introduction to this work:

> *Here one may certainly admire man as a mighty genius of construction*, who succeeded in piling up an infinitely complicated dome of concepts upon an unstable foundation, and as it were, on running water. Of course, in order to be supported by such a foundation, his

DOI: 10.4324/9781032647616-7

construction must be like one constructed by spiders' webs: delicate enough to be carried along by the waves, strong enough not to be blown apart by every wind. As a genius of construction man raises himself far above the bee in the following way: whereas the bee builds with wax that he gathers from nature, man builds with the far more delicate conceptual materials which he first has to manufacture from himself. In this he is greatly to be admired, but not on account of his drive for truth or for pure knowledge of things.[3] [emphasis mine]

What is noteworthy in this paragraph is that when Nietzsche says 'In this he is greatly to be admired, but not on account of his drive to truth or for pure knowledge of things', he is basically exposing his anti-Kantian stance.

In what follows, I examine the notion of 'constructivism' in Kant that must be related to his so-called 'Copernican Revolution' discussed before. I mainly follow Tom Rockmore, who points out that Kant's 'Copernican Revolution' is a *constructivist* approach to the theory of knowledge.[4] Related to this, we should also note that Kant's constructivism is based on his mathematical thinking and theory of science. I briefly return to Kant's mathematical thinking to discuss constructivism before examining its specific philosophical implications. The point of departure is Kōjin Karatani's statement in *Architecture as Metaphor*, as previously mentioned, on the triadic concept in Kant, that is, 'thing-it-itself', 'phenomenon', and '*Schein*'. This triad forms a structure that must be grasped *transcendentally*. It is this triadic structure that Kant called 'architectonics'. To reiterate, Kant's critical philosophy, as Karatani tells us, is marked by the 'omnipresence of the "metaphor"', and it is in his figurative use of language that Kant employed the term architectonic as a *metaphor*. At the center of this examination is the problem of the theory of knowledge—epistemology—in the background of which stand 'rationalism' and 'empiricism', between Descartes and Hume. Kant's position between them must be understood, in Karatani's term, as we have seen, by a 'pronounced parallax'.

In his *Kant's Metaphysics and Theory of Science*, Gottfried Martin writes that

The constructive character of geometry provides Kant with a second reason for calling judgments synthetic. The constructive character of geometry and of mathematics in general is according to Kant a fundamental feature of mathematics which distinguishes it from Philosophy.[5]

Kant made this distinction in *Critique of Pure Reason*. He wrote:

> **Philosophical** cognition is **rational cognition** from **concepts**, mathematical cognition that from the **construction** of concepts. But to **construct** a concept means to exhibit *a priori* the intuition corresponding to it. For the construction of a concept, therefore a **non-empirical** intuition is required, which consequently, as intuition, is an *individual* object, but that must nevertheless, as the construction of a concept (of a general representation), express in the representation universal validity of all possible intuitions that belong under the same concept.[6]

As Martin points out, 'The meaning of construction becomes apparent if we consider proofs and definitions', and that 'When the mathematician wants to prove a proposition he always does so by means of construction'.[7] Kant first wrote the following in *Critique of Pure Reason*:

> Now Philosophy as well as mathematics does deal with magnitude, e.g., with totality, infinity, etc. And Mathematics also occupies itself with the difference between lines and planes as spaces with different quality, and with continuity of extension as a quality of it. But although in such cases they have a common object, the manner of dealing with it through reason is entirely in philosophical than in mathematical consideration. The former confines itself solely to general concepts, the latter cannot do anything with the mere concepts but hurries immediately to intuition, in which it considers the concept *in concreto*, although not empirically, but rather solely as one which it has exhibited *a priori*, i.e., constructed, and in which that which follows from the general conditions of the construction must also hold generally of the subject of the constructed concept.[8]

And further:

> Give a philosopher the concept of a triangle, and let him try to find out in his way how the sum of its angles might be related to a right angle. He has nothing but the concept of a figure enclosed by three straight lines, and in it the concept of equally many angles. Now he may reflect on this concept as long as he wants, yet he will never produce anything new. He can analyze and make distinct the concept of a straight line, or of an angle, or of the number there, but he will not come upon any other properties that do not already lie in these concepts. But now let the geometer take up this question. He begins at once to construct a triangle. Since he knows that two right angles

together are exactly equal to all of the adjacent angles that can be drawn at one point on a straight line, he extends one side of this triangle, and obtains two adjacent angles that together are equal to right ones. Now he divides the external one of these angles by drawing a line parallel to the opposite side of the triangle, and sees that there arises an external adjacent angle which is equal to an internal one, etc. in such a way, through a chain of inferences that is always guided by intuition, he arrives at a fully illuminating and at the same time general solution of the question.[9]

As Martin tells us, the significance of Kant's reflection on construction came to light 'through modern inquiries into the foundations of mathematics'.[10] It is useful to reiterate what was said before about Kant's attitude to the non-Euclidean geometry. Many Kantians, as Martin points out, strongly disputed the possibility of non-Euclidean geometry, and there are good reasons why Kant was right to be careful about non-Euclidean geometries, as Karatani has also brought out. But, as Martin states,

there can be no doubt that it was clear to Kant that in geometry the field of what is logically possible extends far beyond that of Euclidean geometry. There was, however, one thesis to which Kant held firm—presumably in error. What goes beyond Euclidean geometry may be constructed in intuition, and this in turn means for Kant that it does not exist mathematically, that it is a mere figment of thought. Only Euclidean geometry exists in the mathematical sense and all non-Euclidean geometries are mere figments of thought.[11]

Martin goes on to mention what Kant in *Critique of Pure Reason* said about the Postulate:

The postulate of the possibility of things thus requires that their concept agree with the formal conditions of experience in general. This, however, namely the objective form of experience in general, contains all synthesis that is requisite for the cognition of objects. […]. That in such a concept no contradiction must be contained is, to be sure, a necessary logical condition; but it is far from sufficient for the objective reality of the concept, i.e., for the possibility of such an object as is thought through the concept. Thus in the concept of a figure that is enclosed between two straight lines there is no contradiction, for the concept of two straight lines and their intersection contain no negation of a figure; rather the impossibility rests not on the concept in itself, but on its construction in space, i.e., on the conditions of space and its determinations; but these in turn have their objective reality, i.e., they pertain to possible things, because they contain in themselves *a priori* the form of experience in general.[12]

Martin comments that

> Kant thus denies the mathematical existence of a closed figure composed of two straight sides; it is indeed logically possible because it is free from contradiction, but it cannot be constructed and given in intuition. Kant's conception of non-Euclidean geometries in general has to be understood in the same way. Non-Euclidean geometries are logically possible but they cannot be constructed; hence they have no mathematical existence for Kant and are mere figments of thought.[13]

Martin in his further examination of Kant's views on the 'ontological' status of space and time says that, for Kant, they are 'transcendentally ideal and empirically real'. As Kant said, 'We assert therefore the empirical reality of space … yet at the same time its transcendental reality', and of time, 'What we assert is therefore the empirical reality of time … but on the contrary we deny all claim to the absolute reality of time … and that is what transcendental ideality consists of'.[14] And, just as a reminder of what Kant said about the term 'transcendental' in the context of the 'science of critique of pure reason' in the 'Introduction B' to *Critique of Pure Reason*: 'I call all cognition transcendental that is occupied not so much with objects but rather with our mode of cognition of the object insofar as this is to be possible *a priori*' and that 'A system of such concepts would be called **transcendental philosophy**'.[15]

Martin points out that Kant's 'transcendental ideality of space and time' is a thesis that he shares with Leibniz. But, when he asserts that transcendental ideality of space and time has its origin in a human mode of knowledge, he parts company with Leibniz. Martin writes:

> From the Kantian point of view a transcendental inquiry into the transcendental ideality of space and time must be directed primarily to the origin of space and time; that is to say, from the Kantian point of view a transcendental enquiry must be an enquiry into the human mode of knowledge.[16]

In this regard, Kant in *Critique of Pure Reason* wrote:

> We have therefore wanted to say that all our intuition is nothing but representation of appearance; that the things that we intuit are not in themselves what we intuit them to be, nor are their relations so

constituted in themselves as they appear to us; and that if we remove our own subject or even only the subjective constitution of the senses in general, then all the constitution, all relations of objects in space and time, indeed space and time themselves would disappear, and as appearances they cannot exist in themselves, but only in us.[17]

As Martin summarizes the matter,

> for Kant space means Euclidean space, and in particular Euclidean geometry. Both Kant and Leibniz assert the objective validity of Euclidean geometry. Leibniz grounds the objective validity of Euclidean geometry in God's thinking, Kant grounds it on human thinking. The transcendental ideality of Euclidean space then means that the being of Euclidean space consists in its being thought by man. This, that the being of Euclidean space consists of its being thought by man, is what Kant means by the transcendental ideality of space.[18]

Moreover,

> In the sense of mathematical existence re-defined by Kant as constructability, there only is three dimensional Euclidean space. [...] The objective validity of geometry can be proved by Kantian arguments only for appearances and not for the things in themselves.[19]

I can now turn to the examination of constructivism in relation to the 'Copernican Revolution'. In his incisive and concise study entitled *After Parmenides: Idealism, Realism, and Epistemic Constructivism*, Rockmore lucidly identifies two approaches to the problem of cognition: One holds that to know is to cognize the real, reality, or the world, which is the 'standard view'. And the other, the modern alternative, is the view that he identifies as 'epistemic constructivism'. He traces these two approaches to cognition from Parmenides to Kant. The standard view is attributed to Parmenides's thesis that 'thought and being are the same', and the alternative, the epistemic constructivism comes to Kant with a 'twofold claim' that 'we do not and cannot know the real, and we know only what we construct'.[20] Significantly, Karatani directly relates Parmenides's thesis to Kant, without getting into the discussion on constructivism, to which I will come later, at the end of this chapter.

Epistemic constructivism, in Rockmore's words, suggests that 'though we do not know the real, we know what we construct. This cognitive approach turns away from the ongoing effort to know the real; but it remains Parmenidean in arguing for knowledge of the "real for us"—that is, for a recognizable version of the Parmenidean thesis that thought and being are the same.'[21] After a comprehensive treatment of idealism and realism in relation to epistemic constructivism, Rockmore examines modern philosophy and a host of modern thinkers with Parmenides and Plato in the background. He comes specifically to discuss Kant's constructivism in relation to the 'Copernican Revolution' in a chapter entitled 'Kant on Causality and Epistemic Constructivism'. He initially mentions that Kant believed that critical philosophy is the 'first philosophical theory to demonstrate its cognitive claims', which, by implication, Kant 'suggests that if the problem of knowledge is central to philosophy, then philosophy both begins and ends in his position'.[22] According to Kant, as Rockmore reminds us, critical philosophy is different from any prior theories. As a transcendental theory 'the critical philosophy claims to provide the only possible approach to cognition. As an a priori theory, it formulates a position independent of time and place.'[23] He also points out that modern rationalism and empiricism both failed to overcome the cognitive problem in properly 'representing what it takes to be real'. He instructively writes:

> Representationalism and constructivism are incompatible cognitive alternatives. Platonism, which denies the backward cognitive inference from appearances to ideas, is antirepresentational. But the way of ideas, which depends on the distinction between primary and secondary qualities, is representational. The way of ideas employs a threefold cognitive model, including a subject, an object, and an idea or representation that in principle correctly depicts the real object.

and further, 'Constructivism presupposes the failure of representationalism. It denies the backward anti-Platonic causal inference by claiming, as the mature Kant later claims, that we know only objects that we "construct"'.[24] Rockmore usefully reminds us that representationalism, which is still widespread in modern philosophy that began with Descartes, and which continues to the present, had in fact been replaced in the second edition of *Critique of Pure Reason* by Kant's turning to constructivism. Kant changed his position for an important reason. Rockmore notes that

> according to him, we cannot infer from the appearance—that is, from an effect—to its cause (the noumenon or thing in itself). If it were possible to infer from the effect to the cause, then the real could be represented. Yet, Kant like Plato, rejects the backwardness inference from an effect to its cause, hence rejects the idea that the object, or the real, can be represented. Hence Kant rejects representationalism understood as correctly depicting or grasping the noumenon.[25]

We can now examine the relation of constructivism to the Copernican Revolution. First, a point about the nature of the Copernican theory: Thomas Kuhn in his *The Copernican Revolution* points out that the Copernican theory is not a 'typical scientific' theory and remarks that 'few scientific theories have played so large a role in non-scientific thought' and adds that this is not unique:

> In the nineteenth century, Darwin's theory of evolution raised similar extrascientific questions. In our own century, Einstein's relativity theories and Freud's psychoanalytical theories provide reorientation of Western thought. Freud himself emphasized the parallel effects of Copernicus' discovery that the earth was merely a planet and his own discovery that the unconscious controlled much of human behavior. Whether we have learnt their theories or not, we are the intellectual heirs of men like Copernicus and Darwin. Our fundamental thought processes have been reshaped by them, just as the thought of children or grandchildren will have been reshaped by the work of Einstein and Freud. We need more than an understanding of the internal development of science. We must also understand how a scientist's solution of an apparently petty, highly technical problem can on occasion fundamentally alter men's attitude toward basic problems of everyday life.[26]

However, as Kōjin Karatani points out, Kuhn is in error in his point on the Freudian unconscious:

> the revolutionary aspect of Freudian psychoanalysis was not in the idea of the "unconscious controlling much of human behavior"; as presented as early as in *Interpretation of Dreams* (and this idea had existed since antiquity), it was in his attempt to see what exists in the gap between consciousness and unconscious vis-à-vis the form of language. In the course of this attempt, he came to extract the unconscious qua transcendental structure.[27]

Now returning to the relation between constructivism and the Copernican Revolution, it is important to note that in the center of this relation is the same question of cognition and the knowledge of the real, which, as Rockmore says, at least since Parmenides has constituted the main cognitive theme. Against skepticism, epistemic constructivism is an attempt to understand the cognitive link between 'construction and the cognitive object'. It is in this relation that we must understand Kant's epistemic constructivism, otherwise known as the Copernican turn in philosophy, as discussed previously.[28] Now, to reiterate, the Parmenidean thesis is about the cognition of the real. And in this respect, according to Kant, all the attempts to know the real, or mind-independent, object are a problem unlikely to be resolved. Thus the Copernican Revolution in philosophy

> centers in Kant's revolutionary insight that if we give up a representa- tional approach, then the most promising approach lies in the assumption that the cognitive object depends on the subject. In other words, Kant's suggestion consists in reversing the relation of the object to the subject, becoming a relation of subject to object.[29]

Rockmore states that although numerous observers are committed to reconciling the critical philosophy with the Parmenidean thesis, only few are ready to admit that 'Kant's Copernican turn breaks with a long tradi- tion of fruitless efforts to grasp the real', and the fact is that many would not concede that it is 'apparently only well into the critical period that Kant turns his back on the traditional epistemic approach in turning to epistemic constructivism'.[30] All attempts to know the real, according to Kant, always fail: 'we cannot know the real'.

The word 'revolution' in the term 'Copernican Revolution', at the time of Kant, was understood in both astronomical and political senses. According to the dictionary definition, the term comes from the Middle English through Old French or Latin 'revolutio (n)' from *revolvere*, or 'roll back'.[31] Further, '*revolvere* refers to moving in a circle on a central axis, as in the supposedly circular orbit through which the earth revolves around the sun.'[32] At present, as Rockmore notes, 'revolution' is defined in three ways:

> politically as the forcible overthrow of a government or social order in favor of a new system; then astronomically as "an instance of revolving, for instance one revolution a second," to which Kant adds a third meaning, associated with a basic change in the understanding of science, such as the Copernican Revolution in astronomy.[33]

Thus the Copernican turn changes the cognitive strategy, from an old view in which the subject depends on the object, to a new view, an epistemic constructivism in which we know *only* what we construct. In the Preface to the second edition of *Critique of Pure Reason*, Kant wrote:

> Up to now it has been assumed that all our cognition must conform to the objects; but all attempts to find out something about them *a priori* through concepts that would extend our cognition have, on this presupposition, come to nothing. Hence let us once try whether we

do not get farther with the problems of metaphysics by assuming that the objects must conform to our cognition, which would agree better with the requested possibility of an *a priori* cognition of them, which is to establish something about objects before they are given to us. This would be just like the first thoughts of Copernicus, who, when he did not make good progress in the explanation of celestial motions if he assumed that the entire celestial host revolves around the observer, tried to see if he might not have greater success if he made the observer revolve and left the stars at rest. Now in metaphysics we can try in a similar way regarding the **intuition** of the objects. If intuition has to conform to the constitution of the objects, then I do not see how we can know anything of them *a priori*; but if the object (as an object of the sense) conforms to the constitution of our faculty of intuition, then I can very well represent this possibility to myself.[34]

And further:

As for objects insofar as they are thought merely through reason, and necessarily at that, but that (at least as reason thinks them) cannot be given in experience at all—the attempt to think them (for they must be capable of being thought) will provide a splendid touchstone of what we assume as the altered method of our way of thinking, namely that we can cognize of things *a priori* only what we ourselves have put into them.[35]

In Rockmore's commentary,

Kant clearly thinks Copernican heliocentric astronomy constitutes a revolutionary step forward to a new cognitive perspective that will not and cannot later be refuted, nor ever require modification. In other words, the modern turn to Copernican astronomy solves the cognitive problem without later need for correction of any kind

and according to Kant, 'his constructive approach resembles the Copernican view in that what we know is not independent of, but rather centrally depends on, the subject'.[36] 'In broadest terms', Rockmore concludes,

Kant's view of epistemic constructivism includes three conditions. First, there is the inability to justify the cognition of mind-independent object that Kant concedes as his central reason to turn to epistemic constructivism. Second, there is the a priori construction of the cognitive object that, in imitation of mathematics, Kant thinks is a necessary condition of a priori knowledge, or knowledge in his specific sense of the term ...[37]

Rockmore later in his *After Parmenides* traces the pre-German idealism and post-Kantian German idealism in relation to the Copernican turn and states that 'If Leibniz is not an idealist, then idealism begins with the pre-German idealists such as Hobbes, Bacon, and Vico, and German idealism begins with Kant's Copernican turn.'[38] He reiterates that the term 'Copernican turn' refers to 'epistemic constructivism' which runs through this period. He points out that the term 'post-Kantian German idealism' refers to the 'effort in Kant's wake by different hands and from different perspectives to carry the Copernican turn beyond the critical philosophy in perfecting the constructive approach to cognition'.[39]

Before I turn to Karatani's novel reflection on the link between Parmenides and Kant, I should here come to the summary that Rockmore has put forward in his outstanding *After Parmenides*. A review of tradition of the Western philosophy, according to Rockmore reveals two points. First, the problem of knowledge, and second, the fact that the main 'cognitive criterion' has been consistently the 'grasp of the real' on the Parmenidean thesis that thought and being are the same, notwithstanding the persistence of the difference between 'the real' and 'the real with us'. Rockmore is of the opinion that

> Philosophy that aspires to grasp the real has, despite numerous ingenious contributions, never been equal to the task. The pre-Socratic efforts to demonstrate the Parmenidean thesis that began in ancient Greek thought continues today. This effort reached an early high point in Platonism—a peak that has arguably never been surpassed—before collapsing in the modern tradition, above all with Kant. Since that time, it has continued to repeat, though perhaps without ever advancing beyond the point at which Kant left it.[40]

The ancient debate takes a new turn in modern philosophy: 'This new turn, though not invented by Kant, is later solidly linked to critical philosophy. Kant transformed the failed Platonic effort to grasp the real into an anti-Platonic effort, based on epistemic constructivism, to know the real for us.'[41] Further, Plato and Kant are the two main turning points in the post-Parmenidean debate: 'The tradition fails to demonstrate either the Parmenidean claim about knowledge of the real or Platonism. It is better understood as pointing to a kind of anti-Platonism that is not knowledge of the real, but rather, as the Copernican turn suggests, of the real for us.'[42] Rockmore remarks that

> The Parmenidean effort to grasp the real never later waned. It continues in the modern view of rationalism and empiricism. [...] Ancient Platonic idealism depends on grasping the real; modern idealism depends on knowing what one constructs. Those attracted to idealism are often countered by different forms of the claim that idealism is incompatible with realism in all its forms, above all with metaphysical realism.[43]

And more importantly:

> Constructivism is a modern form of idealism that is committed to different forms of realism within the limits of human experience. As Kant already noted, observers fail to grasp the qualities of the thing that merely appears but cannot be known since "through the senses we cannot cognize it at all as it is in itself". Kant is an idealist. Idealism that denies we know the real is not antirealist since it accepts that we can and do know the real for us—the real we construct.[44]

I now come to Karatani and his illuminating commentary on the confluence of the ideas between Parmenides and Kant, which touches in different ways on the same notion of constructivism without explicitly mentioning the term itself. In his groundbreaking *Isonomia and the Origins of Philosophy* he gets to the bottom of the Parmenidean saying 'it is the same to think and to be'. He discusses the method of 'indirect proof' essayed by Parmenides, which is 'understood to have overturned the premises of natural philosophy', and mentions that Parmenides actively placed himself in the lineage of the Ionian school.[45] Karatani cites the following fragment that 'appears to establish the supremacy of thinking over being'[46]:

> For the same thing is there for thinking and for being. If nothing existed, there would be nothing to think about. If being did not exist, the thought would not even exist. In fact, without being ... you will not find thinking.[47]

Karatani explains that

> it is a statement of idealism to the effect that thinking determines being. What Parmenides is saying, though, is the opposite. Being exists, and all thinking deals with being. When there is no coherence

in thinking, it means that the object of thinking cannot be existent, as for example with Pythagoras's kenon or void.[48]

He insightfully remarks that:

> At one time, the natural philosophy rejected personified gods. They used reason (logos) to clear away a sensible and imaginative world of illusion. However, the illusion Parmenides sought to clear was rather one born of reason, as in Pythagoras's notion of a realm of truth that transcends the senses. For Parmenides, this realm of truth is nothing (nonexistence), and therefore an illusion. This illusion is different from that produced by the senses. Illusion produced by the senses can be rectified by reason. However, it is difficult for reason to rectify illusion born of reason. The only possibility is to demonstrate how thinking falls into self-contradiction. If we are to see something really ground-breaking in Parmenides, it is this critique of reason.[49]

With this passage, Karatani leaves to doubt that he has of course Kant in mind and goes on to explain that 'Whereas older philosophy set as its task to critique a sensibility-based illusion by way of reason, Kant sought to critique the kind of illusion (*Schein*) that reason itself generates', and we must importantly remember that 'This kind of illusion is actually indispensable for reason, and therefore reason cannot easily displace it.'[50] And we are already informed by Karatani that Kant called this world of illusion 'transcendental illusion', which goes to the heart of the notion of 'critique' in Kant, by which is meant the 'critique of reason by reason'. Karatani remarks that, in fact, Parmenides is the forerunner of this notion of critique, or to put it conversely, Kant is the inheritor of Parmenides. In the following, Karatani clearly explicates this point:

> Kant made the distinction between three things: the thing in itself, phenomena, and illusion. Kant is a materialist who affirms that things reside externally. However, what we capture is not the thing in themselves but subjectively constructed phenomena. In this case, phenomenon effectively means scientific cognition. Thus, phenomenon is different from illusion; while phenomenon is rooted in human sensible intuition, illusions not. Further, some illusions are formed by pure reason; they are transcendental illusions.[51]

As we know, these difficult notions were the target of Kant in his *Critique of Pure Reason*, as Karatani reminds us. Shedding light on these illusive terms, Karatani first notes that the distinction between phenomenon and thing in itself may appear to be another version of the dual-world theory, with its illusory world of sense, and the true world of reason. Of course this is not the case; Kant's target was illusion, but especially the illusion of the true world. Notwithstanding, the thing in itself has been understood as true world. This misunderstanding arises because Kant presented the thing in itself directly and actively.[52]

Kant had originally conceived of beginning his *Critique of Pure Reason* with a discussion of antinomy, or dialectic, that is to say, in Karatani's words,

> to begin by demonstrating that if the distinction between phenomenon and thing in itself is not maintained, one falls into paradox, or in other words, to give an indirect proof of the existence of the thing in itself. Kant's concern was that, by omitting this step of indirect proof and launching straight into discussion, the thing in itself might be taken for an idealistic realm that transcends the sense, and this concern proved well founded.[53]

Departing from this point, one needs a

> tripartite distinction of the form: phenomenon, thing in itself, and illusion, to understand Parmenides as well. In Parmenides's extant philosophical treatise in verse, *On Nature*, the goddess tells of two 'ways of inquiry for thinking,' first 'the path of Persuasion (Truth),' and second the 'inscrutable track.' The path of persuasive Truth consists in recognition: 'What-is is, for being is, and nothing is not.' However, it does not rest there as the goddess also advises he must follow the 'inscrutable track'. Here I cease from faithful account and thought about truth; from this point on learn moral opinions, hearing the deceptive order of my words.[54]

Karatani poses the question 'whence comes this necessity for one who knows truth to learn moral opinions?' and follows it by his explication: 'Moral opinions, though, for Parmenides, do not mean illusion. In Kant's organization this would be phenomena, that is to say, thinking through the use of sensible intuitions.'[55]

In conclusion, I bring out *architectonic* in relation to what was said previously about Copernican theory in Kant that must go by the term 'transcendental' through the act of constructivism. As Karatani reminds us, Kant by getting around the contradiction in the philosophy of his time, that is, rationalism and empiricism, introduced forms of sensibility or categories of understanding, calling them 'transcendental' structures.

'What is crucial is this *architectonic* that is called "transcendental". And even if these particular words or concepts are not always used in various post-Kantian contexts, the same architectonic can be found there.'[56] To reiterate, as Karatani puts it:

> Kant's Copernican turn is not a turn toward philosophy of subjectivity, but that toward the thing-in-itself by a detour of the scrutiny of subjectivity. It was for this objective and nothing else that Kant elaborated the transcendental structure of subjectivity.[57]

Notes

1 Karl Marx, *Capital, Volume I*, trans. Ben Fowkes (London: Penguin Classics, 1990), 284.
2 Marx's concern in the passage cited previously was of course the question of human labour in relation to nature. Prior to the passage cited, Marx wrote:

> Labour is, first of all, a process between man and nature, a process by which man, through his own actions, mediates, regulates and controls the metabolism between himself and nature. He confronts the material of nature as a force of nature. He sets in motion the natural forces which belong to his own body, his arms, legs, head and hands, in order to appropriate the materials of nature in a form adapted to his own needs. Through this movement he acts upon external nature and changes it, and in this way simultaneously changes his own nature. He develops the potentialities slumbering within nature, and subjects the play of forces to his own sovereign power.
>
> (*Capital*, 283)

3 See Freidrich Nietzsche, *Philosophy and Truth: Selection from Nietzsche's Notebooks of the Early 1870s*, ed. and trans. Daniel Breazeale (Amherst: Humanity Books,1999), 85.
4 See Tom Rockmore, in *Kant's Wake: Philosophy in the Twentieth Century* (Malden: Blackwell, 2006). For what follows I am basically relying on the incisive analysis of Rockmore. Also see Tom Rockmore, *After Parmenides: Idealism, Realism, and Epistemic Constructivism* (Chicago and London: The University of Chicago Press, 2021). I return to this excellent work later below.
5 See Gottfried Martin, *Kant's Metaphysics and Theory of Science*, trans. P. G. Luca (Westport: Greenwood Press, 1974), 21. This important book was originally published in German in 1951, and the first English edition came out by Manchester University Press in 1955.
6 Immanuel Kant, *Critique of Pure Reason*, trans. and ed. Paul Guyer and Allen W. Wood (Cambridge: Cambridge University Press, 1998), A 713/B 741, 630; quoted in different translation in Gottfried Martin, *Kant's Metaphysics and Theory of Science*, 21.
7 Gottfried Martin, *Kant's Metaphysics and Theory of Science*, 21.
8 Immanuel Kant, *Critique of Pure Reason*, A715/B743, A716/B744, 631.
9 Immanuel Kant, *Critique of Pure Reason*, A716/B744, A 717/B745, 631–632, also partially quoted in different translation in Gottfried Martin, *Kant's Metaphysics and Theory of Science*, 21. Martin mentions that Kant, in order to avoid any misunderstanding,

at once points out that algebraic procedure must also be regarded as construction, though of a symbolic kind. Operating with symbols in the processes such as addition and subtraction corresponds to the drawing of straight line in Geometry (A 717, B 745). People have tried to interpret these remarks of Kant to mean that intuition is used in geometry as an additional help; but in reality being tied in this way to construction means limitation. Of all possible proofs only those are to be admitted which can be supported by a construction.

(21–22)

10 Gottfried Martin, *Kant's Metaphysics and Theory of Science*, 22.
11 Gottfried Martin, *Kant's Metaphysics and Theory of Science*, 23–24.
12 Immanuel Kant, *Critique of Pure Reason*, A220/B268, A221, 322–323; also see the partial citation of the same passage in Gottfried Martin, *Kant's Metaphysics and Theory of Science*, 24.
13 Gottfried Martin, *Kant's Metaphysics and Theory of Science*, 24.
14 Quoted partially in Gottfried Martin, *Kant's Metaphysics and Theory of Science*, 37. The fuller passage in *Critique of Pure Reason*, in regard to 'space', goes as follows:

Our expositions accordingly teach the **reality** (i.e., objective validity) of space in regard to everything that can come before us externally as an object, but at the same time the **ideality** of space in general to things when they are considered in themselves through reason, i.e., without taking account of the constitution of our sensibility. We therefore assert the **empirical reality** of space (with respect to all possible outer experience), though to be sure at the same time its **transcendental ideality**, i.e., that it is nothing as soon as we leave out the condition of possibility of all experience, and take it as something that grounds the things in themselves.

(A28/B44, 160)

In regard to 'time':

Our assertions accordingly teach the **empirical reality** of time, i.e., objective validity in regard to all objects that may ever be given to our senses. And since our intuition is always sensible, no object can ever be given to us in experience that would not belong under the condition of time. But, on the contrary, we dispute all claim of time to absolute reality, namely where it would attach to things absolutely as a condition of or property even without regard to the form of our sensible intuition. Such properties, which pertain to things in themselves, can never be given to us through senses. In this therefore consists the **transcendental ideality** of time, according to which it is nothing at all if one abstracts from the subjective conditions of sensible intuition, and cannot be counted as either subsisting or inhering in the objects in themselves (without their relation to our intuition).

(A35/B52, A36, 164)

15 Immanuel Kant, *Critique of Pure Reason*, A12/B26, 149.
16 Gottfried Martin, *Kant's Metaphysics and Theory of Science*, 38.
17 Immanuel Kant, *Critique of Pure Reason*, A41/B59, 168; also quoted in Gottfried Martin, *Kant's Metaphysics and Theory of Science*, 38.
18 Gottfried Martin, *Kant's Metaphysics and Theory of Science*, 39.
19 Gottfried Martin, *Kant's Metaphysics and Theory of Science*, 40. Martin in the meanwhile points out that

It has often been said that there is a gap here in the Kantian proof. But the gap is not in the proof but in the formulation. Kant should not really have said that spatial properties are only attributable to appearances and not to things in themselves. He should only have said, it does not necessarily follow from the fact that appearances necessarily have Euclidean character that things in themselves also have Euclidean character. He thus really ought only to have said, it need not follow from the fact that appearances are in space and time that things in themselves are also in space and time.
(40–41)

20 See Tom Rockmore, *After Parmenides*, 1. Rockmore explains that

Parmenides neither demonstrates nor attempts to demonstrate this thesis, which since pre-Socratic philosophy, continues to function as a criterion of knowledge, and never more so than at present. Rationalists like René Descartes and empiricists like John Locke are both committed to versions of the traditional view that to know is to know the real. They are countered by dissenters who, like the author of critical philosophy, believe there has never been any progress toward this goal.
(1)

21 Tom Rockmore, *After Parmenides*, 4.
22 Tom Rockmore, *After Parmenides*, 83.
23 Tom Rockmore, *After Parmenides*, 85. Moreover, Rockmore points out that

The same thinker, who suggests his position is independent of the history of philosophy and is hence ahistorical, appears to contradict this claim by suggesting the various ways the critical philosophy depends on the prior debate. In this text, Kant refers to, interprets, and often replies to a large number of thinkers. They include Hume, who is a central influence, but also Leibniz, Christian Wolff, Locke, Berkeley, A.G. Baumgarten, perhaps Plato, Aristotle, Fichte, Salomon Maimon, K.L. Reinhold, and many others.
(85)

24 Tom Rockmore, *After Parmenides*, 84. Rockmore further remarks that

Modern representationalism arises through the Cartesian inference from ideas in the mind to the world. Kant favored representationalism until the so-called critical period, when he later abandoned this approach for constructivism. The German thinkers were steadily committed to Newtonianism, hence to modern science, which he thinks is undermined by Hume's attack on causality. Kantian representationalism relies on a causal connection that Hume denies and that Kant, in answering Hume, seeks to reestablish.
(84)

25 Tom Rockmore, *After Parmenides*, 90.
26 Thomas Kuhn, *Planetary Astronomy in the Development of Western Thought* (Cambridge: Harvard University Press, 1957), 4.
27 See Kōjin Karatani, *Transcritique: On Kant and Marx*, trans. Sau Kohso (Cambridge: Cambridge University Press, 2005), 32.
28 In this respect Rockmore importantly notes that 'Copernican Revolution' is a

term Kant never used to refer to his position, but one that is often mentioned in the literature. However, since it is rarely discussed in detail, it remains mysterious and little understood, even in light of immense and rapidly growing Kantian literature. The present state of the debate can perhaps be indicated by the fact that what is apparently the most detailed account concludes that Kant probably never read Copernicus.

(Tom Rockmore, *After Parmenides*, 91)

29 Tom Rockmore, *After Parmenides*, 91.
30 Tom Rockmore, *After Parmenides*, 91.
31 In Tom Rockmore, *After Parmenides*, 92.
32 Tom Rockmore, *After Parmenides*, 92.
33 Tom Rockmore, *After Parmenides*, 92. Rockmore writes:

> Kant's conception of revolutionary cognitive change is linked to his normative view of science. There are different types of knowledge, including logic, pure mathematics, pure natural science, and the future science of metaphysics. But knowledge itself of whatever kind presumably is not mutable but permanent. Understood in this way, knowledge becomes possible only in following what Kant calls the secure path of science. At present we live in a historical period that at least on the scientific plane is dominated by general relativity and quantum mechanics, though this may later change through new discoveries. Kant, who is a Newtonian, thinks Newton has in effect brought pure natural science to a high point and an end. He does not believe that the problem of knowledge can be dealt with for a particular period only, such as our time or specific historical moment. His reference to secure path of science suggests knowledge is neither limited in time nor historical, and will not later be abandoned for another path. On the contrary, he is proposing through a conceptual revolution to solve (or resolve) the problem of knowledge—not, say, for our time or for a historical period, but rather permanently.
>
> (92–93)

34 Immanuel Kant, *Critique of Pure Reason*, B xvi, B xvii, 110; also quoted in Tom Rockmore, *After Parmenides*, 93.
35 Immanuel Kant, *Critique of Pure Reason*, B xviii, 111.
36 Tom Rockmore, *After Parmenides*, 94.
37 Tom Rockmore, *After Parmenides*, 105.
38 Tom Rockmore, *After Parmenides*, 111–112.
39 Tom Rockmore, *After Parmenides*, 112. Rockmore further explains that

> If we abstract from Leibniz (who is arguably a special case), then 'German idealism' has three main characteristics. To begin with, it abandons the ancient efforts to know the world, or the world as it is. Second, German idealism favors knowing the human world over knowing the world. Finally, in Kant's wake, German idealism modifies the role of the subject that constructs what it knows. Individually and as a group, the German idealists all turn away from the bi-millennial efforts to know the real and toward the effort to know the real for us. Constructivism (or epistemic constructivism) and modern idealism are closely related. German idealism is a form of epistemic constructivism. Kantian Copernicanism is both idealist and constructivist. Post-Kantian German idealism builds on the critical philosophy in turning from the a priori to the posteriori plane.
>
> (112)

40 Tom Rockmore, *After Parmenides*, 163. Rockmore further reflects that

> Parmenides, Plato, and Kant are among the main actors in the cognitive debate. Early in the Greek tradition, the Parmenidean view that thought and being are the same led to a lively effort to know the real, eventually

extending through the entire later tradition. This debate reaches an early peak in Plato that was never later surpassed, that Kant claims but fails to bring to an end late in the eighteenth century, that still continues at the time of this writing, and that was basically transformed by the emergence of epistemic constructivism in the modern discussion.

(163–164)

41 Tom Rockmore, *After Parmenides*, 164.
42 Tom Rockmore, *After Parmenides*, 164.
43 Tom Rockmore, *After Parmenides*, 165.
44 Tom Rockmore, *After Parmenides*, 165–166.
45 See Kōjin Karatani, *Isonomia and the Origins of Philosophy*, trans. Joseph A. Murphy (Durham and London: Duke University Press, 2017), 94. I am only touching on a small part of this important text which is a tremendous contribution to the current philosophical debate on the relation between Socrates and Plato and its political implications from a Marxist point of view, which I will be dealing with more comprehensively in my forthcoming book devoted to Karatani's reading of Marx.
46 Kōjin Karatani, *Isonomia and the Origins of Philosophy*, 94.
47 Quoted in Kōjin Karatani, *Isonomia and the Origins of Philosophy*, 94.
48 Kōjin Karatani, *Isonomia and the Origins of Philosophy*, 94.
49 Kōjin Karatani, *Isonomia and the origins of Philosophy*, 94.
50 Kōjin Karatani, *Isonomia and the Origins of Philosophy*, 94–95.
51 Kōjin Karatani, *Isonomia and the Origins of Philosophy*, 95.
52 Kōjin Karatani, *Isonomia and the Origins of Philosophy*, 95. Karatani notes that

> Kant himself was aware of the possibility of misunderstanding. After the publication of the *Critique of Pure Reason*, he wrote to a friend that he had originally conceived of the work under a different plan, and it would have been better if he had stuck with it.
>
> (95)

See Kant's letter to M. Hertz, May 11, 1781, in *Immanuel Kant: Philosophical Correspondence 1759–1799*, ed. Arnold Zweig (Chicago: University of Chicago Press, 1967).
53 Kōjin Karatani, *Isonomia and the Origins of Philosophy*, 95.
54 Kōjin Karatani, *Isonomia and the Origins of Philosophy*, 95–96.
55 Kōjin Karatani, *Isonomia and the Origins of Philosophy*, 96. He further explains that

> Aristotle, as we saw before, characterizes Parmenides as saying, "what-is is one"; however, "being forced to follow the observed facts," he proceeds to an investigation of sensible reality. However, Aristotle has the sequence backward. Parmenides, by first introducing the path of Truth, cleared away any illusion of a true world that transcends the senses. With this process, he opened up the path to the investigation of phenomena.
>
> (96)

Karatani concludes his reflections by saying that

> Illusion is represented more than anything by the kind of Pythagorean thought that would reject the sensible realities and discover the origin of the world in number. What Parmenides advises is to first clear away this kind of illusion and move on to inquiry into mortal opinions (phenomena). Put another way, clear away Pythagorean philosophy, and return to the path of understanding of nature opened by the Ionian school, and

proceed further down its path. And in fact the next generation of Eleatic philosophers would carry out that task—and from their effort would come the atomic theory.

(96)

56 Kōjin Karatani, *Transcritique: On Kant and Marx*, 31.
57 Kōjin Karatani, *Transcritique: On Kant and Marx*, 34.

7

MARX AND ARCHITECTONICS

How can science be a work of art, how can art and science together constitute an architectonic system, and how can this architectonic system attain to a literary *style* of a high caliber? Who meets the standards of this stylistic ideal? According to Ludovico Silva, that figure is Marx. Marx's work, Silva suggests, must not only be *read* but has to be *studied* under the twin notions of *architectonic* and *style*. Silva's book *Marx's Literary Style*, originally published in 1971 and belatedly translated into English in 2023, is a groundbreaking work. It is a crown jewel of the vast literature on Marx we have inherited. Silva's work was written earlier than Karatani's *Marx: Toward the Center of Possibility* but surprisingly shares the same concern with the latter on two major counts: the Kantian architectonic on the one hand and the role of *metaphor* in the language of philosophy on the other. What is refreshing in Silva's text is that he offers a unique application of both notions to Marx's oeuvre. Silva's work indirectly and independently affirms Karatani's attribution of Marx's work to be a continuation of Kant's 'transcendental critique'. Karatani and Silva come wonderfully close to each other, both confirming the same point about Kant's figurative and rhetorical uses of language in his architectonic philosophy, which, for Silva, is the foundation on which the work of Marx should be studied. Silva is the only Marxologist who has explicitly suggested that we must read Marx *stylistically*. Moreover, Karatani and Silva both engage the 'architecture metaphor' in the language of philosophy, which, in the case of Silva, as we will see subsequently, is specifically applied to Marx's work, thus putting to rest the much misunderstood so-called relation between 'base' and 'superstructure' in a sustained and a decisive analysis. In a precise sense, Silva advises us to view Marx, all along and at the same time, as a *philosopher*, as a *scientist*, and as an *artist*, whose work from the vantage point of this study can *also* be grounded in the *will to architecture*, as I claim. In what follows I try to follow Silva's argument step by step as to how Marx's work should be

DOI: 10.4324/9781032647616-8

studied under the Kantian notion of 'architectonics', treating him as a philosopher and his work as a scientific corpus *and* also a *work of art*. Silva's analysis in this regard is unprecedented and an illuminating view of Marx we have never had before. Here I want to express that I wish Karatani had referenced Silva's book, written more than twenty years before Karatani published his analysis of Kant in relation to Marx, as we have seen, first in *Architecture as Metaphor* and later in *Transcritique: On Kant and Marx*. Elsewhere, I will attempt to read Silva's *Marx's Literary Style* in tandem with Karatani's *Marx: Towards the Center of Possibility* that was published in original Japanese in 1974 and later in English translation in 2022. I would like to think that Karatani would have highly appreciated Silva's study of Marx, grounded as it is in the same philosophical approach as his own.

Before we get to the employment of the term 'architectonics' in Silva's analysis, it is useful first to understand the way he discusses the term 'metaphor' with its subtle relation to the notion of 'analogy' along with the 'consistent, periodic reappearances of certain great metaphors' Marx used in his oeuvre. According to Silva, it is the 'matrix-metaphors that encompass all of his literary figures and that serve as their totality', which 'are the metaphors with which he illustrates his conception of history and they also often allow him to formulate the impeccable criticism of bourgeois ideologues and economists'.[1] Silva reminds us that the presence of these vast metaphors 'do not play a merely literary or ornamental role in Marx's work; beyond their aesthetic value, they achieve a cognitive value as the expressive support of his science'.[2]

Silva says the followings on the meaning and uses of the term 'metaphor':

Those who believe that metaphors are not a source of knowledge are wrong; metaphors may not represent exact knowledge, but they have a cognitive value. The foundation of any metaphor is analogical reasoning, and ever since Aristotle we have known that we understand many things by analogy, which he defined as 'equality of shares'. To establish the equal shares that exists between two sets of phenomena (for example, between the lungs and the air and gills and water) is to take an important step in the study of these phenomena. Along with these reasons are those wielded by the poets: every suitable metaphor expands the expressive power of language, and every science needs a powerfully expressive language; therefore, every appropriate metaphor is an excellent companion to science, just as all appropriate examples are. Nietzsche affirmed, when it comes to expressing thoughts, sometimes metaphors and examples are everything.[3]

Silva identifies three basic metaphors in Marx that he will study, namely, (1) the 'superstructure' metaphor, (2) the 'reflection' metaphor, and (3) the metaphor of religion. I will attend to these, with a more specific attention paid to the 'superstructure' metaphor. Here I first examine Silva's invocation of architectonics, in relation to Marx's work, as a 'stylistic feature', which he innovatively calls as '*architectonic of science* or the *scientific work as a work of art*'.[4]

To begin with, Silva makes it clear that he uses the word 'architectonic' in the precise sense that Kant defined it in his *Critique of Pure Reason*. He cites the key passage that I also have cited in a previous chapter, and it is useful to refresh our mind again to reinforce the point. Kant, in the third chapter of 'The Transcendental Doctrine of Method', entitled 'The Architectonic of Pure Reason', wrote:

> By an **architectonic** I understand the art of system. Since systematic unity is that which first makes ordinary cognition into science, i.e., makes a system out of a mere aggregate of it, architectonic is the doctrine of that which is scientific in our cognition in general, and therefore necessarily belongs to the doctrine of method. Under the government of reason our cognitions cannot at all constitute a rhapsody but must constitute a system, in which alone they can support and advance its essential ends. I understand by a system, however, the unity of the manifold cognitions under one idea. This is the rational concept of the form of a whole, insofar as through this the domain of the manifold as well as the position of the parts with respect to each other is determined *a priori*. The scientific rational concept thus contains the end and the form of the whole that is congruent with it. The unity of the end, to which all parts are related and in the idea of which they are also related to each other, allows the absence of any part to be noticed in our knowledge of the rest, and there can be contingent addition or undermined magnitude of perfection that does not have its boundaries determined *a priori*. [...] For its execution the idea needs a *schema*, i.e., an essential manifold and order of the parts determined *a priori* from the principle of the end. A schema that is not outlined in accordance with an idea, i.e., from the chief end of reason, but empirically, in accordance with aims occurring contingently (whose number one cannot know in advance), yields **technical** unity, but that which arises only in consequence of an idea (where reason provides the ends *a priori* and does not await them empirically) grounds **architectonic** unity.[5]

Pointing out that whatever position we adopt toward Kant, Silva says that 'no one can reasonably doubt two things: that it is a monument to reason, and that it is stocked with valuable methodological observations, many of which still retain their usefulness'. He goes on to reiterate Kant's points:

> *The art of constructing a system!* What is scientific in our understanding is so because it possesses a systematic, architectonic unity in which all its parts correspond to one another and in which none is true without respect to the whole.

adding that

> today, structuralism refers to this as 'the logical precedence of the whole to the parts', but in Kant the *a priori* was logico-transcendental, not merely logical. If we set aside the "transcendental" implication, we are left with a perfectly valid methodological schema.[6]

Silva repeats that 'According to Kant, the architectonic is the art of system', and says that here he is in agreement with Paul Valéry, who spoke of '*la plus poétique de idées: l'idée de composition*' and explains that

> In this, Valéry was surely following in the steps of his equally great teacher Mallarmé, for whom each verse was *a musical score*, a minimal orchestra through which—to put it in the terms of everyone's teacher, Baudelaire—'les parfums, les couleurs et les sons se répondent': they are architectonic 'correspondences'.[7]

In this regard Silva goes on to remark:

> The general method of science and general method of art thus coincide in this idea: *for there to be science, and for there to be art, there must be architectonics.* For thought to be science, it must be systematic; for experience to be art, it must be architectonic and be governed by the art of system.[8] [my emphasis]

In a precise manner of mathematical logic Silva deduces the following:

> And if science implies architectonics, and architectonics implies art, then science implies art. This is the logical skeleton of this reasoning: if p implies q, and q implies r, then p implies r by the simple and clear

law of transitivity. The material skeleton of this reasoning: if a structural condition of science is its architectonic character, and if by the same token, a structural condition of art is its architectonic character, then science and art have at least one structural condition in common, 'r', which is a variable in the formal expression, and becomes a constant in the non-formal expression: the architectonic character. Is it any wonder, then, that the architectonic dimension of a scientific system is also its beautiful side?[9]

And thus, according to Silva,

> Karl Marx had a true lifelong obsession with constructing an *Economy* that had an architectonic structure and appearance. He was also conscious that this needed to be accomplished *in the same way as the creation of a work of art.*[10]

And, moreover,

> not just in terms of the general form of the scientific edifice—its broader and most general structure lines—but also in its smaller details: in the moulding of the expressions, the beadwork of its phrasing, the firm curves of its verbal vaults, in its metaphorical bas-relief, its conceptual pilasters and, in the end, its foundation in erudition.[11]

Marx needed, according to Silva, to have his artistic and perfect 'whole' before it could be sent to the publisher. We have, therefore, 'two halves' in 'Marx's oeuvre', one which went to press during his lifetime and the other which is in fact 'incomplete manuscripts'. The second half is 'stylistically imperfect', Silva says. 'From the point of view of architectonic', Silva notes, 'there is a stylistic abyss' between the *Contribution to the Critique of Political Economy*, published in 1859, and the *Grundrisse*, drafted between 1857 and 1858. While busy writing *Grundrisse*, Marx finished *Contribution to the Critique*. They are entirely different in terms of 'style', as Silva tells us.

> One can sit down and *read* the *Critique*; one must sit down and *study* the *Grundrisse*. The latter is a brilliant draft, but only a draft; the former, on the other hand, is one of the most perfect models of scientific literature, of science as a work of art, of scientific architectonics,

and 'the same difference separate works like *Critique of Hegel's Philosophy of Right* from *1844 Manuscript*, or Volume 1 of *Capital* from the *Theories of Surplus Values*'.[12] Marx aspired and adhered to scientific work that encompasses *every* conception of history, as Silva emphasizes, and in this respect, the 'celebrated Preface' to the *Critique* of 1859 is an important case which, as Silva puts it, 'includes both the structural features of the social edifice (*struktur*) as well as the appearance of the structure itself (*Überbau*)'.[13] These terms are related to Silva's analysis of the metaphor of the 'superstructure' to which we now come. First it is useful to remind ourselves of the well-known passage in the Preface which has caused so many complaints about the alleged 'mechanical' relationship between 'base' and 'superstructure'. Marx wrote the followings in the Preface:

> In the social production of their lives men enter into relations that are specific, necessary and independent of their will, relations of production which correspond to a specific stage of development of their material productive forces. The totality of these relations of production forms the economic structure of society, the real basis from which rises a legal political structure, and to which correspond specific forms of social consciousness. The mode of production of material life conditions the social, political and intellectual life-process generally. It is not the consciousness of men that specifies their being, but on the contrary their social being that specifies their consciousness.[14]

Concerning this passage, Silva affirms that Marx in fact revised the French translation of Volume 1 of *Capital* personally in which he quotes the fragment from his Preface. Given the importance of this text, Silva points out that 'Marx must have granted it extra attention in his revision. In the French version, *Überbau* is not given as "superstructure" but as "edifice" (*édifice*), and *Basis* and *Grundlage* are translated as *fondation*'.[15]

Now we must confront all the misunderstandings, legitimate or just simplifications, in the interpretations of this passage and the Preface in its entirety. We must do this in the light of Silva's novel and sophisticated study on the meaning of the notion of 'superstructure' in Marx. And it must be understood under the leading concept of *architectonics* that underlies the 'architectural metaphor'. In the section '"Super structure" as metaphor' in *Marx's Literary Style*, Silva admits at the very outset that this topic presents a 'tremendous difficulty'. To

> treat what the great majority of Marxists, Marxologists, and Marxians consider to be a complete scientific *explanation* as a metaphor—or, more accurately, as an analogy that grounds a great metaphor—can easily sound like heresy, or like a 'bourgeois subtlety' meant to

undermine Marx's theoretical edifice; Moreover, to engage polemically with the distinct number—small though it may be—of authors who see 'superstructure' as a scientific explanation and not a metaphor would take us so far afield that we would have to abandon our goal of discussing Marx's style and turn our essay into an exercise in Marxist theory.[16]

Silva's initial response is that with Marx or, for that matter, with any scientific theory 'it is absolutely impossible to separate out *signs* from *meanings* (signified), or, as was once said in an aestheticizing vein, "form" from "content"'.[17] He judiciously draws an analogy and asserts that

> If a writer like Marx has style, and a brilliant style at that, it is because, in his prose, signs and meanings march in tandem, in a balance of forces, and together can engage in any number of pirouettes, just as consummate athletes with perfectly calibrated weights, power and movement can accomplish aerial feats that, for all that daring, do not contravene the laws of physics but rather play with them.[18]

What is '*superstructure*'? With the variation of the term 'superstructure', referred to in Spanish as 'supra-structure' or 'over-structure', Silva informs us that Marx had two designations for the term. 'Sometimes, employing a Latin etymology, he says *Superstruktur*; in others, employing a German one, he says *Überbau*, which literally refers to the upper (*über*) part of building or structure (*Bau*)'.[19] Like an educated architect, Silva reminds us that

> In strict architectural terms, however, it is not appropriate to use *Überbau* or superstructure to refer to the upper part of a building— the whole thing is, after all a single structure. *Überbau* really refers to the scaffolding or framework that is attached to a building during its construction and that is, logically, removed upon completion. An architectonically complete building is a structure, with no trace of superstructure, *Überbau*, or scaffolding.[20]

This is nothing short of an ingenious observation on the part of Silva, from which Marxists and Marx's scholars have to learn. He explains that

> Neither of the above-mentioned words appears with any frequency in Marx's writings, contrary to what one might infer from so much of the literature on ideological superstructures. It is true that Engels does insist on the term—in some letters from the 1880s in particular—but Marx only mentions it on very rare occasions.[21]

Silva further informs us that Marx analyzed *theory* to the point of its
exhaustion, when, for example, he used it in relation to 'theory of labour-
power' or the 'theory of surplus-value'. 'On the other hand,' Silva makes
it clear that, 'when he employed a metaphor, he knew to be discrete and
he used it on few occasions, because he was well aware that metaphors,
when used properly, demand the strictest stylistic economy', and in this
regards he cites the following passages from *The German Ideology*:

> The form of intercourse determined by the existing productive forces
> at all previous historical stages, and in its turn determining these, is
> *civil society* ... [it] has as its premise and basis the simple family and
> multiple, called the tribe ... Already here we see that his civil society
> is the conception and theatre of all history, and how absurd is the
> conception of history held hitherto, which neglects the real relations
> and confines itself to spectacular historical events.
>
> [...]
>
> Civil Society embraces the whole material intercourse of individu-
> als within a definite stage of the development of productive forces ...
> The term 'civil society' [*bürgerliche Gesellschaft*] emerged in the
> eighteenth century, when property relationships had already extri-
> cated themselves from the ancient and medieval communal society.
> Civil Society as such only develops with the bourgeoisie; the social
> organization evolving directly out of production and intercourse,
> which in all ages forms the basis [*Basis*] of the state and of the rest of
> idealistic superstructure [*idealistischen Superstruktur*], has, however,
> always been designated by the same name.[22]

Silva asks: 'the "superstructure" to which the text refers—is it an explanation or a metaphor?' His answer goes by this reasoning:

> If it were an explanation, it would have to make explicit the concrete
> way in which social, material relations—the "civil society" of which
> Hegel spoke—produce ad hoc ideological formations: legal bodies
> that use torturous casuistry to justify private property as an 'inaliena-
> ble right'(!); religious beliefs that give celestial foundations to earthly
> misery by extolling the wonders of material property; phenomena like
> the state which, while *products* of specific material situations, consti-
> tute themselves as *producers* and preservers of those situations; and
> finally, the celebrated 'principles' of the philosophers, products of
> history which identify themselves as its motors. None of this is
> explained with the mere mention of a 'superstructure' built upon a
> 'base'.[23]

Silva comes to chastise Marxists:

> Marx knew what Marxists seem to ignore: that it's one thing to give a schematic introduction to a history by means of illustrative metaphors and quite another to explain that same theory scientifically and positively. Precisely because his work goes beyond pure metaphor, Marx was well within his rights as a writer when he employed metaphors in the sense we have noted. The same thing happens with *alienation*, which began as an ethical metaphor and progressively became a socio-economic explanation. The claim that the worker is 'alienated from himself' is, at first, a metaphor; it turns into an explanation when, guided by Marx, we realize that in becoming a *commodity* (as it must [be] due to the social regime of production), the worker's labour-power becomes the worker's own worst enemy.[24]

Silva's complaints about 'Marxists' get harsher:

> Just as there are those who make tendentious attempts to reduce alienation to its metaphorical qualities and speak of a phantom 'human essence' that is separated from the worker (and in so doing arbitrarily reduce Marx's entire corpus to a few passages from the *1844 Manuscripts* that Marx never authorized), there is a whole legion of ostensible Marxists who reduce the theory of ideological formations to the pure metaphor of the 'ideological superstructure', a metaphor that, isolated from the whole theoretical *designatum* which it is meant to merely *illustrate*, flips Marx's whole theory on its head and leaves upside down everything he worked so hard to put on firm ground.[25]

Silva continues:

> let us suppose, for a moment, that 'superstructure' is an explanatory and not merely a metaphorical term—what would it 'explain' to us? It can explain no more than the following: society, as a material structure, has an ideal superstructure *constructed* upon itself; but, if this superstructure is constructed in the same way as a scaffolding it can be separated from the structure—all scaffolding can be removed, after all—and can thus be considered an independent entity. If Ideology is *truly*, and not just metaphorically, a 'superstructure', what prevents us from taking it as its own celestial body, as an autonomous framework?[26]

This would put us in a position of 'ideologue', as Silva notes, a position Marx relentlessly attacked. Did he not in fact reproach those ideologues, Silva remarks, for 'thinking of ideas, beliefs, religions and philosophical "postulates" as realms apart that exist independently of civil society, that is, of the material life of society?'[27] 'In other words,' as Silva pointedly puts it, 'to accept "superstructure" as a scientific explanation is to turn Marx himself into an *ideologue*, if not into a shameless Platonist believer in a *topos hyperouranios*, in a home for the ideas found beyond the sky'.[28]

Here, going back to the passage quoted previously from the Preface to *A Contribution to the Critique of Political Economy*, it is proper and instructive to cite Silva's comments in affirmation of the argument he has forcefully advanced that he perspicuously relates to his employment of 'building analogy'. He writes:

> No one will deny, sensibly at least, that these terms possess greater authority than the much-touted 'base' and 'superstructure' that contemporary Marxism talks so much about. But our goal here is not to lock ourselves into a merely terminological question. Mostly for the worse, 'base' and 'superstructure' tend to say the same thing as the other terms, in the sense that they can play a role as terms in an analogy. But they fulfill this role less successfully, from the literary point of view, because Marx's point is to compare the economic structure of society to the foundations of a building on the one hand, and, on the other, to compare that society's ideological formation (that is, its legal and political 'façade'—the 'state') to the building itself which rests on those foundations. An *ideologue* is the one who, with crude provincial reasoning, thinks that if the foundations are not visible, they must not exist; that is, one who confuses society with its legal-political façade, forgetting or denying—like an intellectual ostrich—the real economic groundwork that sustains the whole façade. And, if he sees an inverted world, with his head on the ground, it is because he believes that the building holds up the foundation, and not the other way around—he judges societies according to what they think about themselves, by the intellectual clothing they wear, and not by the real relations sustained by the individuals who make them up. This takes on an exceedingly concealing and misleading cast as soon as one thinks of these relations as relations of exploitation.[29]

Here I am reminded of what Sebastiano Timpanaro in his *On Materialism*, originally published in 1970, wrote. He compared the position of contemporary Marxists to a person who lives on the first floor of a house and turns to the tenant of the second floor and says:

> 'You think you're independent, that you support yourself by yourself? You're wrong! Your apartment stands only because it is supported on mine, and if mine collapses, yours will too'. And on the other hand to

the ground floor tenant he says: 'What are you saying? That you support and condition me? What a wretched illusion! The ground floor exists only in so far as it is the ground floor to the first floor. Or, rather, strictly speaking, the real ground floor is the first floor, and your apartment is only a sort of cellar, to which no real existence can be assigned'.[30]

Timpanaro comments that

> To tell the truth, the relations between the Marxist and the second floor tenant have been perceptibly improved for some time, not because the second-floor tenant has recognized his own 'dependence', but because the Marxist has reduced his pretensions considerably, and has come to admit that the second floor is very largely autonomous from the first, or else that the two apartments 'support each other'. But the contempt for the inhabitant of the ground floor has become increasingly pronounced.[31]

Silva in a diagram makes an analogy between 'The Economic Structure (*Struktur*) and Ideology (*Ideologie*) to Foundations (*Basis*) and Edifice (*Überbau*)' respectably to say that there is an '*equality of share*', which according to Aristotle, '*makes up an analogy*'. But he makes the stipulation that the fact that there is an analogical equality does not mean in any way that the 'terms in the second pair can *truly* substitute for those in the first', noting that 'They can only substitute for them *metaphorically*'. Making a subtle distinction between analogy and metaphor, he goes on to say

> Every metaphor is made up of such a transposition. If we say 'old age is to life as evening is to the day', we articulate an analogy; but if we substitute the positions and say 'the evening of life' in order to refer to old age, we articulate a metaphor. In the same way, if we say 'the base or foundation of society', we enunciate a metaphor. And the same is the case if we say ideological *superstructure* or *edifice*.[32]

Silva draws certain conclusions stating the following:

> Marx's oeuvre is outfitted with many metaphors of this type, which possess an eminently literary value—and, if you will, also a scientific one, seeing as these metaphors help illuminate his theories. Marx's theory is that the social relations of society govern and determine every ideological aspect of society, that is the legal-political corpus, the state and the diverse set of social beliefs. His theory's metaphor is this: the economic base or foundation sustains the enormous ideological superstructure or

edifice. Let us do justice to Marx's literary style by respecting his meta-phors as metaphors. And let us do justice to his scientific theories by not confusing them with their metaphorical auxiliaries. A good many of the charges of 'Determinism' and 'schematism' that bourgeois theorists level at Marx arise from these kinds of confusion, which are sadly prop-agated by Marxists themselves. It is Marxists, and not bourgeois ideo-logues, who have turned 'superstructure' into a scientific theory; what they have succeeded in doing is inverting Marx's theory and turning it into an ideology.[33]

I now come to Silva's treatment of the second metaphor named previ-ously as 'reflection as metaphor'. Silva reminds us that in the 1859 Preface Marx introduces a 'verbal dichotomy' that serves as a 'bridge' between the 'superstructure' metaphor and the metaphor of 'reflection'. In terms of analogy, as we have seen, there are two pairs: 'the first of these, *Economic Structure/Ideology*, is the scientific expression of the-ory, while the second, *Base/Edifice*, which has a linear correspondence with the first, is its metaphorical expression'.[34] As we are reminded on the subject of the German terms employed by Marx: 'Economic Structure' is *ökonomische Struktur*, while 'edifice' or 'superstructure' is *Überbau*, which is not *Superstruktur*. Silva writes that 'it is symptomatic that in the scientific expression Marx uses *Struktur*—a Latin-derived word designat-ing a *concrete epistemological concept* that has an enormous theoretical importance in Marx's mature work, especially in *Capital*'.[35] Silva contin-ues to remark that:

> All of this makes us wary of the danger of thinking of Marxist theory in terms of 'superstructure', a word that forces us to imagine the world of ideology as superior and apart from, as an independent realm float-ing above the social structure. The inverse is true: ideology lives and develops *in the social structure itself*: it is its interior continuation and plays, within it, an active everyday role. In concordance with an eco-nomic structure dominated by exploitation, ideology has until now justified this exploitation; it is also a form of exploitation itself, if one accepts the idea of *ideological surplus-value*.[36]

'The fact that ideology', Silva argues,

> is a product of the material situation in no way implies that it, ideol-ogy, is constituted in a world that lies 'above' the material situation: ideology remains tied to the social skeleton or, to use a metaphor of Althusser's, it acts as social 'cement'.[37]

Silva notes that as it has been 'popular' for some time to speak of 'ideological superstructure', it has been 'no less popular' to label Marxist theory of ideology as 'ideological reflection'. The interpreters of Marx, Silva argues, have upended the 'verbal dichotomy' in Marx, as the latter have preferred

> to stick to the metaphor of ideology as a "reflection" of the material structure of society and, in the process, have missed the scientific terms with which Marx develops the problem, centered on the word *Ausdruck* or 'expression', which defines ideology as the *expression* of material relations.[38]

To make his point, he goes on to cite from *The German Ideology* where the reflection metaphor is expressed by famously using the term *camera obscura*. It is a well-known passage which goes as follows:

> If in all ideology men and their relations appear upside-down as in a *camera obscura*, this phenomenon arises just as much from their historical life-process as the inversion of objects on the retina does from the physical life-process. In direct contrast to German philosophy which descends from heaven to earth, here it is a matter of ascending from earth to heaven. That is to say, not of setting out from what men say, imagine, conceive, nor from men as narrated, thought of, imagined, conceived, in order to arrive at men in the flesh; but setting out from real, active men, and on the basis of their real life-process demonstrating the development of the ideological reflexes and echoes of this life-process. The phantoms [*Nebelbildungen*, 'nebulous pictures'] founded in the brains of men are also, necessarily, sublimates of their material life-process, which is empirically verifiable and bound to material premises. Morality, religion, metaphysics, and all the rest of ideology as well the form of consciousness corresponding to these, thus no longer retain the semblance of independence. They have no history, no development; but men, developing their material production and their material intercourse, alter, along with their actual world, also their thinking and the products of their thinking.[39]

As Silva points out, Marx after *The German Ideology* abandoned his 'reflection' metaphor. But the same is not true in the case of his friend and coauthor, Engels, who in *Anti-Düring*, as Silva notes, used the same metaphor many times. After an extended analysis of ideology in relation to 'reflection' and 'expression' along with his reflections on the problem of 'alienation', which we do not need to get into here, Silva comes to reiterate his point:

> All of this shows us why contemporary Marxism needs to review its 'reading' of Marx's works and why it needs to see his oeuvre from a *Stylistic* point of view. The careful examination of style, after all, is the primordial method for distinguishing what is metaphor, wordplay, illustration or ornament from what is properly theoretical in a given style. Such a study of Marx's oeuvre is all the more important. Marx belongs to a class of scientific writers who are rare today. His determination to overcome every division of labour in his own person led him to tackle every aspect of scientific labour, beginning with the literary aspect. Why do we insist on denying Marx something that always preoccupied him—his literary style?[40]

And more pointedly:

> So, given that he was an omnidimensional, omnilateral scientist, who devoted as much care to his calculations as to the precision of his metaphors, why denigrate and divide him? Why take his metaphors for what they are not? This is a comparable, if inverse, error to that committed by bourgeois, one-dimensional scientists who, irritated by Marx's metaphors, insist that his whole oeuvre is a metaphor, and that the theory of surplus-value is the product of a feverish, messianic imagination.[41]

We finally come to the last metaphor, namely, 'religion as metaphor'. As a reminder, 'superstructure' and 'reflection' are the metaphors Marx frequently used in all of his work. They are exemplars of his 'scientific theory', that is, 'the theory of ideology, which is intimately connected to Marx's general materialist theory' as Silva informs us.[42] Marx returned to the metaphor of religion over and over again in almost all of his work. Silva notes that this metaphor has not been a casualty of 'mysticism' in Marx's work, because it was used as a means to confront or 'destroy' that mystification in the first place. By way of a definition of this metaphor, it was Marx's intention to use it as an 'analogy' that would illuminate, through a comparison to 'religious alienation', the notion of the 'alienation of labour' and 'historical and social alienation' in general. As Silva points out, 'This is how we find it in the *1844 Manuscript* and so it remains in major works such as the *Grundrisse, Capital* and *Theories of Surplus Value*'.[43] In the manuscript it is written that

Just as in religion the spontaneous activity of the human imagination, the human brain and the human heart detaches itself from the individual and reappears as the alien activity of a god or of a devil, so the activity of the worker is not his own spontaneous activity. It belongs to another, it is a loss of his self.[44]

Silva comments on this passage that

This is a perfect analogy: A:B::C:D, that is, *the same relationship* obtains between the mental activity of religion and the mind itself on the one hand, and between the productive activity of the worker and the worker himself on the other. This relationship is one of alienation.[45]

Now it is in a famous passage in the chapter on 'The Commodity' in *Capital* that Marx offers his 'Metaphor *as analogy*'. Marx wrote:

In the act of seeing, of course light is really transmitted from one thing, the external object, to another thing, the eye. It is a physical relation between physical things. As against this, the commodity form, and value-relation of the products of labour within which it appears, have absolutely no connection with the physical nature of the commodity and the material [*dinglich*] relations arising out of this. It is nothing but the definite social relation between men themselves which assumes here, for them, the fantastic ['phantasmagoric' is the correct translation] form of a relation between things. In order, therefore, to find an analogy we must take a flight into the misty realm of religion. There the products of the human brain appear as autonomous figures endowed with a life of their own, which enter into relations both with each other and with the human race. So it is in the world of commodities with the products of men's hands. I call this the fetishism which attaches itself to the products of labour as soon as they are produced as commodities, and is therefore inseparable from the production of commodities.[46]

On the relation between 'alienation' and 'fetishism', Silva properly comments, they

are not the same thing: while every instance of commodity fetishism involves alienation, not every form of alienation involves commodity fetishism. Here, however, we are dealing with what Marx in 1844 called the 'alienation of the product'. Is it not significant that, in order to describe it, he uses the exact same analogy in 1867 as he did in 1844? The analogy now looks like this: the relationship between the religious products of the mind and the mind itself *is the same as the relationship* between commodity products of man and man himself. The 'equal shares' that make up the analogy are nothing more than the alienation that exists in both cases. It is as if we said: 4:2::6:3. The arithmetical relation is the same. Religious alienation serves as a perfect metaphor for the alienation of labour.[47]

It is noteworthy that, as Silva points out, in another way, Marx, in his *1844 Manuscript* and *Grundrisse*, used religion as a metaphoric comparison between Christ and money. From *1844* we find money

defined as an *alienated mediator*: what is established is the *mediating activity* itself (a precursor of "commodity fetishism", in which money appears as the ultimate form of alienation). Money, which is nothing but social relation, seems to become a *material thing* possessing mediating powers over the relations between people and leading them to become things insofar as money becomes personified.[48]

Marx wrote:

Christ originally represents (1) man before God, (2) God for man and (3) man for man. In the same way *money* originally represents (1) private property for private property; (2) society for private property; (3) private property for society. But Christ is God *alienated* and *man* alienated. God continues to have value only in so far as he represents Christ, man continues to have value only in so far as he represents Christ. Likewise with money.[49]

'Following this analogy', Silva writes,

we find that man has value in this society insofar as he represents money. Marx measures the *value* of commodities according to the labour *time* that is socially necessary for their production—what would he say of the contemporary phrase "time is money"? The comparison with Christ is even stronger insofar as Christ has always been represented as the spirit of material poverty.[50]

In *Grundrisse*, the initial 'Christ–money' metaphor attains to the subtle 'Christ–exchange-value' metaphor. As Silva explains:

Both possess a double value: Christ is not just God, he is man, and exchange-value is both itself and a use-value that *incarnates* it, the same way that God is *incarnate* in man. And, just as in the God–man unity the first member or "God" becomes the mediation between God and man, that is, his own mediation, so too in the use–value-exchange–value unity, this last term strangely arises as the mediator between use and exchange, that is, as its own mediator.[51]

Silva incisively continues to reflect more, emphasizing the 'metaphorical' use in *Grundrisse*:

> And so, Christ, as mediator, becomes even more important than God, who, after all, lives in celestial solitude. In the same way, exchange-value, as mediator becomes more important than use-value. This is a metaphorical representation of an entire economy based on exchange-value, in which the market is more important than man, in which production serves the needs of the market rather than the needs of man, just as religion attends more to the administrative needs of the Church than to the needs of God. And, just as the economy is founded on the competition of all against all and not distribution according to need, so religion is based on the fear of hell rather on the love of heaven.[52]

On this note, I bring this investigation into Silva's highly significant *Marx's Literary Style* to a conclusion. This chapter has been only an incomplete examination of his extraordinary book. It is appropriate to sum up referencing his own 'A Stylistic Appraisal of Marx's Oeuvre' by which he summarizes his thoughts:

> The expression of an architectonic vision of society; a verbal reflection of dialectical thought; vast analogical metaphors complete in their designs; a virtuosic writing full of the spirit of concreteness, of criticism, polemic and mockery: such are the most prominent features of the style achieved by Marx, who got his start in poetic meditations, who conceived of prose as a work of art, and whose apex consists of a scientific corpus literarily blessed with a prodigious expressive power.[53]

And, I must add what he has to say in the last chapter of his book entitled 'Epilogue on Irony and Alienation' where Silva cites *The Class Struggle in France* (1850) to say that Marx 'in golden letters' writes: 'The mortgage the peasant has on heavenly possessions guarantees the mortgage the bourgeois has on peasant possession', which for Silva summarizes 'all of the stylistic characteristics' that he has tried to examine in his book. He further remarks:

> Architectonically speaking, the sentence is perfect. It also participates in what we have called the "dialectic of expression", which is also an

"expression of the dialectic". It features a combination common in Marx: Irony mixed with indignation. How many have tried to imitate Marx's style, only to copy the indignation while forgetting the irony! To be able to imitate Marx's style gracefully, one would need to recall that the entire machinery of his indignation is mounted on the serrated gear of his irony.[54]

And,

It is therefore, necessary to engage in a radical critique of ideology. A critique which in Marx is stylistically paired with irony. No critique is as devastating as that which goes from irony to denunciation and from denunciation to irony.[55]

Notes

1 Ludovico Silva, *Marx's Literary Style*, 43.
2 Ludovico Silva, *Marx's Literary Style*, 43.
3 Ludovico Silva, *Marx's Literary Style*, 43.
4 Ludovico Silva, *Marx's Literary Style*, 23.
5 Immanuel Kant, *Critique of Pure Reason*, trans. and ed. Paul Guyer and Allen W. Wood (Cambridge: Cambridge University Press, 1998), 691–692; partially quoted in Ludovico Silva, *Marx's Literary Style*, 24.
6 Ludovico Silva, *Marx's Literary Style*, 24.
7 Ludovico Silva, *Marx's Literary Style*, 24–25.
8 Ludovico Silva, *Marx's Literary Style*, 25.
9 Ludovico Silva, *Marx's Literary Style*, 25.
10 Ludovico Silva, *Marx's Literary Style*, 25.
11 Ludovico Silva, *Marx's Literary Style*, 25. Silva narrates that

> Responding to Engel's insistence that the first volume of *Capital* be published at once, Marx replied 'I cannot bring myself to send anything off until I have the whole thing in front of me. Whatever shortcomings they may have, the advantage of my writings is that they are an artistic whole, and this can only be achieved through my practice of never having things printed until I have them in front of me *in their entirety*'.
>
> (25–26)

12 Ludovico Silva, *Marx's Literary Style*, 28.
13 Ludovico Silva, *Marx's Literary Style*, 28.
14 Karl Marx, 'A Contribution to the Critique of Political Economy, Preface' in *Marx, Later Political Writings*, ed. Terrel Carver (Cambridge: Cambridge University Press, 1996), 159–160.
15 Ludovico Silva, *Marx's Literary Style*, 51.
16 Ludovico Silva, *Marx's Literary Style*, 46.
17 Ludovico Silva, *Marx's Literary Style*, 46. Silva informs us that

> A truly literary style exists where signs express meanings most exactly— plastically, musically, and in terms of prosody; that is, where there is no dissonance or disproportion between the signs deployed and their intended meanings. As Antonio Machado said, to say what happens in the

street, one must say 'what happens in the street', or something like it—'what happens in the street everyday', for instance; one should never say 'the customary events that transpire in the throughfare'. This last example exhibits dissonance or disproportion: in it, there is an absence of agreement between sign and meaning. There is style: the verbal scalpel's incision on the conceptual torso is not exact.

(46–47)

18 Ludovico Silva, *Marx's Literary Style*, 47.
19 Ludovico Silva, *Marx's Literary Style*, 47.
20 Ludovico Silva, *Marx's Literary Style*, 47.
21 Ludovico Silva, *Marx's Literary Style*, 47. Silva further points out that as far as it can be remembered, Marx 'employs *Superstruktur* only three times and *Überbau* only once', and adds that

> We might well be wrong about these numbers, but, in any case, it is clear that Marx hardly ever used these expressions. This is the first reason for thinking that, while it may illustrate a scientific theory, *for Marx* the famous 'superstructure' was nothing more than a metaphor, used with stylistic discretion on a couple of occasions but more often replaced by other metaphors or, better yet, *theoretical expressions*.

(47–48)

22 Ludovico Silva, *Marx's Literary Style*, 48.
23 Ludovico Silva, *Marx's Literary Style*, 49. Silva continues to remark:

> In other parts of *The German Ideology*—as well as in other works of his—Marx gives us explanations like the ones alluded to above, but it is *precisely then*, when he moves to *explain*, that he abandons the metaphor of the "superstructure" and dedicates himself to giving detailed explanations of ideological formations and their relationship to the structure of society.

(49)

24 Ludovico Silva, *Marx's Literary Style*, 49.
25 Ludovico Silva, *Marx's Literary Style*, 50.
26 Ludovico Silva, *Marx's Literary Style*, 50.
27 Ludovico Silva, *Marx's Literary Style*, 50.
28 Ludovico Silva, *Marx's Literary Style*, 50.
29 Ludovico Silva, *Marx's Literary Style*, 51–52.
30 See Sebastiano Timpanaro, *On Materialism*, trans. Lawrence Garner (London: Verso, 1975), 44.
31 Sebastiano Timpanaro, *On Materialism*, 44–45.
32 Ludovico Silva, *Marx's Literary Style*, 52.
33 Ludovico Silva, *Marx's Literary Style*, 52–53. Silva continues with his analysis of the second and the third metaphor, namely, 'Reflection as Metaphor' and 'Religion as Metaphor' in the rest of his book, making a number of wonderful points, equally important and illuminating, which I do not have space in this work to discuss.
34 Ludovico Silva, *Marx's Literary Style*, 53.
35 Ludovico Silva, *Marx's Literary Style*, 53. In this relation, Silva mentions Maurice Godelier in his essay 'System, Structure and contradiction in *Capital*' categorizes Marx as a forerunner of contemporary structuralism. Silva then remarks that

it is no less symptomatic that in metaphorical expression Marx employs a German term, *Überbau*, which is not scientific. Given that Marx, at the beginning of *Capital* and elsewhere, makes a point of spotting verbal dichotomies of this kind in the English authors of the seventeenth century—who tended to use a German-derived term, 'worth', for use-value, and a Latinate one, 'value', for exchange-value—what keeps us from making these same kinds of observations about Marx's own?

(53–54)

36 Ludovico Silva, *Marx's Literary Style*, 54. Silva mentions that he has explored the idea of 'ideological surplus-value' in a book titled *La plusvalía ideológica*. In this regard, he mentions Marcuse as having said that 'the ideology comes to be embodied in the process of production itself', and adds that

all he is doing is correctly restating the Marxist theory of ideology as something not separate from, but immanent within, the social structure; something produced by that structure and active in the interior. When, for example, the state applies the legal ideology of private property to justify the accumulation of wealth in the hands of the few and its unequal distribution, is this not a case of ideology acting within and from the social structure?

(54)

37 Ludovico Silva, *Marx's Literary Style*, 54–55.
38 Ludovico Silva, *Marx's Literary Style*, 55.
39 Quoted in Ludovico Silva, *Marx's Literary Style*, 55–56.
40 Ludovico Silva, *Marx's Literary Style*, 63–64.
41 Ludovico Silva, *Marx's Literary Style*, 64.
42 Ludovico Silva, *Marx's Literary Style*, 64. In this respect, Silva complains,

That so many commentators of both yesterday and today speak of supposed 'reflection theory' and of 'superstructure theory' is nothing but a sign of intellectual laziness; after all, it is much easier and more comfortable to avoid scientific explanations and to stick to their metaphorical substitutes. This is one of the reasons for the notorious 'schematicism' of the manuals.

(64–65)

43 Ludovico Silva, *Marx's Literary Style*, 65.
44 Quoted in Ludovico Silva, *Marx's Literary Style*, 65.
45 Ludovico Silva, *Marx's Literary Style*, 65.
46 In Karl Marx, *Capital, Volume I*, trans. Ben Fowkes, intro. Ernest Mandel (New London: Penguin Classic, 1990), 165.
47 Ludovico Silva, *Marx's Literary Style*, 66.
48 Ludovico Silva, *Marx's Literary Style*, 67. Silva adds that '"Man becomes poorer as man"—that is, separated from this mediator—"the richer this mediator becomes"', 67.
49 Quoted in Ludovico Silva, *Marx's Literary Style*, 67; also See Marx, 'Excerpt from James Mill's Elements of Political Economy', in *Early Writings* (Legare Street Press, 2022), 261.
50 Ludovico Silva, *Marx's Literary Style*, 67. And further,

it is more curious, however, if we remember an ancient tradition, expressed in Augustine, that gave Christ the name *Mediator*. Saint Augustine writes in his *Tractates on the Gospel of John* that Christ was *homo manifestus, Deus occultus* and that therefore: *Unus enim Deus, et unus mediator Dei et hominum homo Christus Iesus* [For there is one God, and the Mediator between God and Men, the man Christ Jesus.] Christ's dual nature—man on the outside and God inside—inspires the metaphor of money, which is use-value on the outside and exchange-value on the inside. And, just as Christ the man is alienated into omnipotent God, so in man money is alienated into an omnipotent thing.

(68)

51 Ludovico Silva, *Marx's Literary Style*, 69.
52 Ludovico Silva, *Marx's Literary Style*, 69.
53 Ludovico Silva, *Marx's Literary Style*, 81.
54 Ludovico Silva, *Marx's Literary Style*, 93.
55 Ludovico Silva, *Marx's Literary Style*, 96.

8

THE ARCHITECT AND THE PHILOSOPHER-KING

A Reading of Paul Valéry

ARCHITECTS: All idiots; they always forget to put staircases in houses.[1]
—Gustave Flaubert, *The Dictionary of Received Ideas*

Is the architect a 'philosopher-king'? I will come to this question after presenting a reading of the '*Socratic*' dialogue of Paul Valéry's *Eupalinos, or the Architect*. The context for my reading here is the complex philosophical debate on the *difference* between Socrates and Plato, a time-honored debate that harkens back to a more fundamental problem which concerns the question of 'origins' of philosophy in a special sense. Kōjin Karatani in his groundbreaking *Isonomia and the Origins of Philosophy* has posed a formidable challenge to the reception of this difference and has a unique presentation of the concept of the philosopher-king to which I come later in this chapter. My aim in reading Valéry's dialogue is thus grounded in Karatani's thesis on the notion of the philosopher-king. It preliminarily prompts certain questions to be asked: 'Who is the architect' and 'who is the philosopher'? Can an architect be a 'philosopher'? And what are their *political* relations to power and, in particular, to *private* and *public* affairs? These questions will have to wait until after a long detour when we come to Valéry's dialogue later. Here I would like to return, one more time, to Karatani's *Architecture as Metaphor* with a special reference to the title of the first chapter, 'The Will to Architecture', where Karatani, before bringing up Plato's notion of the 'philosopher-king', examines the etymological root of the word 'architecture' in respect to Plato's view of the figure of the 'architect'. Hence we are back to the *will to architecture* that, in this context, has to be addressed by taking care of the term *arché*, the first component in the word 'architecture' itself.

The etymological root of the term *architectonicé* (architecture) 'is constructed from *architectonicé techné*', which in ancient Greek 'signifies *techné* of *architectón*', with

DOI: 10.4324/9781032647616-9

architectón being a compound of *arché* (orgin, principle, primacy) and *tectón* (craftsman). Among the Greeks, architecture was considered not merely a skill of craftsmen but an art practiced by those who possess a principal knowledge and mastery of all technologies, and who therefore plan and lead other craftsmen.[2]

What is important to note is that the word *techné* refers not only to technology but also to making, but more precisely to *poiēsis* that applies to any production or creation. This is what Plato said in the *Symposium*:

> Well, you know, for example that 'poetry' [*poiēsis*] has a very wide range. After all, everything that is responsible for creating something out of nothing is a kind of poetry [*poiēsis*]; and so all the creations of every craft and profession are themselves a kind of poetry [*poiēsis*], and everyone who practices a craft is a poet.[3]

Now it must be noted here that this statement in the *Symposium* must be understood in the context of the discourse on *Love* to which the whole dialogue is devoted, into which we need not enter here. What is important to bear in mind though is what Karatani states: that Plato in his use of architecture as metaphor 'discovers a figure that under the aegis of "making" is able to withstand "becoming"'.[4] More important, before we proceed with more on the etymology of the word 'architecture', is Karatani's comment that an etymological account is nevertheless inadequate to explain why 'Plato regarded architecture as a figure of philosophy par excellence, or to explain why this figure is obsessively repeated in philosophical and theoretical discourse' and the fact that Plato 'disdained both architecture and the real-life architect'.[5]

Now what does *archi*, the first component in the term 'archi-tecture' signify? Heidegger once said, 'Philosophy inquires into the *arché*'.[6] It primarily means to seek 'being'.[7] *Arché* brings out the metaphor of architecture into philosophy in search of a 'solid ground', to build an edifice on a stable foundation, which always remains unstable. The Greeks meant by the word all of the following: 'beginning, origin, sources, basic principle, foundational principle, first principle, original or elemental constituent'.[8] Metaphysics, in this sense, is an incessant search for origins. At its core is the desire for incessantly building anew—that is, 'primordial foundations from which to spring again'.[9]

But *arche* in the Greek thought has an expanded connotation. To learn more about it, it is proper to go to Jean-Pierre Vernant and his classic *The Origins of Greek Thought*. Vernant associates *arché* with the political thought and the constitution of *polis*, but also with 'command', 'power', 'law', and 'sovereignty'. He begins by remarking that the 'institution of the city-state and the birth of rational thought' are intrinsically intertwined: 'a period of decisive mutation that laid the foundation for the government of the *polis* at the very moment when Orientalizing style was triumphant, and which secured the advent of philosophy by secularizing political thought'.[10] He writes: 'Once the notion of *arche*, command, had been severed from *basiliea* [royal palace], it becomes independent and determined by the province of a strictly political reality'.[11] Vernant informs us that a Greek would say that

> certain deliberations, certain decisions must be brought *es to koinon* [to the common], that the ancient privileges of the king and *arche* itself were set down *es to meson*, in the middle, at the center. The recourse to a spatial image to express the self-awareness that a human group has acquired, its sense of existing as a political unit, is of value not only as a comparison; it also reflects the creation of a social space that was altogether new. Indeed, urban buildings were no longer grouped, as before, about a royal palace ringed by fortification. The city was now centered on the agora, the communal place and seat of the *hestia koine* [the central or public hearth], a public area where problems of general interest were debated. The city itself was now surrounded by walls, protecting and delineating the entire human group of which it was composed. On the spot where the royal citadel once rose—a private and privileged dwelling—the city erected temples that were open to the public worship. On the ruins of the palace, that acropolis which was henceforth consecrated to its gods, the community itself was now projected on the sacred plane, just as at the profane level it found its proper place in the expanse of the agora. What this urban framework in fact defined was a mental space; it opened up a new spiritual horizon. Once the city was centered on the public square. It was already a *polis* in every sense of the word.[12]

With the *polis*, Vernant observes, 'social life and human relations took a new form, and the Greeks were fully aware of its originality' and that

> The system of the *polis* implied, first of all, the extraordinary preeminence of speech over all other instruments of power. Speech became the political tool par excellence, the key to all authority in the state, the means of commanding and dominating others.[13]

In this state *arche*, that is, 'sovereignty', was submitted to the art of oratory and had to be resolved only by debate. 'There was thus a close connection, a reciprocal tie, between politics and *logos*'.[14] A second feature is attributed to *polis* and it was the

> full exposure given to the most important aspects of social life. We can even say that the polis existed only to the extent that a *public* domain had emerged, in each of the two differing but interdependent meanings of the term: an area of common interest, as opposed to private concerns, and open practices openly arrived at, as opposed to secret procedure.[15]

Vernant discusses how the hierarchical system of relations of submission and dominance was replaced by the notion *homoioi*, meaning 'men who were alike', who share the state as equals, *isoi*. And in this relation, he significantly bring out the notion of *Isonomia*. He writes:

> In the sixth century this image of the human world was precisely expressed in the concept of *Isonomia*—that is, the equal participation of all citizens in the existence of power. But before it had acquired this fully democratic meaning, and before it had inspired such institutional reforms as those of Cleisthenes, the ideal *isonomia* was able to convey or to extend communal aspirations that went back to the very origins of *polis*. There is some evidence that the terms *isonomia* and *isocratia* served in aristocratic circles to define an oligarchical regime that contrasted with the absolute power of one man (the *monarchia* or *tyrannis*). In this regime, arche was reserved for a small number of the exclusion of the majority, but was divided equally among all members of that elite group.[16]

However, Vernant does not make it explicit enough for the reader that *isonomia* originated in Ionia and not in mainland Greece. There is also an exact definition for the notion of *isonomia* which we owe to Karatani and his *Isonomia and the Origins of Philosophy*, as mentioned. I will come to this in a moment. It suffices here to conclude that Vernant helpfully reminds us that

> *Arche* in reality belongs exclusively to the law. Any individual or faction that tried to secure a monopoly on *arche* threatened the *homonoia* [unanimity] of the social body by such an attack on the balance of all other forces, and thereby put the city's very existence at risk.[17]

In Plato's *Timaeus* we read Timaeus saying:

> As I see it, then we must begin in making the following distinction:
> What is *that which always is* and has no becoming, and what is *that
> which becomes* but never is? The former is grasped by understanding,
> which involves a reasoned account. It is unchanging. It comes to be
> and passes away, but never really is. Now everything that comes to be
> must of necessity come to be the agency of some cause, for it is
> impossible for anything to come to be without a cause. So whenever
> the craftsman looks at what is always changeless and, using a thing of
> that kind as his model, reproduces its form and character, then of
> necessity, all that he so completes is beautiful. But were he to look at
> a thing that has come to be and use as his model something that has
> been begotten, his work will lack beauty.[18]

As Leslie Kavanaugh notes,

> Timaeus states that anyone with the least amount of sense must begin
> with the invocation of the gods. Any undertaking, great or small,
> begun or having no beginning must begin with the beginning, an
> invocation, beginning at the 'proper place', 'according to nature'.
> After the invocation, he begins: First then, in my judgment, we must
> make a distinction and ask, What is that which always is and has no
> becoming, and what is that which is always becoming and never is?'
> The *is*, being, is eternal and unchanging, the *same*. The *becoming* on
> the other hand, is never fully real according to Timaeus, but is con-
> stantly coming-to-be and then passing-away.[19]

And further, 'The eternal idea is "apprehended by intelligence and reason" (*logos*), whereas the changing becoming is merely an object of
opinion (*doxa*), apprehended through perception'.[20] Furthermore, 'The
beginning, the *arché* of becoming', Kavanaugh notes,

> is generated in this account (*logos*) by the unchanging forms (*eidos*)
> generating the sensible things that are likeness (*eikon*) of eternal
> being. But how does the unchangeable provide an impulse for gener-
> ation? This problem is precisely what leads Plato to propose the third
> term, the *chora* as intermediary, further on in the dialogue.[21]

Karatani informs us that Plato belonged to the 'minority of the Greek
thinkers who represented the view that the world is a product of *making*,
as opposed to those who held the world is *becoming*. 'His belief, Karatani

remarks, 'that architecture could stave off becoming must have appeared abruptly and completely out of context of Greek thought in general—it must have come from Greece's exterior, from Egypt, where immortality of spirit, monotheism, and state-controlled planning originated.'[22] It is here at this point that Karatani also notes that the Platonic notion of the philosopher-king itself can be traced back to Egypt.[23] On this note, I now examine the notion of the philosopher-king that Karatani fully discusses in his *Isonomia and the Origins of Philosophy*. But first we should consider the following passage in Plato's *Republic*:

> Until philosophers rule as kings or those who are now called kings and leading men genuinely and adequately philosophize, that is, until political power and philosophy entirely coincide, while the many natures who at present pursue either one exclusively are forcibly prevented from doing so, cities will have no rest from evils, Glaucon, nor, I think, will the human race. And, until this happens, constitution we've been describing in theory will never be born to the fullest extent possible or see the light of the sun. It is because I saw how very paradoxical this statement would be that I hesitated to make it for so long, for it is hard to face up to the fact that there can be no happiness, either public or private, in any other city.[24]

Plato's theory of ideas and the concept of the philosopher-king, Karatani says,

> are presented as if they are Socrates's position. However, this is not Socrates, but clearly Pythagorean thinking. What Plato inherited from Pythagoras is not merely mathematics nor the concept of transmigration. Pythagorean consciousness rather lies at the core of Plato's political thought.[25]

Plato inherited the idea of 'dual world' from Pythagoras. In the dual world we confront the 'distinction between reason and sensibility, of knowledge and non-knowledge, and of truth and illusion'.[26] Although Plato was an admirer of Socrates, he inherited every idea from Pythagoras, including mathematics. In Ionia, as Karatani informs us, there was no 'distinction between philosopher and non-philosopher, the dual world was never established'.[27] Pythagoras, for that matter, is the first philosopher. As we will see subsequently, Karatani establishes the fact that Socrates, who never left Athens, has more affinity with Isonomia, which accepts no special status or privileged position. There was no dual world in Ionia, no distinction between sensibility and reason, or between the real and the truth. This is importantly related to the conception of *arché* (the principle of things) that Pythagoras located in number:

> at the same time this conforms with the basic attitude of Ionian natural philosophy, it is a fundamental rejection of it. This is because what Pythagoras discerned as fundamental was not physis. Pythagoras viewed numbers as reality. Numbers are about relationships, and their mode of existence is not the same as that of individual material things. To see relations as more real notwithstanding, and then locate in them arche, is to identify abstraction as reality. In Pythagoras, Ionian natural philosophy was converted de facto to a form of idealism.[28]

In the section 'The Philosophical-King' in *Isonomia*, in order to establish that the notion of the philosopher-king originates in Pythagoras, Karatani quotes a passage from Book 6 of *The Republic*, which goes as follows:

> And this was what we foresaw, and this was the reason why truth forced us to admit, not without fear and hesitation, that neither cities nor States nor individuals will ever attain perfection until the small class of philosophers whom we term useless but not corrupt are providentially compelled, whether they will or not, to take care of the State, and until a like necessity be laid on the State to obey them; or until kings, or if not kings, the sons of kings or princes, are divinely inspired with a true love of true philosophy.[29]

Karatani immediately informs us that 'this kind of thinking cannot possibly come from Socrates'. He explains:

> For Socrates, service to the state was strictly proscribed. That the idea of a philosopher-king is Plato's own is also clear from *The Seventh Letter*, where Plato voices the identical opinion. 'And I was forced to say, when praising true philosophy that it is by this that men are enabled to see what justice in public and private life really is. Therefore, I said, there will be no cessation of evils for the sons of men, till either those who are pursuing a right and true philosophy receive sovereign power in the States, or those in power in the States by some dispensation of providence become true philosophers'.[30]

Karatani emphasizes again that the influence of Pythagoras on Plato is not on the matters of mathematics or transmigration. Rather, at the root it was a political problem. He traces the itinerary Plato traveled along to arrive at his opinions.[31] Karatani points out that Plato associated himself with Socrates toward the end of his life but never considered living like him, and he never gave up the aspirations to get involved in the affairs of the state. But, 'once the democratic faction brought capital charges against Socrates', Plato was suspected by both sides of the political factions. And, expecting further retaliation by the democratic faction against the aristocratic side, after Socrates's death (399 BCE), he had to flee Athens. It was during this time that, as Karatani tells us, 'Plato forgoes politics and becomes a philosopher', citing what Plato said in *The Seventh Letter*:

> Finally, it became clear to me with regard to all exiting communities, that they were one and all misgoverned. For their laws have got into a state that is almost incurable, except by some extraordinary reform with good luck to support it. And I was forced to say, when praising true philosophy that it is by this that men are enabled to see what justice in public and private life really is.[32]

It is then that he arrived at the statement of the philosopher-king:

> 'With these thoughts in mind,' Plato writes, 'I came to Italy and Sicily on my first visit.' With the hope of putting his idea about the philosopher-king into practice, Plato crossed over to Italy in 388 BCE, deepened his exchange with the Pythagoreans, and met their leader Archytas. Subsequently, Plato crossed to the island of Sicily and visited the tyrant of Syracuse, Dionysius I. But there he also met Dionysius's brother-in-law Dion, a beautiful youth who loved philosophy, and formed the hope that a government by a philosopher-king might be realized in Syracuse.[33]

But everything proved to be disastrous for him there, not being able to achieve his intended goal, and he had to return to Athens where he established his academy. He subsequently returned to Syracuse a couple of times but was still unsuccessful; this was predictable, as Karatani says, because in practice it was too difficult to realize the rule of a philosopher-king.

The attraction of Plato to Pythagoras was more than philosophical reason.

> Democracy in Athens sent Socrates to his death. When Plato fled after this incident and commenced a period of wandering, he would have reflected on the nature of democracy. The doubt that presented itself was that, if the support of the majority is sufficient to legitimize a government, any degree of despotism can be allowed in their nature. Here is how he expresses the problem …

and Karatani here cites *The Republic*:

> The excess of liberty, whether in States or the individual, seems only to pass into excess of slavery. Yes, the natural order. And so tyranny naturally arises out of democracy, and the most aggravated form of tyranny and slavery out of the most extreme form of liberty? As we might expect.[34]

'What then, is to be done?' Karatani asks. He offers the following explanation:

> During the period he was mulling over this question, Plato came into contact with the school of Pythagoreans. Here he found rule by philosophers. And, as discussed above, it was likely from this that he received the idea of philosopher-king. However, this was not simply a matter of copying the influence. Given the political troubles he experienced in Athens, and the ten years of wandering after, Plato's understanding of Pythagoras's thought was honestly earned.[35]

If you want to be a philosopher, you must transcend the sensible world of appearance:

> The problem Pythagoras came face to face with first was the people. Left to their own devices, the freedom of the people ends in tyranny. The reason for this, according to Pythagoras, is that they are not truly free. They need to be released from the prison of their flesh. For this, an order is required. Second is the problem of the leader. Pythagoras's close friend Polycrates ended up a tyrant because of a problem residing within himself. The leader as well must become free from the yoke of the flesh. He must become a being that recognizes the true world that transcends the sensible world of appearance. That is to say, he must be a philosopher. Hence Pythagoras built an order ruled by a philosopher, through which he hoped to transform the society.[36]

We come to the crux of the matter, which concerns the position of Socrates in what was said previously. As Karatani reminds us, Plato relates the idea of philosopher-king to Socrates, but in fact it comes from Pythagoras and has little to do with Socrates. Karatani writes:

> There was no way that Socrates, who declined public service all his life, would become king. Socrates rejected any thought that placed public affairs over private or spiritual matters over the physical. That is

to say, he questioned both the Athenian and the Pythagorean versions of the 'dual world', which is a division between the public and private, and Socrates sought to overcome it as a private citizen.[37]

In this regard, Karatani observes the following:

> Plato aimed at a condition where the soul ruled over the body. What Socrates aimed at, though, was the abolition of rule itself, that is to say, isonomia. Plato used the fact that Socrates was put to death by a democracy as a trump card. All through his career he championed Socrates and spoke in his name. However, this was a reverse implementation of Socrates's orientation. Socrates, whether unconsciously or not, recuperated the Spirit of Ionian thought. Plato utilized this character as the greatest weapon in his own battle.

Plato turns the thinking of Socrates upside down. Karatani argues and explains that 'The philosopher is the one who transcends the sensible world of semblance and grasps the truth. Further, this philosopher is active in public affairs, and through possession of political power realizes truth in the political world.'[38] Karatani cites what Plato said in *The Republic*:

> Until philosophers are kings, or the kings and princes of this world have the spirit and power of philosophy, and political greatness and wisdom meet in one, and those commoner natures who pursue either to the exclusion of the other are compelled to stand aside, cities will never have rested from the evil—no, nor, the human race.[39]

Karatani then states that:

> In Plato, the ideal state will be realized when a philosopher like Socrates comes to rule. For him, 'the truth is that the State in which the rulers are most reluctant to govern is always the best and most quietly governed'. However, this is not the sublation of rule. It is government by rulers who reject rule. In sum, the pursuit of a state of no-rule (isonomia) in Socrates becomes rule by the philosopher-king in Plato.[40]

Karatani continues his perceptive analysis for the rest of his *Isonomia and the Origins of Philosophy*, leading to a complex and thought-provoking conclusion concerning the whole notion of 'democracy' and 'state' related to the same difference between Plato and Socrates. The reflections above on the notion of the philosopher-king must be sufficient to get to Paul Valéry's 'Socratic' dialogue of *Eupalinos, or the Architect*.

First, who was the real Eupalinos? Historically, little is known about Eupalinos. He was an ancient Greek engineer who built the Tunnel of Eupalinos on Samos Island in the sixth century BCE.

> The tunnel, presumably completed between 550 and 530 BC, is the second known tunnel in history which was excavated from both ends and the first with a methodical approach to doing so. Being also the longest tunnel of its time, the Tunnel of Eupalinos is regarded as a major feat of ancient engineering. It was constructed for the tyrant Polycrates of Samos, and was a remarkable 1,036 meters (3,399 ft) long. It brought water to the city, passing through limestone at the base of a hill; this tunnel still exists.[41]

The Greek historian Herodotus describes the tunnel briefly and names Eupalinos of Megara as its 'architect':

> I have dwelt rather long on the history of the Samians because theirs are the three greatest works (*ergasmata*) of all the Greeks. One is a tunnel (*orygma amphistomon*) through the base of a nine hundred foot high mountain. The tunnel's length is seven stades, its height and length (width) both eight feet. Throughout its length another cutting (*orygma*) has been dug (*ororyktai*) three feet wide and three feet deep, through which the water flowing in pipes is led into the city from an abundant spring. The builder (*architekton*) of the tunnel was the Megarian Eupalinus, son of Naustrophus.[42]

Valéry's dialogue is staged between Phaedrus and Socrates in *Eupalinos, or the Architect*. I cite in part passages with which I am concerned most, and I interrupt them inserting my comments. They go as follows:

Phaedrus

One day, dear Socrates, I spoke of this very thing with my friend Eupalinos.

'Phaedrus,' he was saying to me, 'the more I mediate on my art, the more I practice it; the more I think and act, the more I suffer and rejoice as an architect—and the more I feel my own being with an ever surer delight and clarity.'

'I lose myself in long spells of expectation; I find myself again by the surprises I gave myself; by means of successive steps of my silence,

I advance in my own edification; and I approach to such an exact correspondence between my aims and my powers, that I seem to myself to have made of the existence that was given me a sort of human handiwork.'

'By dint of constructing,' he put it with a smile, 'I truly believe that I have constructed myself.'

Socrates

To construct oneself, to know oneself—are these two distinct acts or not?[43]

Here I cite Nietzsche from his 'On the Truth and Lies in a Nonmoral Sense' where, as we saw before, he addressed the 'man', or rather the philosopher, as a 'mighty genius of construction':

Here one may certainly admire man as a 'mighty genius of construction', who succeeds in piling an infinitely complicated dome of concepts upon an unstable foundation, and, as it were, on running water. Of course, in order to be supported by such a foundation, his construction must be like one constructed of spiders' webs: delicate enough to be carried along by the waves, strong enough not to be blown apart by every wind. *As a genius of construction*, man raises himself far above the bee in the following way: whereas the bee builds with wax that he gathers from nature, man builds the far more delicate conceptual material which he first has to manufacture from himself. In this he is greatly to be admired, but not on account of drive for truth or for pure knowledge of things[44] [emphasis mine].

However, Nietzsche in *Twilight of the Idols* had railed against Socrates and rationality:

If one needs to make a tyrant of *reason*, as Socrates did, then there must exist no little danger of something else playing the tyrant. Rationality was at that time divined as a *saviour*; neither Socrates nor his "invalids" were free to be rational or not, as they wished—it was *de rigueur*, it was their *last* expedient. The fanaticism with which the whole of Greek thought throws itself at rationality betrays a state of emergency: one was in peril … The moralism of the Greek philosophers from Plato downwards is pathologically conditioned: likewise their estimation of dialectics. Reason = virtue = happiness means merely: one must imitate Socrates and counter the dark desires by producing a permanent *daylight*—the daylight of reason. One must be prudent, clear, bright at any cost: every yielding to the instincts, to the unconscious, leads *downwards* …[45]

I imagine Nietzsche to be in rage hearing Valéry portraying Socrates cast as a great 'Constructor'—belonging to the same family of the 'mighty genius of construction'. Here I recall Karatani's naming Nietzsche in relation to Plato and Socrates. After stating that 'Plato carried his project out from first to last under the name of Socrates', Karatani writes:

> As a result, from the time of Plato on, the origins of philosophy have been taken to reside in Socrates. And by extension, from the time of Nietzsche on, the critique of Plato has taken the form of an attack on Socrates, with the key to transcending Platonic philosophy taken to reside in the pre-Socratic. However, if one wants to properly consider the pre-Socratics, one must include Socrates in their number.[46]

The philosopher aspires to be an architect, but he is to be reminded that he is an architect in *death*. The philosopher 'assassinated' the architect in himself. Let us see how Valéry conveys this point by staging the scene where Phaedrus and Socrates exchange pleasantries:

Phaedrus

You seem to have been won over yourself to the adoration of architecture! Here you are, unable to speak without borrowing from the major art its images and its firm ideal.

Socrates

I am still steeped in the sayings of Eupalinos that you were recalling. They have aroused within me something that is akin to them.

Phaedrus

So there was an architect in you?

Socrates

Nothing can beguile, nothing attract us, nothing makes us prick up our ears, or holds our gaze, nothing by us is chosen from among the multitude of things, and causes a stir in our souls, that was not in some sort pre-existing in our being or secretly awaited by our nature. All that we become, even fleetingly, was prepared beforehand. *There was within me an architect whom circumstances did not fashion forth.*[47] [my emphasis]

And further:

Socrates

[...] Chance placed in my hand the most ambiguous object imaginable. And the infinite reflections that it caused me to make were equally capable of leading me to that philosopher that I became, and to the artist that I have never been ...

Phaedrus

It was an object that solicited you so variously?

Socrates

Yes. A paltry object, just something I found as I was walking. It was the origin of a thought divided, of itself, *between constructing and knowing.*[48] [emphasis mine]

Pausing on the statement 'It was the origin of a thought divided, of itself, between constructing and knowing', I am tempted to say here that Socrates is a Kantian philosopher, a thinker of *architectonics*, not of a Platonic kind.

Later on in the dialogue, Phaedrus puts it rather bluntly to Socrates:

Phaedrus

Your own life was spent so! ... But for my part, *I cannot console myself for the death of that architect who was in you, and whom you assassinated by mediating overmuch on the fragment of a shell! With your profundity and prodigious subtleties, Socrates, you would have far surpassed our most famous builders.* Neither Ictinos, nor Eupalinos of Magara, nor Chersiphron of Gnossos, nor Spintharos of Corinth would have been able to rival Socrates the Athenian. [my emphasis]

Socrates

Phaedrus, I beg of you! ...This subtle matter of which we are now made does not permit of our laughing. I feel I ought to laugh, but I cannot ... So refrain![49]

Socrates is not a philosopher-king. But the architect is, who has an eye on power. Besides, as we have learned from Karatani, although Socrates lived in Athens all his life he had more affinity with the Ionian thought of *isonomia*, translated as the principle of 'no-rule'. He cannot be a philosopher-king, he cannot be an architect, because he does not want to deal with public affairs, he does not want to be in the service of Power and State. He was sentenced to death under the 'democratic' majority rule in Athens … No architect is ever sentenced to death for 'corrupting the youth'!

Further down, Valéry seems to secretly make Phaedrus and Socrates exchange in the Vitruvian triadic theory of architecture, that is, '*utilitas, firmitas, venustas*'—utility, solidity, beauty.

Socrates

It is therefore reasonable to think that the creations of man are made either with a view to his body, and that is the principle we call *utility*, or with a view to his soul, and that is what he seeks under the name of *beauty*. But, further, since he who constructs or creates has to deal with the rest of the world and with the movement of nature, which both tend perpetually to dissolve, corrupt, or upset what he makes, he must recognize and seek to communicate to his works a third principle, that expresses the resistance he wishes them to offer to their destiny, which is, to perish. So he seeks *solidity* or *lastingness*.

Phaedrus

Yes, those are indeed the main characteristics of a complete work.

Socrates

Architecture alone demands them, and carries them to their highest point.

Phaedrus

I look upon it as the most complete of the arts.[50]

The philosopher Socrates would not have concurred with the Roman architect, Vitruvius, who in his *Ten Books on Architecture* tried to show off that he knew the Greeks well! Unlike Vitruvius—and every architect coming after him in the last two thousand years—Socrates, in Karatani's definition of him, was a thinker of *isonomia*. No architect—*no architect*—as far as I know has ever adopted the thinking of *isonomia*—at least not yet! I imagine that what Valéry wanted to really say is that perhaps Eupalinos was that *rare* builder who, in Socrates's manner, was on the side of *isonomia*.

In retrospect, and with due respect to Valéry, we perhaps should not impute unconditionally the Vitruvian triadic *utilitas, firmitas, venustas* to Socrates, the great thinker of Isonomia. Towards the end of the dialogue, Valéry nicely takes us back to the figure of the 'dead architect' who resides in the philosopher:

Socrates

[…] I shall make mistakes sometimes, and we shall have some ruins; but one can always very profitably look upon a work that has failed as a step which brings us nearer to the most beautiful.

Phaedrus

It is fortunate for them that you are a dead architect!

Socrates

Must I be silent, Phaedrus? —so you will never know what temples, what theatres, I should have conceived in the pure Socratic style! … I was going to give you an idea how I should have carried out my work. I should first have set out all the problems, evolving a flawless method. Where?—For what?—For whom?—To what end?—Of what size?— And exercising an ever stricter control over my mind, at the highest point I should have realized the operation of transforming a quarry and a forest into an edifice, into splendid equilibrium! … And I was draw-ing up my plan with an eye to the purpose of the humans who pay me; taking into account localities, lights, shadows, and winds; choosing the site according to size, its aspect, its approach, the adjacent lands, and the true nature of the subsoil. …[51] [emphasis mine]

And, finally, we are at the end of the dialogue:

Socrates

Immortal there—relatively to mortals! … But there …. But … there is no *here*, and all that we have been saying is as much as natural sport of the silence of these nether regions as the fantasy of some rhetori-cian of the other world who has used us as puppets!

Phaedrus

It is in this that immortality rigorously consists.[52]

The architect and the philosopher both, to reiterate, must be the thinkers of *architectonics*. Here, at this moment, in the twenty-first century, as I contend, it is the *architect* who must go to the philosopher in order to know how to be a thinker of *architectonics*—strictly speaking in the Kantian sense of the term. Insofar as the human reason is insatiable, we will be confronting the predicament of an intertwined act of 'construction', in both the edifice of knowledge—*philosophy*—and building shelter—*the art of building*. There is a philosopher lying dormant in the architect—this architect is often a shameless *utilitarian*. And the philosopher, who remains an architect only in *death*. It will take a millennium for the architect to become a Socratic 'architect', to learn the lesson of *isonomia*. That has to wait until we arrive at the state of 'world republic' in the full Kantian terms, as Karatani has elsewhere reflected, or what is called communism.[53] That will be a time when we will change our conception of 'democracy' from our received notion of the 'Athenian democracy', the 'rule of majority', that sent Socrates to his death.

The philosopher *and* the architect, both as *constructors*, must, by definition, be thinkers of *architectonic reason*—they *must* both be Kantian. The former is not always, and the latter hardly. But the *will to architecture* must be held by both.

Notes

1 Gustave Flaubert, *Bouvard and Pécuchet with the Dictionary of Received Ideas* (London: Penguin Books, 1976), 294.
2 Kōjin Karatani, *Architecture as Metaphor: Language, Number, Money*, trans. Sabu Kohso (Cambridge: The MIT Press, 1995), 5–6.
3 See Plato, 'Symposium', in *Complete Works*, ed. John M. Cooper, Associated ed. D.S. Hutchinson (Indianapolis: Hackett, 1997), 488.
4 Kōjin Karatani, *Architecture as Metaphor*, 6.
5 Kōjin Karatani, *Architecture as Metaphor*, 6. Karatani here refers to F. M. Cornford who had suggested that 'Greek thinkers can be grouped into two general types. On the one hand, evolutionists consider the world a living, growing form or organism; on the other hand, creationists consider the world a designed work of art', 6. Karatani adds that 'These two types represent two worldviews: one that understands the world as becoming and another that understands the world as a product of making. The latter view was held by a minority of Greek thinkers', to which, according to Karatani, Plato belonged, 6.
6 Quoted in Leslie Jayne Kavanaugh, *The Architectonic of Philosophy: Plato, Aristotle, Leibniz* (Amsterdam: Amsterdam University Press, 2007), 17.
7 In Leslie Jayne Kavanaugh, *The Architectonic of Philosophy: Plato, Aristotle, Leibniz*, 17. Also see, Martin Heidegger, *Nietzsche* ed. David Farrell Krell,

trans. Stambaugh, Krell, Capuzzi, 4 volumes (San Francisco: Harper and Row, 1991). Heidegger wrote:

> Philosophy inquires into *archē*. We translate the word as "principle". And if we neglect to think and question rigorously and persistently, we think we know what "principle" means here. *Archē* and *archein* mean "to begin." At the same time, they mean to stand at the beginning of all; hence, to rule. Yet this reference to the designated *archē* will make sense only if we simultaneously determine that *of* which and *for* which we are seeking the *archē*. We are seeking it, not for some isolated event, not for unusual and recondite facts and relationships, but purely and simply for being.
>
> (volume two, 187)

8 Usefully summarized in Leslie Jayne Kavanaugh, *The Architectonic of Philosophy*, 17–18. She further writes:

> Philosophy seemingly begins with wonderment, and yet remains with the never-ending desire to search for the beginning, for the origin, for the first for something solid and basic on which to stand firmly. The oldest philosophical texts also searched for the *arché*. The most elemental was thought to be alternatively various kinds of material—a prime cause, a principle of generation and destruction, the chaos, or the beginning without end. First was the beginning. Yet this beginning is an unceasing grasping into blue vacuous space, an unremitting search for what elusively recedes backwards, an infinite regress, beyond any steadfast hold on what came first.
>
> (18)

9 Leslie Jayne Kavanaugh, *The Architectonic of Philosophy*, 18. She cites Jacques Derrida as saying 'is not the quest for an *archia* in general, no matter with what precautions one surrounds the concept, still the "essential" operation in metaphysics?', 18. Also see Jacques Derrida, *Margins of Philosophy*, trans. Alan Bass (Chicago: Chicago University Press, 1982), 63.

10 Jean-Pierre Vernant, *The Origins of Greek Thought* (Ithaca: Cornell University Press, 1982), 11. Daniel Payot in his much neglected *Le Philosophe et l'architecture* (Paris: Aubier, 1982) also discusses Vernant's book in the section titled 'Archi-tecture'.

11 Jean-Pierre Vernant, *The Origins of Greek Thought*, 41-42. Vernant defines the word *basileus*, in the plural, as designating 'not a single person who concentrated all forms of power in himself, but rather a category of notables who as a group occupied the highest reaches of the social hierarchy', 37.

12 Jean-Pierre Vernant, *The Origins of Greek Thought*, 47–48.

13 Jean-Pierre Vernant, *The Origins of Greek Thought*, 49.

14 Jean-Pierre Vernant, *The Origins of Greek Thought*, 50. Vernant points out that 'Historically, rhetoric and sophistry, by analyzing the form of discourse as the means of winning the contest in the assembly and the tribunal opened the way for Aristotle's inquiries', 50.

15 Jean-Pierre Vernant, *The Origins of Greek Thought*, 51.

16 Jean-Pierre Vernant, *The Origins of Greek Thought*, 61. Vernant further adds

> that the requirement of *isonomia* was able to acquire such strength by the end of the sixth century, that it could justify the popular demand for ready access by the *demos* to all civic offices, may no doubt be explained by the fact that it was rooted in a very old egalitarian tradition, and even responded to certain psychological attitudes of aristocracy of the hippeis.
>
> (61–62)

17 Jean-Pierre Vernant, *The Origins of Greek Thought*, 67.
18 Plato, 'Timaeus', in *Complete Works*, 28 b, 1234–1235. The editors in the footnote clarify that

> 'Becoming' and 'coming to be' here as elsewhere translate the same Greek word, *genesis*, and its cognates; the Greek word does not say, as English 'comes to be' does, that once a thing has come to be, it now *is*, or has *being*.
>
> (n.8, 1234)

Also regarding the word 'craftsman' in the paragraph quoted, they note that 'Greek *dēmiourgos*, [is] also sometimes translated below as "maker" or "fashioner—whence the divine "Demiurge" one reads about in accounts of the *Timaeus*', n. 9, 1234.

19 Leslie Jayne Kavanaugh, *The Architectonic of Philosophy*, 32.
20 Leslie Jayne Kavanaugh, *The Architectonic of Philosophy*, 32.
21 Leslie Jayne Kavanaugh, *The Architectonic of Philosophy*, 36. Kavanaugh goes on to discuss extensively the notion of *chora*, which we do not need to get into.
22 Kōjin Karatani, *Architecture as Metaphor*, 8.
23 Kōjin Karatani, *Architecture as Metaphor*, 8. On this point, Karatani points out that

> Signs of Egyptian influences can also be discovered at the origins of Judeo-Christianity. Freud, for example, in *Moses and Monotheism*, argued that Moses, who was raised Egyptian and monotheistic, was murdered en route from Egypt. Moses's murder initiated a kind of structure of repetition that Freud called the 'return of the repressed.' From a Freudian perspective, these two fundamental tenets of Western thought—Judaism and Christianity—originated in Egypt, and it is their origin that has been so strictly repressed and that continues to obsessively return.
>
> (8)

24 Plato, 'Republic', in *Complete Works*, 473d, 1100.
25 Kōjin Karatani, *Isonomia and the Origins of Philosophy*, trans. Joseph A. Murphy (Durham and London: Duke University Press, 2017), 75.
26 Kōjin Karatani, *Isonomia and the Origins of Philosophy*, 74.
27 Kōjin Karatani, *Isonomia and the Origins of Philosophy*, 74.
28 Kōjin Karatani, *Isonomia and the Origins of Philosophy*, 78.
29 Quoted in Kōjin Karatani, *Isonomia and the Origins of Philosophy*, 127–128.
30 Kōjin Karatani, *Isonomia and the Origins of Philosophy*, 128.
31 Karatani writes that

> In *The Seventh Letter*, Plato describes his experience as a young man in great detail. 'In my youth I went through the same experience as many other men. I fancied that if, early in life, I became my own master, I should at once embark on a political career. And I found myself confronted with certain occurrences in the public affairs of my own city.' These 'certain occurrences' were the despotism of the Thirty Tyrants engineered by his own aristocratic faction, among whom were many of Plato's relatives and friends. They sought to implicate Socrates in their deeds but were refused. Plato too chose not to participate in this order. The reign of Thirty Tyrants shortly collapsed, and before long 'once more, though with more hesitation, I began to be moved by the desire to take part in public and political affairs.'
>
> (Kōjin Karatani, *Isonomia and the Origins of Philosophy*, 128)

32 Quoted in Kōjin Karatani, *Isonomia and the Origins of Philosophy*, 129.

33 Kōjin Karatani, *Isonomia and the Origins of Philosophy*, 129.
34 Quoted in Kōjin Karatani, *Isonomia and the Origins of Philosophy*, 129–130.
35 Kōjin Karatani, *Isonomia and the Origins of Philosophy*, 130.
36 Kōjin Karatani, *Isonomia and the Origins of Philosophy*, 130.
37 Kōjin Karatani, *Isonomia and the Origins of Philosophy*, 130–131. Karatani explains that

> This is a transformation from below, transformation of each individual. Next, to put it in terms of Pythagoras' dual world, Socrates never thought that he attained the world of truth. He felt himself to be ignorant in this sense. And he would attach himself like a gadfly to anyone who claimed to possess knowledge (truth), and engage him in the ceaseless interrogation of his method. What is called irony consists in this method. This is not a process that seeks to arrive at the world of truth. It aims at the idea of truth, knowledge itself, as the premise on which the dual world of ignorance and knowledge is based.
>
> (131)

38 Kōjin Karatani, *Isonomia and the Origins of Philosophy*, 131.
39 Kōjin Karatani, *Isonomia and the Origins of Philosophy*, 131.
40 Kōjin Karatani, *Isonomia and the Origins of Philosophy*, 131.
41 I am extracting this information from https://en.wikipedia.org/wiki/Eupalinos.
42 Cited in https://en.wikipedia.org/wiki/Eupalinos.
43 Paul Valéry, *Eupalinos, or the Architect*, in *Dialogues*, 81.
44 Friedrich Nietzsche, *On Truth and Lies in a Non-Moral Sense*, in *Philosophy and Truth, Selections from Nietzsche's Notebooks of Early 1970s*, ed. and trans. Daniel Breazeale (Amherst: Uumanity Books, 1999), 85.
45 In Friedrich Nietzsche, *Twilight of the Idols and The Anti-Christ*, trans. and intro. R. J. Hollingdale (New York: Penguin Books, 1968), 33.
46 Kōjin Karatani, *Isonomia and the Origins of Philosophy*, 134.
47 Paul Valéry, *Eupalinos, or the Architect*, 109.
48 Paul Valéry, *Eupalinos, or the Architect*, 110–111.
49 Paul Valéry, *Eupalinos, or the Architect*, 125.
50 Paul Valéry, *Eupalinos, or the Architect*, 129.
51 Paul Valéry, *Eupalinos, or the Architect*, 148–149.
52 Paul Valéry, *Eupalinos, or the Architect*, 150.
53 See Kōjin Karatani, *The Structure of the World History: From Modes of Production to Modes of Exchange*, trans. Michael K. Bourdaghs (Durham and London: Durham University Press, 2014), see 'Chapter 12: Toward a World Republic'.

EPILOGUE

Karatani at the end of his *Architecture as Metaphor* has a distinct thesis to advance. He does not need to refer back to the notions of the *will to architecture* and the concept of *architectonics* that he discussed in the earlier chapters of his book. Rather, his concerns are now to bring out the notions of *Idee*, *Schein*, and the 'thing-in-itself' in association with Kantian transcendental philosophy with the purpose of advancing his views that he will fully take up later in his *Transcritique: On Kant and Marx*. His central thesis is that Marx's *critique* is a return to the Kantian 'transcendental critique'. By this Karatani aims to put forward a view of philosophy in relation to 'communism'. He treats these ideas densely in the short 'Afterword' to *Architecture as Metaphor*. He writes:

> Today's debates on postmodernism are fundamentally critiques of the narrative of the Hegelian *Idee*. For Hegel world history is a self-realization of *Idee*, and for many, Marxism is a mere variant of it. Is it possible that what has taken place since 1989 is the disintegration of the *Idee*? I think not.[1]

A reassessment of the Hegelian *Idee* has thus become urgent, as Karatani asserts.

But what is *Idee*? Before Hegel put forward the 'world history' as the 'self-realization' of *Idee*, Kant argued that *Idee* denotes a 'pure concept of reason', for which no object of experience can be given. Kant, employing a building analogy, wrote the following in *Prolegomena to Any Future Metaphysics*:

> As the understanding stands in need of categories for experience, reason contains in itself the ground of ideas, by which I mean necessary concepts whose objects *cannot* be given to experience. The latter are inherent in the nature of reason, as the former are in that of the

DOI: 10.4324/9781032647616-10

understanding. While the ideas carry with them an illusion likely to mislead, this illusion is unavoidable though it certainly can be kept from misleading us.

And then:

> The distinction of *ideas*, i.e., of pure concepts of reason, from the categories, or pure concepts of the understanding, as cognitions of a quite different species, origin, and use is so important a point in founding a science which is to contain the system of all these *a priori* cognitions that, without this distinction, metaphysics is absolutely impossible or is at best a random, bungling attempts to build a castle in the air without knowledge of the materials or their fitness for one purpose or another.[2]

Karatani in a novel way tells us that for Kant, who borrowed the term from Plato, '*Idee* is an imaginary representation of the "thing-in-itself": it is that which can never be grasped and represented by any theoretical approach'.[3] However, he adds, 'what is important is that the concept of the "thing-in-itself" was proposed by Kant less as an account of the world, as with Plato's *idea*, than as the basis upon which to criticize all the ideation as *Schein*'.[4] The latter term *Schein* directly refers to what Kant said in the passages I quoted previously, that 'While the ideas carry with them an illusion likely to mislead, this illusion unavoidable though it certainly is can be kept from misleading us'.[5] What is important, as Karatani tells us, is that 'Kant did not simplemindedly deny *Idee*: he claimed, after all, that *Idee* was a necessary *Schein* that functions "regulatively," though it cannot be proven theoretically and must never be realized "constitutively"'.[6] Karatani rightly points out that after Kant, the 'thing-in-itself' was ignored by philosophers—if not contested or refuted. The result, as he cogently puts it, was the emergence of the Hegelian position that '*Idee* is realistic and the real is ideation'. And significantly, in this regard, Marx, no matter how 'materialistic' he is said to be, in the early years of his philosophical thought belonged to this Hegelian system. Karatani makes a partial reference to what Marx wrote towards the end of his 'Toward a Critique of Hegel's *Philosophy of Right*: Introduction', which I quote here at length.

> As philosophy finds its *material* weapon in the proletariat, the proletariat finds its *intellectual* weapon in philosophy. And once the lightening of thought has deeply struck this unsophisticated soil of the

people, the *Germans* will emancipate themselves to become men. Let us summarize the result: The only emancipation of Germany possible *in practice* is emancipation based on *the* theory proclaiming that man is the highest essence of man. In Germany emancipation from the *Middle Ages* is possible only as emancipation at the same time from the *partial* victories over the Middle Ages. In Germany *no* brand of bondage can be broken without *every* brand of bondage being broken. Always seeking *fundamentals*, Germany can only make a *fundamental* revolution. The *emancipation of the German* is the *emancipation of mankind*. The *head* of this emancipation is *philosophy*, its *heart* is the *proletariat*. Philosophy cannot be actualized without the transcendence [*Aufhebung*] of the proletariat, the proletariat cannot be transcended without the actualization of philosophy.[7]

About the latter phrase in the foregoing passage, Karatani instructively implies 'a causality in which philosophy (*Idee*) is realistic and the real (proletariat) is ideation'.[8] With *The German Ideology*, though, Marx makes a radical break, that Althusser named as an 'epistemological break', which for Karatani is rather a 'return' to the Kantian 'transcontinental critique'. As Karatani explains:

By seeing the philosophical discourse of the Hegelian *die Linke* (including Marx's own) from outside Germany, *The German Ideology* revealed these Hegelian discourses to be merely *Schein*. Moreover, Marx showed that all discourses are possibly only a *Schein*: this was made possible by positing history as the 'thing-in-itself.' And this history is the '*naturwüchsiges* manifold' unstructurable by any form whatsoever. Marx rejected the 'spirit' and 'transcendental ego' that integrate it into the imaginary.[9]

Karatani further remarks that Marx did not deny *Idee* unconditionally, as he acknowledged its inevitability granting that theoretically it is still *Schein*. But he did deny the "constitutive function of Idee. He consistently, Karatani reminds us, criticized the "constitutive" program for the development of a future society—only indirectly in *The Manifesto of the Communist Party* and *Critique of the Gotha Programme*.

Marx persisted in criticizing the "constitutive" use of reason, a kind of reason put into practice by the communism initiated at the Russian Revolution. Communism's collapse, however, has not led to the total disintegration of *Idee*, because *Idee* is, from the beginning, merely a *Schein*. And whatever kinds of *Idee* are preached as substitutes, they too are mere *Schein*.[10]

Marx affirmed the inevitability of *Idee*. The question of *religion* and its critique is a case in point. Religion is also a *Schein*, an illusion with a certain necessity that Kant, as we recall, called 'transcendental illusion'. In this regard, Marx clearly differed from Ludwig Feuerbach and the Hegelian *die Linke*, as is evidenced in the famous passage in his 'A Contribution to the Critique of Hegel's *Philosophy of Right*: Introduction':

> *Religious* suffering is the *expression* of real suffering and at the same time the *protest* against real suffering. Religion is the sigh of the oppressed creature, the heart of a heartless world, as it is the spirit of the spiritless conditions. It is the *opium* of the people. The abolition of religion as people's *illusory* happiness is the demand for their *real* happiness. The demand to abandon illusions about their condition is a *demand to abandon a condition which requires illusions*. The criticism of religion is thus critique in *embryo*, a *criticism of the vale of tears* whose *halo* is religion.[11]

Commenting on this passage, Karatani incisively argues that 'there is no reason to criticize religion theoretically, because it can only be dissolved practically. While Philosophers of the Enlightenment criticized religion through reason, such a "criticism of religion has been essentially completed"'. He further remarks that in Kantian terms 'Religion, albeit a *Schein*, has a certain necessity inasmuch as man is an existence of passivity (pathos); it functions "regulatively" as a protest against reality, if not "constitutively" of reality'.[12]

Coming now to the the question of 'communism' mentioned previously, Karatani ends with the same line of argument:

> Although communism as well is a mere *Schein*, to criticize its 'illusion' means no more and no less than 'to call on [people] to give up a condition that requires illusion.' And religion will be upheld so long as this state of affairs endures. We can never dissolve fundamentalism by the criticisms or dialogues motivated by the enlightenment, precisely because to criticize the 'illusion' of the latter is 'to call on them to give up a condition that requires illusions.' The advocating of the collapse of *Idee* and the insistence on its realization are, in fact, intertwined and inseparable, and both are *Schein* that represent, each in its own way, the real (the thing-in-itself) of world capitalism, of which they themselves are members.[13]

With these remarks I now go back to the beginning of *Architecture as Metaphor* where Karatani discussed the *will to architecture* in relation to Plato and his notion of *Ideal*. To recall, Karatani wrote there:

> Plato did not capriciously pose the being of Ideal, or the foundation of knowledge. Indeed, he failed rather miserably in his attempt to implement his idea of the philosopher-king. Instead, Plato realized the impossible in the imaginaire: he made Socrates a martyr to this impossible-to-achieve idea, in the same way, for example, that St. Paul exalted Jesus.
>
> All of this demonstrates the impossibility of the *being* of the *ideal* and yet, at the same time, it repeatedly invokes the *will to architecture* by asserting that the impossible, the *being* of the *ideal* be realized. This will to architecture is the foundation of Western thought.[14]

With Kant and Marx, Karatani is a thinker of *architectonics*. He is convinced that we can never abandon the *will to architecture*. He thinks that *transcendentalism*, as he has put it, simply casts a light on the *unconscious* structure that precedes and shapes experience. He firmly maintains the tradition of 'transcendental *critique*'. Like Kant and Marx, his thought is grounded in *epistemic constructivism*: to know the object we first have to *construct* it. The relation between subject and object must be reversed. This means that 'objects are constituted by the form that the subject *projects into* the external world'.[15] Here let us recall what Kant said:

> Up to now it has been assumed that all our cognition must conform to the objects; but all attempts to find out something about them *a priori* through concepts that would extend our cognition have, on this presupposition, come to nothing. Hence let us once try whether we do not get farther with the problems of metaphysics by assuming that the objects must conform to our cognition, which would agree better with the requested possibility of an a priori cognition of them, which is to establish something about objects before they are given to us.[16]

The 'will' in the *will to architecture*, to be grounded in the Kantian human *architectonic reason*, involves a practical moral imperative, the categorical imperative in precise Kantian terms. In *Grounding of the Metaphysics of Morals* Kant wrote:

> Everything in nature works according to laws. Only a rational being has the power to act according to his conception of laws, i.e., according to principles, and thereby has a will. Since the derivation of actions from law requires reason, the will is nothing but practical

reason. If reason infallibly determines the will, then in the case of such a being actions which are recognized to be objectively necessary are also subjectively necessary, i.e., the will is a faculty of choosing only that which reason, independently of inclination, recognizes as being practically necessary, i.e., as good.[17]

Kant famously said: 'Act in such a way that you treat humanity, whether in your own person or in the person of another, always at the same time as an end and never simply as means.'[18] As Karatani reminds us Marx, who was not so generous to Kant, was referring to the same 'categorical imperative' when in 'A Contribution to the Critique of Hegel's *Philosophy of Right*: Introduction', he wrote the following:

> The weapon of criticism obviously cannot replace the criticism of weapons. Material force must be overthrown by material force. But theory also becomes a material force once it has gripped the masses. Theory is capable of gripping the masses when it demonstrates *ad hominem*, and it demonstrates *ad hominem* when it becomes radical. To be radical is to grasp things by the root. But for man the root is man himself. The clear proof of the radicalism of German theory and hence of its political energy is that it proceeds from the decisive *positive* transcendence of religion. The criticism of religion ends with the doctrine that *man is the highest being of man*, hence with the *categorical imperative to overthrow all conditions* in which man is a degraded, enslaved, neglected, contemptible, being—conditions that cannot better be described than by the exclamation of a Frenchman on the occasion of a proposed dog tax: Poor dogs! They want to treat you like human beings![19]

As Karatani later in his *Transcritique: On Kant and Marx* wrote, Marx's *Capital* was driven by his 'ethical will'.

> If so, there is no need of searching for Marxian ethics outside *Capital*. For his part, Kant's ethics cannot be sought only in his account of morality. Being theoretical at the same time as being practical—the transcendental stance is itself ethical.[20]

In our *will to architecture*, that must never be abandoned, we persist in a universal *ethical* stance.

Notes

1   Kōjin Karatani, *Architecture as Metaphor: Language, Money, Number*, trans. Sabu Kohso (Cambridge: The MIT Press, 1995), 185.

2 Immanuel Kant, *Prolegomena to Any Future Metaphysics, Second Edition*, trans. and Intro. James W. Ellington (Indianapolis/Cambridge: Hackett, 1977), 65.

3 Kōjin Karatani, *Architecture as Metaphor: Language, Money, Number*, 185.

4 Kōjin Karatani, *Architecture as Metaphor*, 185.

5 Kōjin Karatani, *Architecture as Metaphor*, 185.

6 Kōjin Karatani, *Architecture as Metaphor*, 185–186.

7 See Karl Marx, 'Toward a Critique of Hegel's *Philosophy of Right*: Introduction', in *Karl Marx, Selected Writings*, ed. Lawrence H. Simon (Indianapolis/Cambridge: Hackett, 1994), 38–39.

8 Kōjin Karatani, *Architecture as Metaphor*, 186.

9 Kōjin Karatani, *Architecture as Metaphor*, 186.

10 Kōjin Karatani, *Architecture as Metaphor*, 187.

11 Karl Marx, 'Toward a Critique of Hegel's *Philosophy of Right*: Introduction', 28; also see Kōjin Karatani, *Architecture as Metaphor*, 187.

12 Kōjin Karatani, *Architecture as Metaphor*, 187–188.

13 Kōjin Karatani, *Architecture as Metaphor*, 188.

14 Kōjin Karatani, *Architecture as Metaphor*, xxxv.

15 In Kōjin Karatani, *Transcritique: On Kant and Marx*, trans. Sabu Kohso (Cambridge: The MIT Press, 2005), 29.

16 Immanuel Kant, *Critique of Pure Reason*, trans. and eds. Paul Guyer and Allen W. Wood (Cambridge: Cambridge University Press, 1998), 110.

17 Immanuel Kant, *Grounding for the Metaphysics of Morals*, trans. James W. Ellington (Indianapolis/Cambridge: Hackett, 1993), 2.

18 Immanuel Kant, *Grounding for the Metaphysics of Morals*, 36.

19 Karl Marx, 'Toward a Critique of Hegel's *Philosophy of Right*: Introduction', 34.

20 Kōjin Karatani, *Transcritique: On Kant and Marx*, trans. Sabu Kohso (Cambridge: The MIT Press, 1995), 1210.

BIBLIOGRAPHY

Allison, Henry E., *Kant's Transcendental Idealism: An Introduction and Defence* (New Haven and London: Yale University Press, 2004).

Aristotle, 'Nicomachean Ethics', in *The Basic Works of Aristotle*, ed. Richard McKeon, intro. C. D. C. Beeve (New York: The Modern Library, 2001).

Badiou, Alain, *Manifesto for Philosophy*, trans. and ed. with intro. Norman Madarasz (Albany: State University of New York Press, 1999).

Badiou, *Badiou by Badiou*, trans. Bruno Bosteels (Sandford: Sandford University Press, 2022).

Baumgarten, Alexander, *Metaphysics, A Critical Translation with Kant's Elucidations, Selected Notes, and Related Materials*, trans. and ed. Courtney D. Fugate and John Hymers (London: Bloomsbury, 2013).

Beiser, Frederich C., *The Fate of Reason: German Philosophy from Kant to Fichte* (Cambridge: Harvard University Press, 1987).

Burnham, Douglas, with Harvey Young, *Kant's Critique of Pure Reason* (Bloomington and Indianapolis: Indiana University Press, 2007).

Caygill, Howard, *A Kant Dictionary* (Oxford: Blackwell, 1995).

Derrida, Jacques, 'Mochlos; or, The Conflict of the Faculties', in *Logomachia: The Conflict of the Faculties*, ed. Richard Rand (Lincoln and London: University of Nebraska Press, 1992).

Descartes, René, *Philosophical Writings: A Selection*, trans. and eds. Elizabeth Anscombe and Peter Thomas Geach, intro. Alexander Koyre (Upper Saddle River: Prentice Hall, 1971).

Dolar, Mladen, 'The Legacy of the Enlightenment: Foucault and Lacan', in *New Formations*, 14 (Summer 1991)

Emmanuele, Kant Immanuel, *Critique of the Power of Judgment*, ed. Paul Guyer, trans. Paul Guyer and Eric Mathews (Cambridge: Cambridge University Press, 2000).

Flaubert, Gustave, *Bouvard and Pécuchet with the Dictionary of Received Ideas* (London: Penguin Books, 1976).

Goldstein, Rebecca, *Incompleteness: The Proof and Paradoxes of Kurt Gödel* (New York and London: W. W. Norton, 2005).

Hintikka, Jaakko, *On Gödel* (Belmont: Wadsworth Thomson Learning, 2000).

Hume, David, *A Treatise of Human Nature*, ed. with into. Ernest C. Mossner (Penguin Books, 1969).

Hume, David, *An Inquiry Concerning Human Understanding*, ed. Eric Steinberg, Second Edition (Indianapolis and Cambridge: Hackett, 1993).

Inwood, Michael, *A Hegel Dictionary* (Oxford: Blackwell, 1992).

Jay, Martin, *Reason after its Eclipse: On Late Critical Theory* (Madison: The University of Wisconsin Press, 2016).

Kant, Immanuel *Prolegomena to Ant Future metaphysics*, second Edition, and the Letter to Marcus Herz, February 1772, trans. with into. And notes, James W. Ellington (Indianapolis/Cambridge, 1977).

Kant, Immanuel, 'An Answer to the Question: What is Enlightenment (1784)', in *Perpetual Peace and Other Essays*, ed. Immanuel Kant, trans. Ted Humphry (Indianapolis and Cambridge: Hackett, 1983).

Kant, Immanuel, 'Dreams of a Visionary Explained by Dreams of Metaphysics', in *The Philosophy of Kant, Immanuel Kant's Moral and Political Writings*, ed. and intro. Carl J. Friedrich (New York: The Modern Library, 1993).

Kant, Immanuel, *Critique of Pure Reason*, trans. and eds. Paul Guyer and Allen W. Wood (Cambridge: Cambridge University Press, 1998).

Kant, Immanuel, *Religion Within the Limits of Reason Alone*, trans. and intro. Theodore M. Greene and Hoyt Hudson, with an essay by John R. Silber (New York: Harper and Brothers, 1960).

Kant, Immanuel, *The Conflict of the Faculties*, trans. and intro. Mary J. Gregor (Lincoln and London: University of Nebraska Press, 1992).

Karatani, Kojin, 'Rethinking City Planning and Utopianism', in *The Political Unconscious of Architecture, Reopening Jameson's Narrative*, ed. Nadir Lahiji (Surrey: Ashgate, 2011).

Karatani, Kojin, *Architecture as Metaphor: Language, Number, Money* (Cambridge: MIT Press, 1995).

Karatani, Kojin, *Isonomia and the Origin of Philosophy* (Durham and London: Duke University Press, 2017a).

Karatani, Kojin, *Marx: Towards the Center of Possibility* (London and New York: Verso, 2020).

Karatani, Kojin, *Nation and Aesthetics, On Kant and Freud* (New York: Oxford University Press, 2017b).

Karatani, Kojin, *The Structure of World History, From Modes of Production to Modes of Exchange*, trans. Michael K. Bourdaghs (Durham and London: Duke University Press, 2014).

Karatani, Kojin, *Transcritique: On Kant and Marx* (Cambridge: MIT Press, 2003).

Kline, Morris, *Mathematics for the Nonmathematician* (New York: Dover, 1967).

Kline, Morris, *Mathematics: The Loss of Certainty* (Oxford and New York: Oxford University Press, 1980).

Kuhn, Thomas, *Planetary Astronomy in the Development of Western Thought* (Cambridge: Harvard University Press, 1957).

Lacour, Claudia Brodsky, *Lines of Thought: Discourse, Architectonics, and the Origin of Modern Philosophy* (Durham and London: Duke University Press, 1996).

Lahiji, Nadir, *An Architecture Manifesto: Critical Reason and Theories of a Failed Practice* (Milton Park: Routledge, 2019).

Lahiji, Nadir, ed. *The Political Unconscious of Architecture: Re-opening Jameson's Narrative* (Surrey: Ashgate, 2011).

Kavanaugh, Leslie Jaye, *The Architectonic of Philosophy: Plato, Aristotle, Leibniz* (Amsterdam: Amsterdam University Press, 2007).

Martin, Gottfried, *Kant's Metaphysics and Theory of Science*, trans. P.G. Luca (Westport: Greenwood Press, 1974).

Marx, Karl, 'Toward a Critique of Hegel's *Philosophy of Right*: Introduction', in *Karl Marx, Selected Writings*, ed. Lawrence H. Simon (Indianapolis/Cambridge: Hackett, 1994).

Marx, Karl, 'A Contribution to the Critique of Political Economy, Preface' in *Marx, Later Political Writings*, ed. Terrel Carver (Cambridge: Cambridge University Press, 1996).

Marx, Karl, *Capital, Volume I*, trans. Ben Fowkes (London: Penguin Classics, 1990).

Morgan, Diane, *Kant Trouble: The Obscurities of the Enlightenment* (London and New York: Routledge, 2000).

Nagel, Ernest, and James R. Newman, *Gödel's Proof*, ed. with a new foreword, Douglas R. Hofstadter, Revised Edition (New York and London: New York University Press, 2001).

Nietzsche, Freidrich, *Philosophy and Truth: Selections from Nietzsche Notebooks of the Early 1870's*, ed. and trans. Daniel Breazeale (Amherst: Humanity Books, 1999).

Nietzsche, Freidrich, *Twilight of the Idols and Anti-Christ*, trans. and intro. R.J. Hollingdale (Middlesex: Penguin Books, 1968).

O'Neill, Onora, 'Vindicating Reason', in *The Cambridge Companion to Kant*, ed. Paul Guyer (Cambridge: Cambridge University Press, 1992).

O'Neill, Onora, *Constructions of Reason: Explorations of Kant's Practical Philosophy* (Cambridge: Cambridge University Press, 1989).

Pinkard, Terry, *German Philosophy, 1760–1860: The Legacy of Idealism* (Cambridge: Cambridge University Press, 2002).

Plato, *Complete Works*, ed. John M. Cooper, Associated ed. D.S. Hutchinson (Indianapolis: Hackett, 1997).

Prince, Hal, *The Annotated Gödel: A Reader's Guide to his Classic Paper on Logic and Incompleteness* (Homebred Press, 2022).

Purdy, Daniel, *On the Ruins of Babel: Architectural Metaphor in German Thought* (Ithaca and New York: Cornell University Press, 2011).

Rockmore, Tom, *After Parmenides: Idealism, Realism, and Epistemic Constructivism* (Chicago and London: The University of Chicago Press, 2021).

Rockmore, Tom, and Beth J. Singer, eds. *Anti-foundationalism, Old and New* (Philadelphia: Temple University Press, 1992).

Rockmore, Tom, *Before and After Hegel: A Historical Introduction to Hegel's Thought* (Indianapolis/Cambridge: Hackett, 1993).

Rockmore, Tom, *In Kant's Wake, Philosophy in the Twentieth Century* (Malden: Blackwell, 2006).

Silva, Ludovico, *Marx's Literary Style*, trans. Paco Núññez, Foreword by Alberto Toscano (London and New York: Verso, 2023).

Thorpe, Lucas, *The Kant Dictionary* (London: Bloomsbury, 2015).

Timpanaro, Sebastiano, *On Materialism*, trans. Lawrence Garner (London: Verso, 1975).

Valéry, Paul, *Dialogues*, trans. William McCausland Stewart (Princeton: Princeton University Press, 1989).

Vernant, Jean-Pierre *The Origins of Greek Thought* (Ithaca: Cornell University Press, 1982).

Wilatt, Edward, *Kant, Deleuze and Architectonics* (London: Continuum, 2010).

Yovel, Yirmiyahu, *Kant's Philosophical Revolution: A Short Guide to the Critique of Pure Reason* (Princeton and Oxford: Princeton University Press, 2018).

Žižek, Slavoj *Tarrying with the Negative: Kant, Hagel, and Critique of Ideology* (Durham: Duke University Press, 1993).

Žižek, Slavoj, *The Parallax View* (Cambridge: The MIT Press, 2006).

INDEX